INTERACTIONS IN POLITICAL ECONOMY

In recent years there has been a growing dissatisfaction with standard economic theorizing. This has fostered the development of alternative ways of understanding how economies actually work. Too often though these approaches have been developed in isolation, or even in opposition to each other.

Interactions in Political Economy demonstrates that the different heterodox approaches to economics have much to learn from each other. Economists working within different paradigms, including post-Keynesianism, Marxism and neo-Ricardian economics address a wide range of issues in methodology, the history of economics, theory and policy. The result is a wealth of insight into how economics ought to be done, how various theoretical approaches dovetail, and the effectiveness of various approaches to economic policy.

The volume reflects the diversity and quality of the annual Great Malvern Political Economy conferences. Contributors include some of the leading names in heterodox economics: John Cornwall, Paul Davidson, Kevin Hoover, Philip Mirowski and Ed Nell.

Steven Pressman is Professor of Economics and Finance at Monmouth University, co-editor of the *Review of Political Economy*, and Associate Editor of the *Eastern Economic Journal*. He is the co-editor of *Women in the Age of Economic Transformation* (1994) and the author of *Quesnay's Tableau Economique: A Critique and Reassessment* (1994). His research and writing is primarily in the areas of poverty, public finance, post-Keynesian macroeconomics and the history of economic thought.

ROUTLEDGE FRONTIERS OF POLITICAL ECONOMY

1 EQUILIBRIUM VERSUS UNDERSTANDING
Towards the Rehumanization of Economics within Social Theory
Mark Addleson

2 EVOLUTION, ORDER AND COMPLEXITY
Edited by Elias L. Khalil and Kenneth E. Boulding

3 INTERACTIONS IN POLITICAL ECONOMY
Malvern After Ten Years
Edited by Steven Pressman

4 THE END OF ECONOMICS
Michael Perelman

5 PROBABILITY IN ECONOMICS
Omar F. Hamouda and Robin Rowley

INTERACTIONS IN POLITICAL ECONOMY

Malvern After Ten Years

Edited by Steven Pressman

ROUTLEDGE

London and New York

First published 1996
by Routledge
11 New Fetter Lane, London EC4P 4EE

Simultaneously published in the USA and Canada
by Routledge
29 West 35th Street, New York, NY 10001

Routledge is an International Thomson Publishing company

Typeset in Garamond by Routledge
Printed and bound in Great Britain by T J Press (Padstow) Ltd,
Padstow, Cornwall

British Library Cataloguing in Publication Data
A catalogue record for this book is available from the British Library

Library of Congress Cataloguing in Publication Data
Interactions in political economy: Malvern after ten years/edited by Steven Pressman.
p. cm. – (Routledge frontiers of political economy) Includes bibliographical references and index.
1. Economics. I. Pressman, Steven. II. Series.
HB171.157 1996 330–dc20
95–47075 CIP

ISBN 0–415–13393–9

For John Pheby, who made Malvern possible

John Pheby

CONTENTS

ILLUSTRATIONS

FIGURES

TABLES

CONTRIBUTORS

John Cornwall is McCulloch Emeritus Professor of Economics at Dalhousie University in Halifax, Canada. His publications include *Growth and Stability in a Mature Economy* (Martin Robertson, 1972), *Modern Capitalism: Its Growth and Transformation* (Martin Robertson, 1977), *The Conditions for Economic Recovery* (Martin Robertson, 1983), *Economic Recovery for Canada: A Policy Framework* (James Lorimer, 1984; with Wendy Maclean), *The Theory of Economic Breakdown* (Blackwell, 1990) and *Economic Breakdown and Recovery* (M. E. Sharpe, 1994). He is a Fellow of the Royal Society of Canada.

Wendy Cornwall is Professor of Economics at Mount Saint Vincent University in Halifax, Canada. Her publications include *Economic Recovery for Canada: A Policy Framework* (James Lorimer, 1984; with John Cornwall) and *A Model of the Canadian Financial Flow Matrix* (Statistics Canada, 1989; with J. A. Brox). She has published articles on the flow of funds, applied econometrics and economic growth, both in journals and in books.

Allin Cottrell is Associate Professor of Economics at Wake Forest University. He is author of *Social Classes in Marxist Theory* (Routledge & Kegan Paul, 1984) and, with Paul Cockshott, *Towards a New Theory of Socialism* (Coronet, 1993). He has published numerous articles on economics and philosophy, socialist planning and the history of macroeconomic thought.

Paul Davidson holds the Holly Chair of Excellence in Political Economy at the University of Tennessee in Knoxville. He is also the editor of the *Journal of Post Keynesian Economics*. Davidson's many books include *Money and the Real World* (Macmillan, 1972), *International Money and the Real World* (Macmillan, 1982), *Economics for a Civilized Society* (Norton, 1988; with Greg Davidson) and *Post Keynesian Macroeconomic Theory* (Elgar, 1992).

Peter E. Earl is Professor of Economics at Lincoln University in New Zealand. His research output includes many books and articles (written from subjectivist, behavioural or post-Keynesian standpoints) on consumer behaviour and economic psychology, the economics of the firm, monetary economics and economic method. His latest major work is a text entitled *Microeconomics for Business and Marketing* (Elgar, 1995), which covers both mainstream and behavioural/new institutionalist theory.

Kevin D. Hoover is Professor of Economics at the University California, Davis. He is the author of *The New Classical Macroeconomics: A Skeptical Inquiry* and numerous articles in macroeconomics, monetary economics, economic methodology and the philosophy of science. He is an editor and the chairman of the board of editors of the *Journal of Economic Methodology*. He previously served on the board of editors of the *American Economic Review*, and serves currently on the boards of the *Review of Political Economy* and the *Journal of Economic Surveys*.

John E. King is Reader in Economics at La Trobe University in Melbourne, Australia. He is the author of *Labour Economics* (Macmillan, 1972) and *Labour Economics: An Australian Perspective* (Macmillan Australia, 1990). With M.C. Howard he is the author of *The Political Economy of Marx* (Longman, 1975), and the two-volume *History of Marxian Economics* (Macmillan, 1972). His latest publications are *Conversations With Post Keynesians* (Macmillan, 1995) and *Post Keynesian Economics: An Annotated Bibliography* (Elgar, 1995).

Philip Mirowski is Carl Koch Professor of Economics and the History and Philosophy of Science at the University of Notre Dame. His most recent books are *Natural Images in Economics* (Cambridge University Press, 1994) and *Edgeworth on Chance, Economic Hazard and Statistics* (Rowman and Littlefield, 1994). He is currently working on a history of the neoclassical theory of supply and demand functions, the economics of science and the prospects for a computational institutionalist economic theory.

Gary Mongiovi is Associate Professor of Economics at St John's University, and is co-editor and book review editor of *Review of Political Economy*. His publications include: 'Sraffa's Critique of Marshall: A Reassessment', *Cambridge Journal of Economics* (1996); 'Keynes, Sraffa and the Labour Market', *Review of Political Economy* (1991); 'Notes on Say's Law, Classical Economics and the Theory of Effective Demand', *Contributions to Political Economy* (1990); 'Keynes, Hayek and Sraffa: On the Origins of Chapter 17 of *The General Theory*', *Économie Appliquée* (1990).

Edward J. Nell is Malcolm B. Smith Professor of Economics at the Graduate Faculty of the New School for Social Research. He is the author of *Transformational Growth and Effective Demand* (New York University Press, 1992), *Prosperity and Public Spending* (Unwin Hyman, 1988) and the forthcoming *The General Theory of Transformational Growth: Keynes After Sraffa*.

Steven Pressman is Professor of Economics and Finance at Monmouth University, co-editor of the *Review of Political Economy*, and associate editor of the *Eastern Economic Journal*. He is the co-editor of *Women in the Age of Economic Transformation* (Routledge, 1994) and the author of *Quesnay's Tableau*

Economique: A Critique and Reassessment (Kelley, 1994). His research and writing are primarily in the areas of poverty, public finance, post-Keynesian macroeconomics and the history of economic thought.

Ingrid H. Rima is Professor of Economics at Temple University. She has written and edited numerous books including *Development of Economic Analysis* (Irwin, 5th edn 1991), the two-volume *The Political Economy of Global Restructuring* (Elgar, 1993), *The Joan Robinson Legacy* (M. E. Sharpe, 1991) and *Measurement, Quantification and the Development of Economic Analysis* (Routledge, forthcoming). Her main research interests are labour economics and the history of economic thought, and she has published numerous articles on these subjects in professional journals.

Claudio Sardoni is Associate Professor of History of Economics at the University of Rome 'La Sapienza'. Among his more recent works are *Marx and Keynes on Economic Recession* (Wheatsheaf and New York University Press, 1987); 'Chapter 18 of *The General Theory*: Its Methodological Importance', *Journal of Post Keynesian Economics* (1990); 'Effective Demand and Income Distribution in *The General Theory*', *Journal of Income Distribution* (1993); '*The General Theory* and the Critique of Decreasing Returns', *Journal of the History of Economic Thought* (1994).

Mark Setterfield is Assistant Professor of Economics at Trinity College, Hartford. His main research interest concerns the concepts of path dependency and the introduction of historical time into economic theory. He has published articles on these topics in the *Review of Political Economy* and the *Journal of Post Keynesian Economics*.

FOREWORD

I am still tickled by the fact that I am (just) the only person under 70 on the academic board of the *Journal of Post-Keynesian Economics* (*JPKE*). Nevertheless, I realized how ancient I had become when I looked through the list of contributors to the volume which commemorates ten years at Malvern. For I found there all friends, many of over thirty years' standing, and some of whom in addition are former or present colleagues, relatives and students, both undergraduate and graduate. This, of course, is one of the many joys of growing old.

I have had the privilege and pleasure of attending several Malvern conferences. I agree with the editor of the present volume that the atmosphere – in the Harcourt Room, where else?– has been friendly and constructive and that serious issues have been tackled in a profound manner and in the best of humours. That is *not* to say that the debates have not been intellectually vigorous; with such outstanding practitioners of the art as Phil Mirowski, Ed Nell and Ingrid Rima, for example, how could they be otherwise? But what is refreshing about all the chapters in the present volume is that they have one ultimate aim, to wit, to understand and then to improve the world, or rather, the lot of its citizens (not, note, agents but real people). This is so whether the contribution of their chapters is to put us right on our methods, or to bring us up to date on the phenomenon of hysteresis in uncertain environments, or to rid Keynes's theory of investment of flaws in its details.

Naturally, reflecting on ten years of Malvern conferences leaves us sad for we shall never see again in the flesh Ken Boulding, John Hicks, George Shackle or Lorie Tarshis. Their spirits, however, are very much alive in this volume, and for that alone I count it a signal honour and act of love to be able to write the foreword to this volume.

Now read on!

G.C. Harcourt

1

POLITICAL ECONOMY AT MALVERN

Steven Pressman

In August 1987, John Pheby organized the first Malvern Political Economy conference. It was attended by over thirty economists from ten different countries, and twelve papers were presented on a wide range of topics. The individual papers and the ensuing discussion were both highly stimulating and rather contentious. Many of the papers presented were subsequently collected and published as a conference volume (Pheby 1989).

Every August since 1987 another Political Economy conference has been held at Malvern. Each conference has been different, but each has been equally stimulating. Thus far more than 200 different economists have attended the Malvern conferences, and around 100 different economists have presented papers there. Two Nobel laureates (John Hicks and James Meade) have come to Malvern, and many other luminary figures in the profession have presented papers at Malvern.

Over the past decade Malvern has become renowned for the excellent food (served by the gracious staff of the Mount Pleasant Hotel), and for the camaraderie that has developed among conference participants. As an added plus, we have had the beautiful Malvern Hills in our backyard. This provided plenty of fresh air, pleasant surroundings and enjoyable places to walk and talk when not listening to the stimulating papers. Even a die-hard New Yorker like myself managed to enjoy 'the idiocy of rural life' in our bucolic haven.

When I think back and reflect on the past Malvern conferences several themes stand out as being especially prominent. One is a dissatisfaction with standard economic theorizing. A second theme involves the search for alternative ways of understanding how economies actually work and alternative solutions to the problems faced by real economies. But perhaps the dominant theme running through Malvern has been a belief that heterodox economic paradigms have much to teach one another, and that economists with different perspectives can learn from one another if given the right environment. Malvern has provided that environment. It has been a place where all approaches to economic analysis have been welcomed and respected, and where the insights from one tradition have met up with what Latakos has called 'the hard core' beliefs from other paradigms. The results have been frequently contentious and sometimes synergistic, but they have always been illuminating.

The twelve chapters that follow were all written by people who have attended past Malvern conferences. In many instances, the individual authors have returned to Malvern again and again. The papers themselves were selected to reflect the diverse array of heterodox economics at Malvern and the cross-fertilization among these perspectives that has made Malvern a very special place over the past ten years.

METHODOLOGICAL ISSUES

Methodological questions have been one major area of concern and interest at Malvern. While these debates may appear overly abstract and abstruse to some, they do have real-world consequences. It is rather certain that mistaken views on how to do economics will lead to both bad economics and bad economic policy.

In Chapter 2 Philip Mirowski looks at the Santa Fe Institute, home of complexity theory. He examines the relationship between the hard scientists and the economists associated with Santa Fe. This study of Santa Fe is placed against the backdrop of the Cowles Commission, and yields a number of interesting similarities and differences. Both institutions were funded to engage in statistical research on stock prices, and both projects were then shifted onto another track by the major researchers and participants. But here the similarities end. The Cowles Commission was taken over by economists interested in formalizing and axiomatizing the structure of Walrasian general equilibrium theory. Their vision was to make economics a hard science like physics. The Santa Fe Institute, in contrast, has been taken over by natural scientists who are more interested in their own experimental work than in economics. Moreover, their vision is a historical one. They look to biology, more than they look to physics, as a model of science; and their view is evolutionary and organicist. In another striking contrast to the Cowles Commission, the physicists at Santa Fe have expressed disdain for the formalist programme that drives much of neoclassical economics.

From this comparative analysis Mirowski draws several methodological lessons. First, and perhaps most important, he sees in Santa Fe support for a Romantic conception of science, which is holistic and historical in outlook, which stresses indeterminacy and diversity, and which is experimental rather than formal and axiomatic. Second, Santa Fe shows the importance of cross-fertilization among disciplines and theories, of cultural images of change over time, and of the personal computer as a simulation tool. These approaches, rather than deductive proofs, lie at the forefront of contemporary science according to Mirowski; and economists would do well to emulate these approaches.

SEMINAL FIGURES IN POLITICAL ECONOMY

At Malvern, history has mattered as well as methodology. With considerable regularity conference participants have looked to the work of seminal figures for ideas about how real economies work and for insights into how to escape from an ahistorical neoclassical framework. The chapters contained in Part II reflect this appreciation for the importance of history.

Peter Earl explores the views of George Shackle concerning entrepreneurship and the firm. Shackle is best known for his view that the world is kaleidoscopic, and that uncertainty plagues any investment decisions that a firm or entrepreneur makes. This radical uncertainty, for Shackle, reduces investment and effective demand, thereby creating macroeconomic problems. Yet, in his work on entrepreneurship and the economics of the firm (especially his 1970 textbook on the theory of the firm), Shackle failed to make use of key ideas from Coase and Schumpeter on entrepreneurship that would have complemented his better-known lines of thought. Instead, Shackle focused on the views of Cantillon, who saw the entrepreneur as an arbitrageur rather than someone proceeding into unfamiliar territory and beset with uncertainty. And he failed to see how, by internalizing the market, firms could reduce transaction costs and thus the uncertainty that they face.

Earl concludes with a discussion of why Shackle missed the opportunity to make these connections. Here Earl identifies several possibilities. First, Shackle was an armchair theorist whereas Coase followed the Marshallian strategy of letting empirical matters direct theoretical inquiry. Second, Shackle saw in Cantillon the idea that entrepreneurs face uncertainty about their future revenue streams. Conversely, in the Coasian tradition, transaction costs reduce uncertainty and make the economic system more resilient.

John King, a well-known and prolific historian of Marxian economics, tackles the economic thought of post-Keynesian economist Hyman Minsky in his chapter. King notes a tension in the early work of Minsky, which reflects some acceptance of post-Keynesian doctrines and some acceptance of neoclassical theory. On the one hand, Minsky recognized the dangers of financial instability, and the need for government economic policy and a lender of the last resort. He also accepted the multiplier–accelerator model as the basis for doing macroeconomic analysis. On the other hand, Minsky took a loanable funds approach to the determination of interest rates, and held that savings constrained investment.

King argues that when Minsky discovered Kalecki's theory of profits it helped to liberate him from the anti-Keynesian loanable funds view of savings and investment. It also made Minsky a true post-Keynesian monetary theorist. Kalecki's theory allowed Minsky to analyse cash flows into firms, and to show how these cash flows could be used to help to finance investment. Thus Minsky was able to escape from the neoclassical view that it was savings that determined and constrained business investment.

Allin Cottrell's chapter examines *Monopoly Capital* by Baran and Sweezy, thirty years after its publication. That work argued that the degree of monopoly had been rising in developed capitalist economies; and that with greater monopolistic elements capitalist economies would tend to stagnate, as the growth of labour productivity increased profit rates and reduced effective demand. Baran and Sweezy also expressed scepticism that government economic policies would be put into effect that increased social spending, and thus offset the trend towards reduced private spending.

Cottrell, however, notes a number of 'awkward facts' that cast doubt on this explanation for stagnation and high unemployment. First, the degree of monopoly in the US economy appears to have fallen rather than grown since the publication of *Monopoly Capital*. Second, Cottrell notes that other data seem to contradict the argument of Baran and Sweezy. Over the past thirty years productivity growth has stagnated, as have corporate profits; at the same time, consumption has exhibited a tendency to rise as a fraction of income, rather than fall.

Cottrell concludes his critique by turning the Baran and Sweezy argument upside-down, thereby returning to Marx and classical economics. Rather than high profit rates reducing spending and contributing to stagnation, Cottrell suggests that it may be falling rates of profit that have reduced investment and contributed to our current economic problems.

COMPARATIVE APPROACHES TO POLITICAL ECONOMY

As noted earlier, one of the defining traits at Malvern has been a cross-fertilization among different economic paradigms and an attempt to integrate ideas from various contemporary schools of thought. The chapters in Part III all attempt to bring the insights from one heterodox paradigm to bear on another heterodox paradigm.

Claudio Sardoni's paper examines the investment demand function contained in Chapter 11 of *The General Theory*. Keynes assumed, according to Sardoni, that as businesses invested more and more, the cost of capital goods would increase and the expected returns to investment would fall as capital became less scarce.

Keynes needed a downward sloping investment demand curve, Sardoni points out, to explain why business investment did not expand until full employment was reached. If investment demand did not slope downward, the only limit to investment would be the lack of resources to produce more plants and equipment, and we would be back in the full employment world of classical economics.

Yet, Sardoni argues, the downward sloping investment demand function has some logical problems. First, Keynes assumed pure or perfect competition, where no firm can affect the overall market. Thus, greater investment by one firm should not affect supply prices adversely. Keynes's views about expected profits can be similarly criticized. Since one producer cannot affect aggregate outcomes, there is no reason that expected returns to investment should fall wherever investment increases. Moreover, as investment rises, entrepreneurs may expect greater profits due to the economic expansion and rising prices.

Finally, Sardoni maintains that Sraffa helps to point the way out for Keynes's investment demand function. What is needed is the assumption that imperfectly competitive market forms are the norm. The problem facing a firm wanting to expand thus becomes how to sell the additional output produced by the new investment. As such, investment is limited because the demand for goods is limited; and an unemployment equilibrium becomes possible because of this limit.

In Chapter 7 Gary Mongiovi poses four problems for post-Keynesian macroeconomic theory from a Sraffian perspective. These difficulties, according to Mongiovi, all stem from the failure of the post-Keynesians to pay due attention to questions of value and distribution.

First, Mongiovi argues that the IS-LM model is wrong, but not for the reasons advanced by post-Keynesians. The problem is not that the IS-LM model does not accurately represent the views of Keynes. Rather, the problem is that the model ignores issues of distribution. More important, according to Mongiovi, is the way in which IS-LM ignores distribution. As noted in the Sardoni chapter, Keynes advanced a downward sloping investment demand curve. Mongiovi argues that this curve is grounded in the marginal productivity theory of distribution, a theory discredited in the Cambridge controversy; and that furthermore, this curve forms the basis of the IS curve.

Second, post-Keynesians are wrong about Say's Law, and the importance of overthrowing Say's Law. Say's Law is a red herring, according to Mongiovi, and does not imply a tendency to full employment. Conventional beliefs among economists that there is a tendency to full employment stem from the marginalist theory of distribution. Third, Mongiovi contends that post-Keynesians are wrong that non-neutral money accounts for unemployment; non-monetary economies will not necessarily move towards full employment equilibrium. Finally, Mongiovi argues that post-Keynesians tend to reject equilibrium analysis. This, however, makes it difficult to do any economic analysis, since it becomes impossible to pinpoint the consequences of any changes that affect the economic system.

In the next chapter, Paul Davidson defends Keynes and post-Keynesian economics from the criticisms leveled by Mongiovi. Davidson argues that Keynes does not require a downward sloping investment demand curve. Moreover, he contends that Keynes's investment demand curve is not a traditional, Marshallian demand curve; rather it is a curve showing statistical frequency distributions. Thus it does not ignore the lessons of the Cambridge critique regarding returns to capital.

Davidson agrees with Mongiovi that Say's Law does not entail full employment, but he notes that Say's Law is also *not* a theory of output and employment.

This theory is what Keynes provided, and what makes up the Keynesian revolution. In response to Mongiovi's point about non-neutral money, Davidson argues that uncertainty and the two essential characteristics of money identified by Keynes are necessary to explain unemployment in real-world economies. Finally, Davidson contends that the persistent centers of gravity demanded by Mongiovi and the neo-Ricardians cannot exist in the real economic world where uncertainty is so pervasive.

Mark Setterfield's chapter addresses the consistency of the notions of hysteresis and uncertainty. The former notion, a favourite of the new Keynesian school, involves the idea that the present state of our economy depends upon its past. In contrast, the uncertainty highlighted by Keynes and Frank Knight involves the impossibility of knowing the probabilities of different potential economic states. The past thus tends to be irrelevant if radical uncertainty prevails. Setterfield should therefore be seen as addressing the issue of whether new Keynesian and post-Keynesian economics are consistent in at least one respect.

His conclusion is that the notions of hysteresis and uncertainty are compatible and tend to complement one another. First, he points out that both notions are properties or characteristics of the real economic environment, rather than qualities of the individuals who inhabit that world. Second, Setterfield notes that both concepts are attempts to deal with real-world historical time. For Keynes, and for the post-Keynesians, historical time creates uncertainty. Similarly, hysteresis is an evolutionary process that takes place through historical time and takes place in an uncertain environment. Finally, Setterfield finds pragmatic compatibilities between models of hysteresis and the post-Keynesian research programme. Post-Keynesians seek to develop useful models that improve our understanding of real-world economies, and to set forth economic policies that might help economies to perform better. Since hysteretic models show how increases in aggregate demand can have permanent and positive effects on unemployment, post-Keynesians should accept these models for pragmatic reasons as well as for theoretical reasons.

POLICY ISSUES

Malvern has not been just about methodology and high theory. These aspects of economics are important only to the extent that they lead to improved economic performance. This, after all, is the reason for studying economic principles – or at least the reason that economic principles *should* be studied.

The chapter by Edward Nell addresses the issue of why developed economies have stagnated since the early 1970s. He notes several important factors contributing to poor economic performance over the past twenty-five years – consumption spending, investment and net exports have grown slowly and become more volatile. While the appropriate government policy should have been to counteract these changes, the USA has failed to employ the appropriate economic policies.

Nell goes on to explain why all the components of aggregate expenditure have grown more slowly and become more volatile since the 1970s. The key factor is that changing technology has changed the way that markets have worked. Higher costs for new technology have made investment more expensive and more risky, thus explaining the changes in investment. Through the multiplier–accelerator process, the whole economy has become less stable and less likely to grow; thus consumer spending slows down. Technology has also increased foreign trade, but it has also allowed capital to pick up and move to wherever labour is cheapest. This has made countries more susceptible to balance of payments problems.

Looking at US economic history since the Second World War, Nell argues that expansionary government policies have led to successful economic performance. And he argues that such expansionary policies must be used again, if the current economic stagnation is to be ended.

John and Wendy Cornwall analyse the dynamics of macroeconomic change over time. They reject as unhelpful neoclassical growth models that assume full employment, that ignore demand and that ignore path dependence. Only an evolutionary perspective that incorporates the role of institutions, the Cornwalls argue, can help to understand macroeconomic dynamics. A two-way street runs between institutions and economic performance. Economic performance induces institutional change; but institutional change also impacts the economy. The Cornwalls then use this schema to explain the economic performance of the major OECD countries after the Second World War.

The experiences of the Second World War in ending the Depression led to a commitment to full employment on the part of national governments, and a willingness to expand demand and guarantee full employment. It also led to cooperative industrial relations, so that low unemployment rates would not spill over into higher inflation. In essence, labour and management agreed to split the gains of productivity growth. And generous social welfare benefits were provided just in case something went wrong.

The good times, though, led to a breakdown of these institutions and to a resurgence of inflation. High employment increased labour power at the same time that labour became more willing to use that power in order to obtain higher wages. An inflationary bias was imparted to the world economy. Fearing inflation, governments began to use contractionary policies, and unemployment rose in virtually every OECD country.

Given this analysis, the appropriate policy solution follows directly. Institutional changes that bring back a social bargain between labour and capital are absolutely imperative. Only within an institutional framework that limits wage growth to productivity growth can expansionary policies again be employed to control unemployment without leading to unacceptable levels of inflation.

NEW DIRECTIONS IN POLITICAL ECONOMY

It is especially fitting to end this volume with the notion of new directions; the very first Malvern conference resulted in a volume entitled *New Directions in Post-Keynesian Economics* (Pheby 1989). And this theme has continued to be important at Malvern over the ensuing years. In fact, more than anything else, Malvern has been associated with an attempt to move economics forward by developing new approaches and modes of analysis. Both chapters in Part V make concerted attempts to push economics along such new lines.

Ingrid Rima argues that traditional economics goes wrong by starting at the microeconomic level and assuming that macroeconomic outcomes will be Pareto optimal. Since microeconomic behaviour can lead to undesirable macroeconomic outcomes, such as Great Depressions, Rima suggests that we need to reverse the direction of our analysis. We need to begin with those macroeconomic outcomes desired by a nation's citizens, and then determine the best means, or the least costly policies, that will let us reach these goals. Rima terms this approach 'instrumentalism', and traces its roots to Adam Smith, John Maynard Keynes, Jan Tinbergen and especially Adolph Lowe.

More important than the historical origins of instrumentalism are its policy implications. First, the transitional economies of central and eastern Europe should not blindly pursue privatization and marketization in the belief that this will lead to the best possible outcome. Rather, a social consensus for reform must be developed that will set out the desired outcomes and the feasible means to achieve these ends. Second, developed capitalist economies must figure out how to move to a more optimal growth path. This will likely involve, among other things, establishing international organizations like a European Central Bank and a European currency in order to keep individual countries from adopting anti-growth policies like 'beggar-thy-neighbour' import restrictions. What it will not involve, however, are the *laissez-faire* economic policies typically championed by neoclassical economists.

Finally, Kevin Hoover's chapter 'Some Suggestions for Complicating the Theory of Money' is advertised as a prolegomenon to future monetary theory. Hoover begins by discussing the uneasy relationship between the theory of money and Walrasian general equilibrium models. Quite simply, in general equilibrium models it is hard to find any role for money. Since barter determines relative prices among goods, money is not needed for this purpose. Furthermore, in a Walrasian economy the auctioneer can set relative prices to eliminate any imbalances in particular markets. This traditional function of money is thus rendered obsolete. Finally, in a Walrasian model it is hard to explain why people hold money, which pays no interest, rather than interest-bearing assets.

Rather than just blaming general equilibrium theorists for these limitations, Hoover also finds fault with monetary theorists who insist on seeing money as a means of exchange or store of value. Hoover then argues that a more appropriate monetary theory must look to the unit of account function of money. Money is important, according to this line, not because it simplifies exchange or provides utility to its holder, but because it is the way that we keep score of who owes how much to whom.

A more appropriate monetary theory, according to Hoover, must begin with the accounting and settlement functions of money, neither of which have a role in general equilibrium models. In addition, Hoover suggests that rather than assuming that money is needed to purchase goods, monetary theory should begin by assuming that goods are purchased with credit, and that money is needed from time to time in order to settle balances. The puzzle of why people hold money is thus solved – people do *not* want to hold money, rather they want to get rid of it (and buy assets) as soon as possible.

CONCLUDING REMARKS

It should be apparent that the fivefold division that I have imposed upon the chapters in this volume is rather arbitrary. Examining methodological issues yields important insights into the directions that economics should follow if it is to be more relevant, as well as insights into the thinking of seminal figures. A study of seminal figures leads to new insights regarding economic methodology, how various theoretical approaches dovetail, and the efficacy of different policy proposals. The chapters that bring together strands from different heterodox paradigms have distinct policy implications, as well as insights into methodological questions such as the nature and importance of uncertainty. The policy-oriented chapters emphasize the limitations of the neoclassical approach, and attempt to build theories that borrow from different heterodox approaches and that also add something new. Finally, the chapters most explicitly addressing new directions build upon the insights from various schools of thought, show sensitivity to methodological issues and consciously seek better policy proposals.

This lack of a neat and orderly division among the chapters here should not really surprise anyone. Nor should it be seen as a criticism of either the chapters or the division that I have imposed upon them. Rather, it should be seen as a reflection of the breadth of each chapter and the breath of fresh air that Malvern has provided to the grand tradition of political economy over the past decade.[1]

NOTE

1 The editor gratefully acknowledges financial support from Monmouth University through a mini-sabbatical to help bring this volume to completion. Many thanks are also due to Diana Prout for typing numerous chapters, and parts of chapters, in this volume. Finally, each author whose paper appears in this volume deserves special thanks for putting up with such a difficult and demanding editor.

REFERENCE

Pheby, J. (ed.) (1989) *New Directions in Post-Keynesian Economics*, Hants.: Edward Elgar.

Part I

METHODOLOGICAL ISSUES

2

DO YOU KNOW THE WAY TO SANTA FE? OR, POLITICAL ECONOMY GETS MORE COMPLEX

Philip Mirowski

Economic theorists are more than a little testy these days. Their allegiance to the Walrasian programme has been a major washout, although the news may not have filtered down to the average economist in the trenches yet. Many economists of the post-war generation placed their bets with game theory as a viable alternative; and while game theory has provided a quick publication route, the intellectual climate there has proven equally stormy. The spectacle of all those rigorous mathematicians wrangling endlessly over philosophical issues such as the nature of rationality, the meaning of common knowledge, the possibility of induction and the like, has begun to seep into the consciousness of lesser folk and bring to mind an earlier débâcle. The inability to agree on a solution concept also signals that something is rotten in the land of von Neumann. These disputes broke out into the open at the 1994 American Economic Association meetings, where a few sessions found advocates of game theory and the Walrasian approach coming into conflict with partisans of a third alternative (sometimes called 'the complexity approach'), often associated with the Santa Fe Institute.

This chapter begins an exploration into the conjunctures and conditions that have led to the impression that there exists this new alternative to orthodox economic theory. It will not be constructed along the lines of a review article – ten years after its conception is too soon to attempt that task – but rather as a meditation upon a remarkable popular book by Mitchell Waldrop (1992), which has placed the word 'complexity' on the intellectual agenda and the tongue-tips of pundits. The book by Waldrop presents a wonderful opportunity not only to discuss the incipient outlines of complexity theory, but also to convey contemporary evidence in a compact form concerning the pragmatic meaning of science in *fin de siècle* economics. In brief, the argument is that as of 1995 'complexity' has no well-defined analytic content. But this is part of its strength, because in our present climate we do not know what science is, or rather, we are not very confident that we know. Nevertheless, there are identifiable structural regularities in how the issue is likely to get resolved. For economists, the resolution is almost always generously provided by our older cousins, the natural scientists, and usually takes the form of unidirectional metaphor transfer.

The reason that Waldrop's book is so ideal for our purposes is that he clearly did not see himself addressing such weighty questions. As a science reporter, his aim was to produce a sequel to James Gleick's bestseller *Chaos* (1987). It seems that he believed that the next great breakthrough in science was happening at the newly founded Santa Fe Institute, and his being present at the creation justified a sort of joint biography of the major players. They must all have been pining for their Boswell, for he got them to make rather revealing comments that help to illuminate their more formal writings.[1]

UPS AND DOWNS IN THE SCIENCE BIZ

People who are looking for a dependable scientific method believe that there is a unique set of principles or procedures to be found, whether now or back in the seventeenth century. Their quest, however, is almost as misguided as those who believe that they discern virtual modern markets in defunct feudal land tenure systems. The antidote for this mad twentieth-century addiction to virtual realities is repeated doses of contextual history of specific practices. For instance, when one learns that the notion of quantitative error in precision physical measurement has changed repeatedly over the last two centuries, and indeed could not be said to have existed prior to that, many pious platitudes concerning the bracing character of stringent quantification lose their patina of cool Olympian clarity.[2] In adopting this more relativist stance, it becomes incumbent to contextualize our own situation and ask who or what sets the agenda for what we regard as science.

There now exists a hallowed tradition in the history and sociology of science that the physical sciences (insofar as one might regard this as a unified category) tend to take on the cast and colouration of their cultural milieux. Such claims range from linking the rise of experimentation to the Restoration settlement in seventeenth-century Britain (Shapin and Schaffer 1985) to shifts from Enlightenment 'balance' to Victorian historicism as influencing the mathematicization of physics (Wise 1993) to the disruption of Weimar Germany opening up a space for fundamental indeterminism in quantum mechanics (Forman 1971). Even some physicists were not adverse to correlating broad cultural epochs with developments in their discipline (Spradley 1989; Prigogine and Stengers 1984: 116; Gleick 1987: 116). Yet these observations arise frequently only in distant retrospect; here we are searching for something to help us understand our own predicament and context, not to mention Waldrop's saga of the Santa Fe Institute. The answer might be found in a concept close to the hearts of macroeconomists – the concept of cycles.

By raising the issue of cyclical movements, I do not mean to evoke something as pretentious as Nietzsche's doctrine of eternal return, nor something quite so mechanical as the erstwhile multiplier–accelerator. Instead, I mean to suggest that science in the West has tended to swing between two polar conceptions, with a certain generational periodicity, for at least the last two centuries. The distinguished historian of physics Stephen Brush has already broached something like this thesis in his underrated book *The Temperature of History* (1978). He asserts there that, at least in the history of thermodynamics, one can discern swings between classicist and Romanticist temperaments of science that consciously evoke terms familiar from literary history. A Romantic view came to predominate around the 1830s, with a classical resurgence beginning in the 1870s, and a swing back to Romanticism after the turn of the century. Using Brush and others, Table 2.1 crudely characterizes the poles of this cyclical movement.

The reader can get a better idea of these categories by consulting a standard survey of literary history. There one would find that the entire package does not remain intact in any specific instance; mixing and matching serves as one of the premier sources of novelty as both the sciences and literatures evolve. Nevertheless, it may prove helpful in our quest for self-understanding to extend the cyclical narrative up to the twentieth century, seeing the build-up from the Great Depression to the 1950s as another period of classical resurgence, with a Romantic revolt playing itself out from the late 1960s up to the present.

There are various landmarks of the classical attitude in mid-twentieth-century science. In physics we might point to Einstein's general theory of relativity, or the search for the fundamental subatomic particle, or the rise of astrophysical cosmology. Much of this was accompanied by a novel sort of theorist, one who valued formal rigour over intuitive application, itself a reflection of a Bourbakist classicism sweeping mathematics (Weintraub and Mirowski 1994). It was, of course, this classical quest for purity that permitted philosophers of science at that time to claim that they codified *the* scientific method once and for all, practically without any reference to the history of science. Power and efficacy were to be explained by an unwavering correct application of a single unified method; order was defined by a rigid determinism of cause and effect.

I do not think it will come as news to most people to point out that most of this programme has now been relinquished in many areas of physics and the

Table 2.1 Romanticism versus classicism

Romanticism	*Classicism*
wholist	atomist
historicist	atemporal
indeterminist	determinist
emotivist	stoic
experimental	formal
diversity	uniformity
aesthetic detachment	interventionist control
organicism	mechanicism
perspectival	aperspectival

other natural sciences. Eminent physicists now openly deride Bourbakist notions of rigour:

> More recently, abstract mathematics reached out in so many directions and became so seemingly abstruse that it appeared to have left physics far behind.... But all that has changed in the last decade or two. It has turned out that the apparent divergence of pure mathematics from science was partly an illusion produced by the obscurantist, ultra-rigorous language used by mathematicians, especially those of a Bourbakist persuasion.... Pure mathematics and science are finally being reunited and, mercifully, the Bourbaki plague is dying out.
>
> (Gell-Mann 1992: 7)

But it goes beyond such simple dichotomies. The effect of the rapid improvement of the computer has been profound upon the physics community. It has elevated simulation as a research procedure to a level somewhat privileged relative to that occupied by mathematical proof procedures. As Mitchell Feigenbaum has commented: 'The whole tradition of physics is that you isolate the mechanisms and all the rest flows. That's completely falling apart. Here you know the right equations but they're just not helpful' (Gleick 1987: 174). It has ushered in a new area of visual aesthetics, as anyone will attest who has seen four-colour glossies (or better yet, animations) of fractals. Attention has shifted from atomist reductionism to solid-state physics, from the ineffably tiny to human-scale phenomena like fluid turbulence, from classical mechanics and relativity to non-linear dynamics and thermodynamics. Sensitive dependence upon initial conditions is the watchword, bringing back in a kind of history. Computation itself has become a metaphor for all manner of physical processes. Indeed, the exemplar of ideal science itself is shifting away from physics and towards biology, with its stress on organicism, evolutionary histories and population thinking.

It is my contention that economics has experienced its own cultural cycles between classical and Romantic inclinations and, perhaps more contentiously, these cycles are out of phase with those in the natural sciences, lagging by perhaps a decade or so. The Romantic origins of British and German historicism are well known; and the genesis of neoclassicism in the 1870s maps fairly directly into Brush's claim of a classical resurgence in physics during the same time period. The fact that neoclassicism (an unfortunate name given our present concerns, but one too widespread to relinquish) was largely appropriated from energy physics certainly helps to cement the connection (Mirowski 1989a). It is not often appreciated that the neoclassical programme ran into severe obstacles at the turn of the last century, and that much of this had to do with a cultural revulsion against the severe formalist mechanism of the programme, only mitigated in the British context by the thin veneer of Marshall's purported organicism. In America the Romantic reaction was best represented by the home-grown institutionalist school. Institutionalist economics, and Romantic inclinations in general, hit their peak during the Depression; after that catastrophe the pendulum of political economy began to swing back towards a more astringent classic temper.

The 1930s and 1940s saw a revival and strengthening of the neoclassical programme (Mirowski 1991). In America, the Cowles Commission was in the vanguard of the neoclassical resurgence, stressing mathematical rigour and a single scientific method, which they claimed to monopolize. This assertion was dramatized in the 'measurement without theory' controversy, striking the death-knell for the institutionalist movement and the defeat of its citadel, the National Bureau of Economic Research (Mirowski 1989b). Adherence to Walrasian general equilibrium theory became the litmus test of economic orthodoxy; linear regression analysis its empirical hallmark; and Bourbakist axiomatization its preferred idiom (Weintraub and Mirowski 1994). Ahistorical atomistic law was pushed to its furthest extreme by Debreu's assertion that the model could handle the passage of time by redefining the commodity to include a date coordinate as part of its specification.

This unforgivably impressionistic sketch of long swings of the pendulum in economics sets the stage for our primary concern, the shaky status of this orthodoxy fifty years later. Now it seems, the Cowles programme is beset on all sides with hesitations, doubts, qualifications and outright contradictions. In many ways, these problems began within Cowles itself. Alfred Cowles offered to bankroll the Econometrics Society and the Cowles Commission in exchange for statistical research into the determinants of stock market prices. Having himself escaped the Great Crash purely by accident, he was distressed that none of his peers in the investment counselling community had done any better in foreseeing the calamity. Over time, and with great skill, the early Cowlesmen weaned him away from these practical concerns and towards the development of structural econometric techniques. Due to Charles Roos and Harold T. Davis, and then in the 1940s, Jacob Marschak and Tjalling Koopmans, Cowles developed its famous structural estimation methods, predicated upon the Neyman–Pearson philosophy of inference. Marschak in particular displayed a real talent for recruiting members with backgrounds in the physical sciences to the project.

But few realize the extent to which the Cowles people were disappointed by the fruits of their endeavours at a relatively early stage. At the very threshold of their triumph over the NBER (circa 1950), without much fanfare they lost faith in their econometric programme (Epstein 1987: 110–13; Mirowski 1993a). After 1950, none of the major Cowles members did much empirical work; nor did they press their econometric techniques further (Christ 1994). Frisch, the first Nobel Prize winner in economics, essentially repudiated his progeny by the 1960s (Epstein 1987: 127). Much of this disillusion can be seen, in retrospect, as presaging the contemporary wave of scepticism about econometrics – ranging from the Lucas critique to uncovering the 'con' in econometrics to the disbanding of large-scale econometric research units.

In the 1950s Cowles opted for pristine Bourbakist mathematical abstraction, best represented by Debreu's *Theory of Value* and Koopmans' *Three Essays on the State of Economic Science* (Mirowski 1993a), in place of structural econometrics. Curiously, the Cowlesmen declined to work on the other possible nascent programmes of mathematical political economy of which they were aware, namely John von Neumann's game theory or Herbert Simon's innovations of bounded rationality and artificial intelligence. Their agenda seemed to consist primarily of rendering the logical structure of the established Walrasian orthodoxy as transparent and impregnable as possible through axiomatization and escalated levels of formalism (Weintraub and Mirowski 1994). In this distinctly classical endeavour they were at first eminently successful, although the quest for certainty took a nasty turn. In effect, the Bourbakist programme of formalization demonstrated that although existence of Walrasian equilibrium could be shown, its uniqueness and stability could not (Ingrao and Israel 1990). Furthermore, the results now regularly cited as the Sonnenschein/Mantel/Debreu theorems demonstrated that conventional assumptions about economic actors placed almost no restrictions upon excess demand functions, thus rendering the whole project of explaining market coordination as the outcome of an invisible hand process increasingly forlorn.

In response to the collapse of the Cowles Commission project, the neglected rivals of game theory and artificial intelligence rushed in to fill the vacuum. And in response to the absence of a legitimate empiricist identity, a new discipline of experimental economics began to sprout.

One might quibble over details, but I think most would agree that the mid-twentieth-century classical-style programme of developing a unified science of economics has run out of steam. True, orthodoxy still attempts to portray a continuity of content; mainstream economists still write down utility and preference functions, still stress some species of optimization, and still assert the existence of a law of demand. But a survey of neoclassical textbooks from Marshall through Henderson and Quandt to Varian and Kreps (Mirowski 1993b) reveals much more discontinuity than even such ahistorical presentations can suppress. When one goes point by point through the Cowles agenda and examines their doctrines, one is led inexorably to the conclusion that there is very little left standing. Thus, when a main figure of the Cowles project, Kenneth Arrow, asserts that what is happening at the Santa Fe Institute is reminiscent of Cowles in the 1950s (Waldrop 1992: 327), it may be time to sit up and take notice.

LOOKING FOR MR RIGHT

The parallels between the Cowles Commission and the Santa Fe Institute are much closer than anyone has previously noticed. The Econometrics Society, founded in 1930 by twelve Americans and four Europeans in a climate of economic contraction and academic hostility to mathematical formalism, might not have gone anywhere had it not found a long-term sponsor in Alfred Cowles. Cowles thought he was buying a better stock market predictor, but the trained physicists and mathematicians that had been taken on board reoriented the centre of research towards their own abstract concerns. Change the numbers a little, move the calendar to 1983, replace widespread hostility to mathematical formalism with a disdain for anything but formalism, replace Alfred Cowles with John Reed, and you have a fair characterization of the inception of the economics programme at the Santa Fe Institute.

Originally, the Santa Fe Institute had nothing to do with economics (Waldrop 1992: 69–89). Founded by a number of distinguished physicists at the Los Alamos National Laboratories, it was initially little more than a rump committee, meeting informally to think up ways to encourage emergent trends in science which they felt were in the air at the time – non-linear dynamics, computational science and collective behaviours in solid-state physics like quantum flow and spin glasses. Of course, like all ambitious academics, they made themselves giddy with dreams of a new Athens; but the practical problem of how to group all these diverse enthusiasms under the rubric of 'complexity' was not getting them much of anywhere. 'The only problem, unfortunately, was that everybody had something different in mind. "Every week", sighs Cowan, "We'd go back to first base, and go round and round again" ' (Waldrop 1992: 72).

George Cowan got two Nobel Prize winners on board – Murray Gell-Mann and Philip Anderson – who in turn helped to attract enough money to run a couple of workshops in late 1984. The workshops did seem to generate interest, but so far there was nothing more than another temporary eddy in the endless stream of conferences and workshops attended by eminent physicists. There was certainly not enough to convince the larger profession that what one had here was 'a new science'. Indeed, after the 1984 workshops money seemed to dry up and intellectual splits re-emerged among members of the board. So in March 1986, the Santa Fe Institute, really no more than a shell, was again trying to figure out how to get the kind of money it wanted. One member, Bob Adams, ran into his friend John Reed, the CEO of Citicorp, at a board meeting of the Russell Sage Foundation.

> During one of the coffee breaks he'd told Reed about the institute, as best as he could explain it, and Reed had been very interested. But he was wondering if the institute might help him understand the world economy. When it came to world financial markets, Reed had decided that professional economists were off with the fairies. Under Reed's predecessor, Walter Wriston, Citicorp had just taken a bath in the Third World debt crisis.... Reed thought a whole new approach to economics might be necessary...and he had asked Adams to find out if the Santa Fe Institute might be willing to take a crack at the problem.

> Reed had even said he would be willing to come out to Santa Fe himself and talk about it.
>
> (Waldrop 1992: 91)

With their usual hubris, the physicists thought that 'it was about twenty years too early to be tackling anything as complex as economics'; but they did need the money, so Philip Anderson was delegated to chaperone Reed out for a visit. Reed enjoyed lecturing to the physicists (no economists welcome as yet), and the physicists enjoyed speculating to Reed about how their pet projects might be recast as some species of economics. A good time was had by all and a deal was cut, although the physicists wanted it made clear they were not being held to deliver anything in particular (Waldrop 1992: 96). So the Santa Fe Institute got a building (only a lease), the board a new research mandate, and the dream a new lease on life. There was just one problem – none of the physicists (and Anderson in particular) wanted to be responsible for this immanent new economics. Indeed, by their own admission they knew very little about the subject, and they were not willing to undergo any formal training.

Under George Cowan's principle of attempting to hire the best and the brightest, Anderson got on the phone to some Nobel laureates in economics. First he called James Tobin, who was not interested, but suggested Kenneth Arrow. Arrow found the project intriguing, but he also had strong opinions about who should be brought on board. He wanted 'people who had a very strong command of the orthodox view of economics. He didn't mind people criticizing the standard model, but they'd better damn well understand what it was they were criticizing' (Waldrop 1992: 97). So Arrow drew up a prospective list of economists, and Anderson a parallel list of physical scientists, for a meeting to be convened at Santa Fe in September 1987 on 'The Economy as a Complex Evolving System'. The results are collected in Anderson, Arrow and Pines (1988).

Waldrop's book is a fascinating chronicle of this interdisciplinary interaction, focusing mainly on five characters – Brian Arthur, John Holland, Stuart Kauffman, Doyne Farmer and Chris Langton. It needs to be remarked, however, that for a book so concerned with economics, it is more than a little odd that no economist besides Arthur is given extended contextual treatment. Partly this may be due to the fact that Arthur was the only economist in long-term residence at Santa Fe at that juncture, but one might also speculate that it has something to do with things not turning out as Waldrop planned. If Waldrop was taking Gleick's *Chaos* as his template, then the narrative should take us from one triumph to the next as ideas cascade upon innovations and back again. However, given the relatively short time frame of the book (it ends for all practical purposes in mid-1990), very little that happened at Santa Fe can be regarded as a breakthrough in the physical sciences. Anderson and Stein on spin glasses, Holland on classifier systems and genetic algorithms, Kauffman on NK models of evolutionary fitness landscapes, and the whole exploding area of chaos and non-linear dynamics all preceded Santa Fe by a good deal. The only novel enthusiasm which might reasonably be laid at their desert door was the startling connections drawn by Langton (described below) between artificial life, cellular automata and regions of order and chaos. So how to write a popular book about an institute that embodied more promise than results? Well, what had much of the early Institute's efforts involved? The answer, thanks to Reed, was economics.

This is why no one should read this book in isolation, without further contextualization both in the direction of more formal scientific outlets, and simultaneously, in tandem with rival popularizing outlets like *Discovery* and *Scientific American*, books like *Eudaemonic Pie*, and the Santa Fe Institute's own *Bulletin*. Also indispensable is a broad familiarity with the history of economics, as indicated above. Without such augmentation, statements reported by Waldrop such as the one by Arthur on page 325 that orthodox economists were 'getting antsy' around 1985, or more significantly, his repeated insistence that 'increasing returns economics' is the key to Santa Fe, slip by without any analysis or understanding.

Given that further analysis will lead ultimately to critique, I want to make it plain at the outset that I do believe that something new is going on, that economics is undergoing profound upheaval and deformation, and that *Complexity* is a valuable documentation of the first nascent tremors. Moreover, since I cannot help but be a product of my own Romantic generation, I am sympathetic to the numerous hints that this economics will be holist rather than atomistic, historic rather than atemporal, will stress diversity of actors rather than proliferate little identical clones, will find order as just another aspect of chaos, and will privilege biology rather than physics. But the historian in me whispers: isn't this really another Cowles? Aren't we just retracing the same old paths that have been periodically opened up between the physical and social sciences over the last century or more (Mirowski 1994a)? Are the physicists really lending us a friendly yet disinterested helping hand, hoisting us up into the late twentieth century, or is there more than a little chaos implicit in the dynamics of this intellectual transaction?

THREE BIOGRAPHICAL STUDIES IN COMPLEXITY

> Complexity is almost a theological concept; many people talk about it, but nobody knows what 'it' really is. There is no universal agreement as to what constitutes a complex system . . . . Some use it to signify systems with chaotic dynamics; others refer to cellular automata, disordered many-body systems, neural networks, adaptive algorithms, pattern-forming systems, and so on . . . . On the surface, many appear to have little in common, and many originate in different areas of science . . . . At the

> heart of many of the problems discussed herein is some kind of non-reducibility.
>
> (Stein 1989a: xiii)

Of course, it would be impossible to provide a survey of everything that gets retailed under the rubric of 'complexity'. Waldrop himself sometimes despairs of the task. As one of the main participants at Santa Fe admits, the movement is held together by some vague inclinations – opposing reductionist strategies, stressing intractable unpredictability, a fascination with new developments in computer and cognitive science, and emergent patterns out of evolving structures. But if one really had to put one's finger on it, the overriding mantra would be almost Hegelian: 'Disorder can flow from order, and order can flow from disorder' (Stein 1989a: xiv). Not every participant attests to each and every component doctrine; but a brief survey of three representative scientists will help to convey the scope of this movement. It may also help us to understand what this all portends for economics.

J. Doyne Farmer

Farmer may well end up the most comprehensively covered (in a journalistic sense) physicist of our generation. Contrary to Andy Warhol, some people really do enjoy more than their allotted fifteen minutes of fame. Farmer's early life and exploits were chronicled in the truly entertaining *Eudaemonic Pie*, a history of the long-term attempt to develop a computer system that could beat the odds at Las Vegas roulette tables. His fame subsequently skyrocketed with the appearance of James Gleick's *Chaos*, where Farmer appears as one of the Santa Cruz 'Dynamical Systems Collective'. Now he plays a strong supporting role in Waldrop's *Complexity*. And of late he has been the subject of stories in the *New York Times* and *Discovery* magazine. These sources seem to agree that he is a larger-than-life character – a sort of cross between Gregory Peck, Abbie Hoffman and Henri Poincaré. He is also an extremely successful physicist, until recently a theoretical group leader at the Los Alamos National Laboratories. More to the point, he has some strong convictions about the economy, and little respect for established disciplines.

Both Farmer and another original member of the Dynamical Systems Collective, Norman Packard, seem to have been strongly influenced in their youth by a charismatic teacher named Tom Ingerson. Among other wisdom, Ingerson told them that: 'Money is the key to freedom. There are two ways to make it, capitalism and theft' (Bass 1992: 29f.). What may appear a homely observation to others seems to loom somewhat larger for Farmer, whose many exploits are bent on finding an elusive third option. The Eudaemonic roulette enterprise may have begun as a lark, but it rapidly became a serious research project into the limits of real-time classical mechanics.

Started in 1977, the Santa Cruz Dynamical Systems Collective did not discover or invent chaos theory, but they outshone other pioneers in three respects: making strange attractors palpable and almost commonplace in their ingenious manifestations; drawing connections between attractors in dynamical systems and mathematical themes in computational theory; and making brazen claims for the philosophical significance of their discovered field. Some examples from Farmer:

> On a philosophical level, it struck me as an operational way to define free will, in a way that allowed you to reconcile free will with determinism. The system is deterministic, but you can't say what it's going to do next. At the same time, I'd always felt that the important problems out there in the world had to do with the creation of organization, in life or intelligence. But how do you study that? What biologists were doing seemed so applied and specific; chemists certainly weren't doing it; mathematicians weren't doing it at all, and it was something that physicists just didn't do. I always felt that the spontaneous emergence of self-organization ought to be part of physics.
>
> (Gleick 1987: 251f.)

> I'm of the school of thought that life and organization are inexorable, just as inexorable as the increase in entropy. They just *seem* more fluky because they proceed in fits and starts, and they build on themselves. Life is a reflection of a much more general phenomenon that I'd like to believe is described by some counterpart of the second law of thermodynamics – some law that would describe the tendency of matter to organize itself, and that would predict the general properties of organization we'd expect to see in the universe.
>
> (Waldrop 1992: 288)

Farmer, always the organizer, also kept his hand in what might be called 'pragmatic economics'. Even when the Santa Cruz Collective started getting attention in 1978, and pressures of fame started to undermine the policy of communal publication with communal support, he did not give up on the roulette project. After completing his thesis (entitled 'Order Within Chaos') in 1981 and accepting a job at Los Alamos, there were still reunions of Eudaemonic Enterprises. Rising quickly through the laboratory ranks, he soon grew tired of the burdens of hustling grants and pleasing the bureaucracy. By the early 1980s, Waldrop (1992: 131) reports, both Packard and Farmer were getting 'downright bored with chaos theory'.

Although Farmer was head of the Complex Systems group at Los Alamos, he began moving increasingly into biology. He was responsible for bringing Stuart Kauffman to Los Alamos before the Santa Fe Institute was a gleam in anyone's eye, and initiated a research project with Kauffman and Norman Packard on simulating the evolution of catalysis of polymer chemistry

(Waldrop 1992: 131). Farmer was also responsible for recruiting Langton for Los Alamos in 1985, later becoming his thesis adviser. Indeed, although Waldrop does not say so in so many words, it is hard not to see Farmer as personally responsible for gathering together many of the inspirational actors (as opposed to the Nobel Prize winners) who later constituted the Santa Fe mainstays. And he was not averse to milking the chaos cow to nurture his vision: 'Farmer had no compunction about channeling most of the group's "general-purpose" money toward Langton and the tiny cadre of artificial life researchers, while making his own nonlinear forecasting work and other efforts pay for themselves' (Waldrop 1992: 285). Providing prediction services for physicists or roulette players was all pretty much the same thing – it bought freedom.

Given that many still associate Farmer with strange attractors and nonlinear dynamics, it is important to get some idea of where he thought the programme should be going. The best short statement can be found in his manifesto 'A Rosetta Stone for Connectionists' (in Forrest 1991). It seems Farmer believes that a truly general theory of evolution should be cast in the format of network theory, at least in part due to the fact that prosecuting the analogy with computation would imply direct recourse to connectionist models. Previous chaotic dynamics models, including his own, dealt with a fixed geometrical object in a fixed-phase space – but that was precisely the problem, especially when trying to encompass phenomena such as living organisms. In the newer approach, he insisted,

> Dynamics occurs on as many as three levels, that of the states of the network, the values of the connection strengths, and the architecture of the connections themselves .... To a first approximation a connectionist model is a pair of coupled dynamical systems living on a graph. In some cases the graph itself may also have a dynamics .... The fast scale dynamics, which changes the states of a system, is usually associated with short-term information processing. This is the transition rule. The intermediate scale dynamics changes the *parameters*, and is usually associated with learning .... On the longest time scale, the graph itself may change.
>
> (in Forrest 1991: 154–5, 157)

It seems Farmer felt that these connectionist models would allow for the subsumption of conventional chaotic dynamics within the framework of evolutionary processes and emergent hierarchical orders. The enthusiasm of Farmer for the work of people such as Holland, Kauffman and Langton stemmed from his conviction that their models exemplified the connectionist approach. Moreover, he asserted that both economics and game theory were 'natural areas of application' for such models, in that they also exhibited such phenomena, but were hampered by a relatively narrow conception of dynamical models (Waldrop 1992: 181).

So how did Farmer react to that eminently pragmatic funding operation engineered by his colleagues at Santa Fe – the Reed-inspired initiative into economics? His response was one of the sharpest at the workshop:

> To someone schooled in nonlinear dynamics, economic time series look very far from equilibrium, and the emphasis of economic theories on equilibrium seems rather bizarre. In fact, the use of the word equilibrium in economics appears to be much closer to the notion of attractor as it is used in dynamics rather than any notion of equilibrium used in physics.
>
> (Anderson *et al.* 1988: 101)

But some economists, including Buz Brock and Michele Boldrin, had done extensive work on discerning fractal dimensions in the phase space of economic variates. Farmer, nodding towards that work, rejected it out of hand (Waldrop 1992: 104). He proposed instead using the forecasting techniques that he had been retailing out of Los Alamos for the last few years. The economists, steeped in the efficient markets hypothesis, responded to this suggestion with disdain. Brian Arthur, the first director of Santa Fe's economics programme, flat-out opposed making chaos theory a substantial portion of the research effort (Waldrop 1992: 244f.). Something seemed awry; the figure most representative of the complexity movement was also the least enthusiastic about its extension to economics.

> Meanwhile, says Farmer, it's even less clear whether the edge-of-chaos idea applies to coevolutionary systems. When you get something like an ecosystem or an economy, he says, it's not obvious how concepts like order, chaos and complexity can even be defined very precisely, much less a phase transition between them.
>
> (Waldrop 1992: 294)

Did this imply washing his hands of economics? Here life becomes even better than fiction. In the spring of 1991, Farmer joined forces with Packard and James McGill to form the Prediction Company. The most telling insight into its motivation is provided by the fact that McGill had to struggle to prevent it from being organized along the lines of a collective, just like Eudaemonic Enterprises and the Santa Cruz Collective (Berreby 1993: 82). Farmer told Waldrop:

> Having reached the end of his limited patience with tight budgets and bureaucratic pettifoggery up at Los Alamos, [he] had recently decided that the only sane way to pursue his real research interests was to go off for a few years and to use his forecasting algorithms to make so much money that he would never have to write a grant proposal again. He felt so strongly about it, in fact, that he'd even trimmed off his ponytail to deal with the business types.
>
> (Waldrop 1992: 358)

When the *New York Times* subsequently did a series of articles on converting the military–industrial complex to civilian purposes, it treated Farmer and the Prediction Company as a major success story (Broad 1992). As is frequently the case in the science biz, the science popularizers got the wrong take on the situation. Farmer was not 'converting' anything at Los Alamos to civilian use; he was skilfully selling some clients the trappings of 'scientific' prediction so that he could pursue his real love – artificial life. (Recall the original Cowlesmen!) Or perhaps, usurping God.

> I almost view it as a religious issue, says Farmer.... As a scientist, my deep-down motivation has always been to understand the universe around me. For me as a pantheist, nature is God.... So when we ask questions like how life emerges, and why living systems are the way they are – these are the kind of questions that are really fundamental to understanding what we are and what makes us different from inanimate matter. The more we know about these things, the closer we're going to get to fundamental questions like, 'What is the purpose of life?'. Now, in science we can never attempt to make a frontal assault on questions like that. But by addressing a different question – like, Why is there an inexorable growth of complexity? – we may be able to learn something about life that suggests its purpose, in the same way that Einstein shed light on what space and time are by trying to understand gravity.
>
> (Waldrop 1992: 319)

The significance of this remarkable turn of events is that the embodiment of complexity theory, the king of chaos, has declared war on economists. Waldrop surely misrepresents the state of affairs when he ends his book by hinting that 'complexity' is slowly and rationally transforming economics with all due scientific prudence. Many of the economists associated with Santa Fe have been willing to deride Farmer's new Prediction Company, including John Geanakopolos and Blake LeBaron[3] (Berreby 1993: 82). James Ramsey is quoted as saying: 'A lot of those chaos guys tend to think economists are dumb and don't know anything. But we do have a greater sense of this amorphous mass of economic information.' The complaint, in a not-so-distant echo of Cowles' position in the 'measurement without theory' controversy, is that Farmer and his confreres have no theory, which must be read as insisting that they are not neoclassicals. But this time, the physicists are arrayed against the neoclassicals, rather than with them. Who is right? Turning the arguments of the rational expectations advocates back upon themselves, Farmer retorts: 'If the point is to make money, though, the question does not need to be answered.'

Stuart Kauffman

Waldrop (1992: 102) writes: 'For Kauffman, order was the answer to the mystery of human existence, an explanation for how we could come to exist as living, thinking creatures in a universe that seems to be governed by accident, chaos and blind natural law.' Kauffman, while not nearly so prominent in biology as Farmer is in physics, does however embody the pretentions of Santa Fe better than any other figure interviewed by Waldrop; and his opinions occupy the vast bulk of the book. A Marshall Scholar at Oxford, he was initially a product of the Philosophy, Psychology and Physiology programme, majoring in philosophy. Like so many other avatars of complexity, he then sharply changed direction in his career, opting for medical school. However, during his medical studies Kauffman kept getting distracted by computer simulations of networks, which he felt were indicative of some neglected aspect of genetics. His search for signs of order in random Boolean networks did not endear him to his medical mentors; and were it not for his work catching the eye of Warren McCulloch his intellectual wanderings might never have found their basin of attraction.

McCulloch was one of the progenitors of the McCulloch–Pitts model of the neuron, and a man whose impact on computational and social theory in the mid-twentieth century is just beginning to be understood. Very important to von Neumann's work on automata and computer design, he was also one of the guiding lights of the cybernetics movement (Heims 1991). Towards the end of his life, in the 1980s, McCulloch put Kauffman in touch with the artificial intelligence community at MIT. Kauffman was then able to land a job in theoretical biology. But contrary to the situation in economics, this was no safe haven. 'The people doing math in biology were the lowest of the low,' Kauffman says. 'It was exactly the opposite of the situation in physics or economics, where the theorists are kings' (Waldrop 1992: 128). So during the 1970s, he threw himself into experimental biology, specializing in the *Drosophila melanogaster* fruit fly. Only in 1982 did he resume work on networks and catalysis – with the encouragement of Farmer. It was at this point, Waldrop tells us, that Farmer and Packard were 'getting downright bored with chaos theory'.

It is important for the economist to understand why Kauffman's work was not gaining much recognition in biology. Waldrop does not perform this service for the reader; however, Lewin (1992), another popular book on complexity, helps here. The major reason for biologists looking askance at his networks is that Kauffman takes the position that the neo-Darwinian evolutionary synthesis is flawed. He does not believe that natural selection is the sole (or even dominant) source of biological order, resisting the orthodox notion of the organism as an *ad hoc* assemblage cobbled together from a sequence of accidents. His insistence upon some principle of order inherent in the physical structure of polymer chemistry or the genetic make-up or morphology verges upon both teleology and vitalism, the two bugaboos of Western population genetics; and his model of connections between evolving species smacks of group selection, another heresy in that same tradition. Cap this all off with the fact that instead of proving mathematical theorems Kauffman runs simulations of highly abstract symbolic networks on computers, only to then assert that the regularities he claims to find there have rough counterparts in amino acids or cell typologies or 'species', and one can understand why his work is not regarded as mainstream, even among the harried band of mathematical biologists. As two philosophers put it, 'there is nothing distinctively biological about the properties of complex systems, or in the properties of their components, on which Kauffman draws in delineating these enabling constraints' (Burian and Richardson 1991: 268). In other words, Kauffman acts like another one of those imperious physicists telling biologists about their own business (Ridley 1994).

But these same 'weaknesses' could easily explain the attraction of his thought for economists and physicists. Kauffman was deeply inspired by R.A. Fisher's artifice of a fixed potential fitness surface defined over the genetic possibilities of the organism. He is also aware of the analogy with a potential energy field in physics, and a field of preferences in orthodox economics. His dissatisfaction with this portrayal, and his claim to innovation, is to admit openly that the potential fitness field cannot be defined as a single-valued function of the individual gene; instead, fitness values of one gene are a function of the other genes internal to the organism; and more intractably, the fitness value of a gene internal to organism A is a function of genes in organisms B to Z. Hence any 'fitness landscape' is continually being deformed by pervasive interdependencies. More often than not, fitness landscapes are rendered rugged and seemingly random by such considerations.

Such pervasive non-linearities and irregularities have defeated previous attempts at analytical modelling. How can any purchase be gained upon the problem? Here is where the computer and the preference for simulation enter in. One might also cite the use of game theory by John Maynard Smith, one of Kauffman's mentors. But another important idea, spelled out by Kauffman (1993) is that certain amounts and types of abstract connectedness, be they between catalytic polymers, between genes, between morphological structures, or between organisms, actually turn out to be superior in terms of maximizing fitness outcomes. Kauffman asserts that because the connectedness property is abstracted out of each individual situation, symbolic networks can actually capture many of the relevant characteristics of order displayed by each biological level of structure. He readily draws the parallel to the notion of basins of attractors in chaos theory: while we may not be able to trace the individual trajectory, we may find structures in the phase space of possibilities in which we can recognize statistical or aggregate regularities.

The other major idea, superimposed upon the first, involves the trademark Santa Fe catchphrase 'the edge of chaos'. It would behove readers to be wary here, since semantics is regularly abused by using the term 'chaos' to refer to something other than the phenomenon noted in the previous paragraph. While the terminology of 'chaos theory' has not yet stabilized, it is conventionally used to designate those non-linear deterministic dynamical systems that display some form of dissipation – the paradigm is fluid turbulence. When Kauffman (and Langton who, as we shall shortly see, deserves credit for formalizing the idea) promote the terminology 'edge of chaos', they are using it in a looser, colloquial sense of a region of phase transition between pure randomness and pure stasis. A common intuitive image is the region of phase transition between ice, which is very structured and rigid, and water, which displays the relative randomness of molecular motion. Between the two is a boundary of melting ice and freezing water, with the identity of both constantly shifting and reforming, and the process producing a species of orderly motion.

How does this translate into abstract networks and fitness landscapes? Very briefly, Kauffman suggests that there exists a small set of tuning parameters wherein one can be transported from a generic set of fitness landscapes where very little change (i.e. motion) is going on to a set of landscapes where so much motion occurs that the outcome looks like a random churning of fitness levels. However, at the boundary between these two sets of states, there are regions of the tuning parameters where movements between stasis and randomness produce a special kind of order: there it is more likely that the system can readily *adapt* to environmental changes. Kauffman likes to compare this region to a strange attractor in chaos theory (note well the semantic shift!). From his perspective, order is inherent in the particularities of the region of fitness landscapes, and not due to the process of selection (although selection will initiate motion in fitness landscapes).

Kauffman's 'NK Boolean network' models exemplify his theses. Imagine a string of symbols with different settings at each symbol. The string is Boolean if $\alpha = 2$; say, each entry can only assume the values 0 or 1. Let N be the number of symbols in a string, and K be the number of other symbols in the same string which cooperate in producing a certain fitness outcome.[4] Given that the thrust of this exercise is to analyse regularities in fitness landscapes, it should be stressed that the definition of fitness is the big black box at the heart of his theory, and that the issue is finessed in practice by randomly assigning fitness 'values' to each permutation of symbols (Kauffman 1993: 37–42).

Kauffman's research does not prove theorems about NK Boolean networks. Rather, it involves running numerous simulations of maximization searches over the networks of such strings, and claims to find that there are certain robust regularities for the primary parameters N and K. Briefly, $K = 0$ is supposed to represent a single-peak fitness landscape (the unique optimum of simple neoclassical models). As $K \rightarrow N - 1$, a situation of pervasive interconnectedness, the fitness landscape grows completely uncorrelated; and as $N \rightarrow \infty$ the large number of fitness determinants causes local optima to fall towards mean fitness. Thus the 'ruggedness' of a fitness landscape occurs somewhere between $K = 0$ and K_{max}, an artefact that Kauffman believes has profound implications for search and evolutionary processes. The unconnected single-peak landscape is written off as implausible in a world where genes and organisms interact. However, as the number of parts and their interactions increase, 'the number of conflicting design constraints among the parts increases rapidly. These conflicting constraints imply that optimization can only attain ever poorer compromises' (Kauffman 1993: 53). Hence, maximum fitness can most often be attained on landscapes of near-maximum ruggedness (Kauffman 1993: 108). Taking a large leap from these computer simulations Kauffman speculates about the nature of biological evolution. He believes that there is an inherent teleology to the very structure of fitness, however defined, which imposes certain regularities upon evolution irrespective of the random and non-teleological character of natural selection.

In other words, fitness landscapes evolve along with the organisms, but only within certain bounds of connectivity, which restricts the achievable range of optimality.

> In coevolution, organisms adapt under natural selection via *metadynamics* where each organism myopically alters the structure of its fitness landscape and the extent to which that landscape is deformed by the adaptive moves of other organisms, such that as if by an invisible hand, the entire ecosystem coevolves to a poised state at the edge of chaos.
>
> (Kauffman 1993: 261)

The 'invisible hand' language should perk up the economists; but it is now also possible to see that Kauffman's work fits rather nicely into Farmer's connectionist programme. Kauffman (1993: 219) is not afraid to use the metaphor of computation for his vision of evolution, as indeed he has done little more than write a computer programme and then interpret it as a meta-model for biological evolution. There are the obvious graph-theoretic aspects, as well as a dynamics defined on the network; further, the network itself also has an implicit induced dynamics. While Kauffman (1993: 202) tends to speak rather loosely of basins of attractors, his work transcends conventional chaotic dynamics – for instance, there is no attempt to write down a Hamiltonian for the process.

This is just one more instance in which Santa Fe scientists seem incapable of being very precise about the meaning of 'complexity'. What Kauffman (1993: 232) seems to mean when claiming that 'Living systems exist in the solid regime near the edge of chaos, and natural selection achieves and sustains such a poised state' is roughly this: unique maxima of objective functions are structurally unlikely, and yet systems with excessively complicated determinants have objective functions that are so 'spread out' that maxima are few and far between and relatively unprepossessing.[5] Hence, only when the determinants are few (N small) and the connections between determinants limited (K small but non-zero) do we find a landscape of multiple optima where a few magnificent peaks are scattered about and there is something valuable for natural selection to locate. This, of course, violates the central dogma of the neo-Darwinian synthesis since Weissman that the environment does not feed back directly onto the genotype, or vice versa. Kauffman violates this quarantine because, like so many others at Santa Fe, he wants to play God and theorize about the origins of life.

Our interest, however, is not how happily Kauffman gets along with biologists, but rather his relationship to economists; and here there is a valuable lesson. Kauffman wants to tell a 'spontaneous order' story, one of Western culture's favourite bedtime tales, and he is not afraid to cite the grandaddy of all economic fables – 'Adam Smith's "invisible hand", slightly reworked' (Kauffman 1993: 263; also Waldrop 1992: 317). But the persistent problem with such bedtime stories is that we heard them so very long ago, and rarely feel that we must reread them in order to recall the plot. In most of *Origins of Order* Kauffman uses economic metaphors in much the same way as did his mentor John Maynard Smith – to lend legitimacy and credibility to his enterprise. There is, of course, no maximization, selection, evolution or Boolean networks in *The Wealth of Nations*; but the invocation of Smith would have been relatively harmless had Kauffman not ended up at the Santa Fe Institute. It is here that our earlier narrative of the place of economists at Santa Fe begins to bite.

According to Waldrop, Kauffman hit it off famously with Brian Arthur. The similarities of fitness landscapes to economists' objective functions should have been patently obvious, and Arthur wanted to introduce an evolutionary component into economics. However, Kauffman was not impressed with economists' level of discourse and, in particular, their fascination with increasing returns. 'I had a hard time understanding why this was new.... Biologists have been dealing with positive feedbacks for years.... Within minutes Kauffman was off, explaining to Arthur why the process of technological change is exactly like the origin of life' (Waldrop 1992: 118, 120). Recalling that one main purpose of the early Santa Fe Institute was to present John Reed with some novel high-tech economics, Kauffman was convinced to contribute to the initial September 1987 economics conference.

The transfer of analogy to economics would involve describing a form of spontaneous endogenous order arising in an economic web or network; but what sort of network should it be? Under the influence of Arthur, Kauffman posited a vaguely physicalist web:

> an economy is a web of transformation of products and services among economic agents. Over time, technological evolution generates new products and services which must mesh together 'coherently' to jointly fulfill a set of 'needed' tasks. It is this web of needed tasks which affords economic opportunity to agents to sell, hence earn a living.... The web

> transforms over time, driven by technological advances and economic opportunity.
>
> (Anderson *et al*. 1988: 126)

But as we have observed, Kauffman remained satisfied with an extremely loose coupling between his NK Boolean networks and any palpable biological phenomenon, so it would only be expected that the relationship to this graph of vague 'needs' in the economic sphere would be comparable. 'Think of each use as radiating need arrows, meaning that the use of the good requires the good or service specified at the termination of the arrow' (Kauffman 1993: 139).

The economists present, needless to say, did not think much of this species of 'need'. They were all neoclassical and were convinced that their theory of preferences was a superior mode of expressing such concepts. Furthermore, they were content that their production functions captured the economic essence of technology. Even worse if you follow the logic of the analogy, Kauffman was heading toward a teleology of the complexity of 'needs' as part of a coevolutionary process with the physical technology. In the subsequent work group, economists preferred to discuss their overlapping generations and prisoner's dilemma models, something that they felt was much more scientific. Arrow warily admitted that Kauffman's work was 'a new perspective not yet absorbed by economists' (Kauffman 1993: 280), but then tried to compare it to recent rational expectations models of learning.

This run-in with economists had the curious consequence of inducing Kauffman to include a section on economics in chapter 10 of *Origins of Order*. Going on the offensive, he attacks general equilibrium models, suggesting that his own models may indicate that markets must be incomplete, that agents must logically be boundedly rational, and that markets may not clear. 'Rather, boundedly rational agents may achieve the edge of chaos, where markets come close to clearing' (Kauffman 1993: 399). Unfortunately, such statements are not well grounded in the text because the nature of the economic webs or networks is left unclear, and worse, there are no explicit prices anywhere to be seen. After renouncing both rational expectations and Nash equilibria (Kauffman 1993: 402), it is not clear where the fitness landscapes are supposed to come from, much less what sort of dynamics might be superimposed upon them. A historian of economics (such as those found in Mirowski 1994a) cannot help but feel a twinge of embarrassment when Kauffman (1993: 402) writes 'our study of the proper marriage of self-organization and selection would enlist Charles Darwin and Adam Smith to tell us who and how we are in the nonequilibrium world we mutually create and transform'. Normally, to have a draft one needs at a minimum an acquaintance with the draftees and an operational form of government.

Chris Langton

Including Chris Langton in our biographical sketches would seem to entertain a paradox. Of our three protagonists he has evinced the least interest (approaching zero) in economics, but it appears that his construction of complexity is having the greatest impact upon the work of economists. This has occurred because Langton has become the figurehead for the burgeoning area of research known as 'artificial life' (AL). But it is worthwhile focusing upon his own innovations in order to gain some perspective on how the programme is being appropriated by some economists.

Langton will probably be regarded in the future as one of the primary heirs to the intellectual legacy of John von Neumann. It is already the case that von Neumann occupies a hallowed place in the history of economic thought – first as innovator of the 'expanding economy' model with its use of fixed-point theorems to prove the existence of general equilibrium, and second as the inventor of game theory (Mirowski 1992; Leonard 1995). But neither of these innovations reflect the concerns of von Neumann in the last decade of his life – the elaboration of the theory of the computer and his work on self-reproducing automata. In particular, it is often forgotten that von Neumann formalized the logic of a biologically replicating system *before* the discovery of the structure of DNA (Waldrop 1992: 218f.), which validated his speculations. The reason that Langton is heir apparent is that he is intent upon distilling out the 'logic of evolution' to complement von Neumann's (1966) original insight.

Von Neumann realized that replication could be viewed as a problem of computation, especially given his appreciation of the significance of Turing's computability theorems (Epstein and Carnielli 1989). Langton wants to carry this further, examining the relationship between computation and evolution. Why should natural selection be able to find genotypes with specific phenotypical traits, especially when one allows that 'the fitness function, the set of criteria that determines whether an organism is "fit" in its environment, should itself be an emergent property of the system' (Langton 1989: 38)? Here Langton differs profoundly from fellow AL travellers like John Holland or John Koza, who are concerned with using various evolutionary concepts and techniques to solve problems of computation in which the fitness function is externally given.[6]

Langton has had a very chequered career, a fact amply documented in Waldrop and Levy. He pursued a doctorate in computer science at the University of Michigan with John Holland and von Neumann's late collaborator Arthur Burks, and he was brought to the Santa Fe Institute by (who else?) Doyne Farmer. In this period, he decided that the best way to attack his rather broad questions was through a relatively narrow area of computer science – cellular automata (CA). This was an inspired choice because narrowness of scope in practice allows greater precision of generalization.

CA are sometimes defined as a regular lattice of finite automata used to formalize the components of self-reproduction, but most people are more familiar with CA through John Horton Conway's 'Game of Life' (Levy 1992: ch. 3). Imagine a virtual chessboard, where each square is either 'dead' or 'alive'. Each square has eight possible neighbours in its immediate vicinity. The rules are simple. If a square is alive it will survive into the 'next generation' if there are either two or three neighbours also alive. It will die if there are fewer than two or more than three live neighbours. Once dead, a square stays dead unless exactly three of its eight neighbours are alive, in which case it experiences 'rebirth' in the next generation. The Game of Life is thus a two-dimensional, eight-state finite cellular automaton.

That's all there is to it. It is so simple that cheap versions are available for the PC. Yet Conway had bigger ambitions for this game than something to fritter away CPU time and make pretty patterns. He wondered whether a universal Turing machine could be embedded in it; in other words, would the patterns produced display enough structure to emulate the main components of an abstract computer, like logic gates, a counter, a clock and memory. By the early 1970s, with some effort, the Game of Life was indeed shown to be a universal Turing machine. It is this fascinating emergent property – universal computation out of such risibly simple and local rules – that caught the attention of Langton and others. Nevertheless, few scientists saw the use of such automata in the early 1980s besides Langton, E.F. Codd, Steven Wolfram and a few computer enthusiasts.

Prior to Michigan, Langton had attempted some computer simulations of actual incidents of natural selection, but 'was unhappy with the experiment. The mechanism he had used was ultimately dependent upon the fitness criterion that he artificially imposed upon the simulation. It was not realistic, not open ended, like real evolution' (Levy 1992: 97). At Michigan, Langton came to recast the problem in the idiom of CA:

> In living systems, a dynamics of information has gained control over the dynamics of energy, which determines the behavior of non-living systems .... Under what conditions can we expect a complex dynamics of information to emerge spontaneously and to come to dominate the behavior of a C[ellular] A[utomaton]?
>
> (Langton, Taylor, Farmer and Rasmussen 1992: 41–3)

Langton's point of departure was a taxonomy of the qualitative dynamic behaviour of CAs developed by Stephen Wolfram (Levy 1992: 66–74; Langton *et al.* 1992: 46f.; Waldrop 1992: 225–35). Wolfram noted that these classes roughly corresponded to classes of motion found in conventional dynamic systems, as shown in Table 2.2.

In something like the Game of Life, Class I would correspond to a mass die-off, II would be a circle winking off and on, III would be seemingly stochastic bedlam, and IV would correspond to the 'glider guns', the only class that would support the existence of universal computation. Langton's strategy was to

Table 2.2 CA behaviour and dynamic systems

Class	*CA behaviour*	*Dynamic systems*
I	Fixed homogeneous state	Limit point
II	Simple periodic structures	Limit cycles
III	Chaotic aperiodic patterns	Strange attractors, chaos
IV	Complex localized structure	**No direct analog**

parameterize the CAs and then ask if any simple regularities govern the transition from one class to another. Using mainly brute force methods Langton did indeed find such regularities. Define the following parameter λ for any cellular automaton with K states and N neighbours. Privilege one state as 'quiescent' and determine the n_q possible modes of transition to this state out of the K^N possible neighbouring states. Then let

$$\lambda = (K^N - n_q)/K^N.$$

This, of course, is just the proportion of states out of the total possible that do *not* lead to quiescence; as a proportion, λ ranges from zero to one. Langton then claimed to have found that transitions between classes of dynamic behaviour were a simple function of λ. As one altered the 'rules' so that λ moved from zero to one, the progression through the spectrum of dynamic behaviours was I→II→IV→III. Further, this behaviour seemed to mimic the behaviour of simple tent maps with a single forcing parameter in the 'transition to chaos' (Ruelle 1991: ch. 11; Bausor in Mirowski 1994a). The difference, notably, was that there was (as yet) no analogue in conventional dynamics for state IV, the transitional state, the state that supported universal computation. Rather than view this as a drawback, Langton drew all sorts of analogies from the regularities of CAs to other kinds of phenomena. In rational mechanics he posited a transition from 'order' through 'complexity' to 'chaos'; in solid-state physics he regarded the intermediate region as similar to the phase transition between solid and liquid; in computation theory he regarded the sequence of classes as halting → 'undecidable' → non-halting; and in the most venturesome flight of imagination, he supposed life (and not just the Game) was poised somehow between static matter and noisy stochastic matter. Another way of thinking about this is to entertain the possibility that most physical phenomena are non-computable, but that somehow organisms have found an opportune perch where computation can actually happen, so that 'It is quite likely that [natural selection] is the *only* efficient general procedure that could find [genotypes] with specific [phenotypical] traits' (Langton 1989: 25). Finally, here is a possible answer to the question of how life could come to exist in a basically random world. One can easily imagine how Doyne Farmer must have regarded this as broad-scale ratification for his connectionist programme – a dynamics defined on a lattice which itself might display an induced emergent dynamics.

One should not claim too much for these findings, a weakness in both the

Waldrop and Levy volumes. First, they are heavily dependent upon tendentious analogies between CAs and other phenomena. They are certainly suggestive; but the hard work of elaborating the metaphor in various empirical fields has not yet happened. Second, there is some semantic slippage here: 'complexity' now means something altogether different to what it meant in the writings of the other denizens of Santa Fe. It is definitely *not* the standard meaning of the Kolmogorov definition of randomness (Chaitin 1987) as Langton and his colleagues (1992: 69) readily admit. Third, and perhaps most troublesome, the change in regimes of CAs does not *exactly* correlate with the λ parameter: 'it is hard to determine whether or not one is precisely at a critical point when working with finite systems. But . . . in most of the experiments on CAs . . . the regime exhibiting the most complex dynamics appears to be just slightly below (the ordered side) of the critical transition itself' (Langton *et al.* 1992: 83). One might think that problems of computability even come to haunt research about computability, in suitably self-referential fashion.

In coming to Santa Fe, Langton did not simply present his results and wait for the world to notice; he became the prime advocate for AL. He convened the first AL conference at Santa Fe in 1987, roughly contemporaneous with the first economics workshop, and has run two additional AL conferences since. He has become a tireless advocate of AL, and explained how life could be thought to reside in a computer.

> AL studies natural life by attempting to capture the behavioral essence of the constituent components of living systems, and endowing a collection of artificial components with similar behavioral repertoires . . . . There is no single program that directs the other programs . . . . There are no rules in the system that dictate global behavior. Any behavior at levels higher than the individual program is therefore emergent.
>
> (Langton 1989: 3)

The very question of the definition of life is being raised once again with a vengeance, now that there are entities like computer viruses that appear to have slipped the control of man (Spafford in Langton *et al.* 1992). To his credit, Langton has been at the forefront of raising the political and moral questions about creating something that will pass for being alive (Levy 1992: ch. 10). To most people, the idea of a computer programme being alive sounds absolutely batty; but like all revolutionary developments, this project opens up the imprecise ideas of life and computation to unprecedented scrutiny and reconceptualization.

At a perhaps less lofty level, Langton has also endowed a large number of participants at Santa Fe with the alluring image of an entire economy captured in the CPU of a computer. This is not the first time that we have had such images – that dates back to Lawrence Klein's model of the US economy unveiled at the Cowles Commission in the 1940s (Epstein 1987: 104–10). But Langton's effect has been more subtle; he and his AL confreres have given greater credibility to the idea that computer simulation is a legitimate tool for discussing the evolution of something so complex as an economy (Lane 1993; Palmer *et al.* 1994). While this has become accepted wisdom at Santa Fe, no one has yet noticed that those engaged there in growing little toy economies seem to have given wide berth to the lessons that Kauffman and Langton draw from their own work. In particular, no one seems to have achieved any analogous results concerning the emergent computational character of trade, nor any evolutionary regularities on a meta-level comparable to Langton's λ-result. Indeed, the historical accident of Arrow packing the Santa Fe economics programme with orthodox neoclassicals has resulted in the major players spending most of their time responding to perceived drawbacks in the rational expectations school of macroeconomics, rather than innovating computational themes.

SOME LESSONS FOR POLITICAL ECONOMY IN THE TWENTY-FIRST CENTURY

The saga of Santa Fe has just begun to be written; and one must acknowledge the possibility that with the wisdom of hindsight it may all be a flash in the pan. Yet, however critical the above survey may seem, I do not believe that this will be the case. Instead, I harbour the conviction that the Romantic trend, mentioned at the beginning of this chapter, is alive and well at Santa Fe, and is destined to have lasting consequences for economics. But the more immediate question is what are the particular lessons and implications of the Santa Fe Institute for those economists less than enamoured with neoclassical orthodoxy? I shall list some answers to this question in cursory fashion, in the hope of generating further reflection on these issues now, rather than fifty years after the fact.

1 It is a mistake to believe that the origin of neoclassical economics in nineteenth-century physics (Mirowski 1989a) is irrelevant for events in the twentieth century. The transfer of metaphor and epistemic authority from physics to economics is unremitting and inexorable. Running the gamut from those innocent of the history of their discipline, like Hal Varian and Herbert Gintis, to those blessed with appreciable historiographic sophistication, like Ingrao and Israel, those who disparage the importance of physics for economics have not been looking in the right places. Arrow is right; Santa Fe is the Cowles of the 1990s.
2 Methodologists looking for a dependable 'scientific method' are also barking up the wrong tree. Cross-fertilization among different disciplines, cultural images of change and growth and chaos, and tools such as the personal computer and computational theory, all jumbled together, define what is intellectually exciting for the self-identified scientist in the late twentieth century.

3 Since 'complexity' has no fixed or well-defined meaning, it may seem presumptuous to berate economists for missing the boat. Nevertheless, a case can be made that those most closely associated with economics at Santa Fe so far (Brian Arthur, Thomas Sargent and Blake LeBaron) do not adequately represent the most innovative or advanced ideas found at Santa Fe in areas such as AL or emergent computation (Weagle 1995; Mirowski 1995b; Sent 1994). This, in turn, is most likely a function of their prior orthodox credentials in combination with the curious history of the Santa Fe Institute.

4 The physical scientists at Santa Fe generally regard chaos theory, by which is usually meant non-linear dynamics in isolation, as uninteresting or a dead end. They have also demoted the idea of optimization over a fixed domain or fitness surface to an elephant's graveyard of old-fashioned nineteenth-century science. Economists, by contrast, still think this kind of optimization and dynamics is the heart and soul of good science (Mirowski 1995b).

5 Economists critical of orthodoxy frequently come to the doctrines they aim to criticize thirty to fifty years too late. At Santa Fe we can observe a version of an apologetics for the twenty first century in its nascent format: it is no accident that most of our protagonists make reference to the 'invisible hand' and to Hayek. But it is important to realize that no physical metaphor has a necessary political or economic content: that is negotiated in tandem with the development of the doctrine in economics. The place to intervene early in the process is here and now; not after the novel formalisms have been ensconced in graduate training as the next Great White Hope.[7]

NOTES

1 Another book on the Santa Fe Institute (Lewin 1992) is considerably inferior, especially when the author adopts the *People Magazine* style of pretending he is good buddies with all the scientists.

2 The lack of an historically transcendent notion of quantitative error is discussed in Mirowski (1994b: 1995a).

3 Both later served as directors of the Sante Fe economics programme.

4 The similarities of the NK Boolean network to the spin-glass model in solid-state physics are explicitly acknowledged in Kauffman (1993: 43); less explicit is the contribution that this similarity made to gaining Nobelist Philip Anderson's support at Santa Fe. Anderson's desire to see spin glasses elsewhere (like the economy) is evident in Anderson *et al.* (1988).

5 I find this last assertion unpersuasive. There are no mathematics to back it up, only an idiosyncratic definition of 'chaos'. 'I shall call such attractors, whose [cycle] length increases exponentially as N increases, *chaotic*. This does not mean that the flow on the attractors is divergent' (Kauffman 1993: 194).

6 Holland and Koza participated more directly in the economics programme at Santa Fe (see Koza 1992: ch. 10; Palmer, Arthur, Holland, LeBaron and Tayler 1994; Weagle 1995; Sent 1994).

7 I would like to thank Steven Pressman, Matt Weagle and the participants of Economics 518 at Notre Dame for giving me the opportunity to clarify some of these issues.

REFERENCES

Anderson, P., Arrow, K. and Pines, D. (eds) (1988) *The Economy as an Evolving Complex System*, Reading: Addison-Wesley.

Bass, T. (1992) *The Eudaemonic Pie*, New York: Penguin.

Berreby, D. (1993) 'Chaos Hits Wall Street', *Discover* March: 76–84.

Broad, W. (1992) 'Defining the New Plowshares Those Old Swords Will Make', *New York Times* 22 February: A1, A12.

Brush, S. (1978) *The Temperature of History*, New York: Burt Franklin.

Burian, R. and Richardson, R. (1991) 'Form and Order in Evolutionary Biology', *PSA 1990*, Vol. II, East Lansing, Mich.: PSA.

Chaitin, G. (1987) *Algorithmic Complexity Theory*, New York: Cambridge University Press.

Christ, C. (1994) 'The Cowles Commission's Contributions to Econometrics at Chicago, 1939–1955', *Journal of Economic Literature* 32,1: 30–59.

Epstein, R. (1987) *A History of Econometrics*, Amsterdam: North Holland.

Epstein, R. and Carnielli, W. (1989) *Computability, Computable Functions, Logic and the Foundations of Mathematics*, Belmont, Calif.: Wadsworth.

Forman, P. (1971) 'Weimar Culture, Causality and Quantum Theory', *Historical Studies in the Physical Sciences* 3: 1–116.

Forrest, S. (ed.) (1991) *Emergent Computation*, Cambridge, Mass.: MIT Press.

Gell-Mann, M. (1992) 'Nature Conformable to Herself', *Bulletin of the Santa Fe Institute* 7: 7–10.

Gleick, J. (1987) *Chaos*, New York: Viking.

Heims, S. (1991) *The Cybernetics Group*, Cambridge, Mass.: MIT Press.

Ingrao, B. and Israel, G. (1990) *The Invisible Hand: Economic Equilibrium in the History of Science*, Cambridge, Mass.: MIT Press.

Kauffman, S. (1993) *The Origins of Order*, New York: Oxford University Press.

Koza, J. (1992) *Genetic Programming*, Cambridge, Mass.: MIT Press.

Lane, D. (1993) 'Artificial Worlds and Economics, pts. I & II' *Journal of Evolutionary Economics* 3: 89–107.

Langton, C. (ed.) (1989) *Artificial Life I*, Redwood City: Addison-Wesley.

Langton, C., Taylor, C., Farmer, J. and Rasmussen, S. (1992) *Artificial Life II*, Redwood City: Addison-Wesley.

Leonard, R.J. (1995) 'From Parlor Games to Social Science: von Neumann, Morgenstern and the Creation of Game Theory 1928–1944' *Journal of Economic Literature*, 33,2: 730–61.

Levy, S. (1992) *Artificial Life*, New York: Vintage.

Lewin, R. (1992) *Complexity: Life at the Edge of Chaos*, New York: Macmillan.

Mirowski, P. (1989a) *More Heat than Light*, New York: Cambridge University Press.

—— (1989b) 'The Measurement without Theory Controversy', *Economies et sociétés* 23,6: 65–87.

—— (1991) 'The How, the When and the Why of Mathematical Expression in the History of Economics', *Journal of Economic Perspectives* 5: 148–58.

—— (1992) 'What Were von Neumann and Morgenstern Trying to Accomplish?', in E.R. Weintraub (ed.) *Toward a History of Game Theory*, Durham: Duke University Press.

—— (1993a) 'What Could Rigor Mean in Mathematical Economics?', *History of Economics Review*, 30: 41–60.
—— (1993b) 'The Goalkeeper's Anxiety at the Penalty Kick', in Neil de Marchi (ed.) *Unnatural Economics*, Durham: Duke University Press.
—— (ed.) (1994a) *Natural Images in Economics: Markets Read in Tooth and Claw*, New York: Cambridge University Press.
—— (1994b) 'A Visible Hand in the Marketplace of Ideas', *Science in Context* 7: 563–89.
—— (1995a) 'Civilization and its Discounts', *Dialogue*, 34: 541–59.
—— (1995b) 'Mandelbrot's Economics after a Quarter Century', *Factals* 3: 581–600.
Palmer, R., Arthur, W., Holland, J., LeBaron, B. and Tayler, P. (1994) 'Artificial Economic Life: A Simple Model of the Stockmarket', *Physica D* 75: 264–74.
Prigogine, I. and Stengers, I. (1984) *Order Out of Chaos*, New York: Bantam.
Ridley, M. (1994) 'Review of Kauffman's *Origins of Order*', *Times Literary Supplement 11 March: 31.*
Ruelle, D. (1991) *Chance and Chaos*, Princeton: Princeton University Press.
Sent, E. (1994) 'Resisting Sargent', unpublished PhD thesis, Stanford University.
Shapin, S. and Schaffer, S. (1985) *Leviathan and the Air Pump*, Princeton: Princeton University Press.
Spradley, J. (1989) 'Historical Parallels in Science and Culture', *American Journal of Physics* 57: 252–8.
Stein, D. (ed.) (1989a) *Lectures in the Sciences of Complexity*, Reading: Addison-Wesley.
Stein, D. (1989b) 'Spin Glasses', *Scientific American* 261,1: 52–9.
von Neumann, J. (1966) *Theory of Self-Reproducing Automata*, Urbana: University of Illinois Press.
Waldrop, M. (1992) *Complexity*, New York: Simon & Schuster.
Weagle, M. (1995) 'Innoculating Neoclassicism against the Genetic Algorithm', University of Notre Dame Economics Department, Discussion Paper.
Weintraub, E.R. and Mirowski, P. (1994) 'The Pure and the Applied: Bourbakism Comes to Mathematical Economics', *Science in Context* 7: 245–72.
Wise, M.N. (1993) 'Mediations', in P. Horwich (ed.) *World Changes*, Cambridge, Mass.: MIT Press.

Part II

SEMINAL FIGURES IN POLITICAL ECONOMY

3

SHACKLE, ENTREPRENEURSHIP AND THE THEORY OF THE FIRM

Peter E. Earl

George Shackle occupies a special place in the minds of those economists associated with Malvern. He presented a paper at the first Malvern conference (Shackle 1989) and attended several subsequent conferences. Malvern participants have been influenced by Shackle's work on Keynes, time, expectations and uncertainty; and several contributed to the *Review of Political Economy* special issue (5,2, April 1993) or the volume edited by Boehm, Frowen and Pheby (1996) in his memory.

This chapter is concerned with one aspect of Shackle's work that has received surprisingly little attention – his views on entrepreneurship and the economics of the firm. Shackle's contribution here turns out to be decidedly enigmatic, for while he has influenced many modern-day researchers in the area of entrepreneurship (particularly those close to the Austrian school), he missed many opportunities to integrate his ideas with the work of others.

In the course of uncovering opportunities that he took up or missed I aim to contribute to this process of integration. First I examine Shackle's most spectacular failure in this area, his 1970 textbook on the theory of the firm. In the second section I explore potential linkages between Shackle and Coase, while in the third section I contrast the attention that Shackle gave to Cantillon's work with his tendency to ignore Schumpeter. The fourth section examines the similarities between Shackle's view of business enterprise and the 'resource-based' view of the firm. The fifth section pulls together threads from the preceding sections, and questions the wisdom of writing about entrepreneurship without simultaneously focusing on internalization and management of activities, issues raised by Coase. The sixth section, which is followed by a concluding discussion, examines some possible reasons that Shackle failed to reach similar conclusions.

SHACKLE'S MISSED OPPORTUNITY

Shackle was given the opportunity to present his perspective on firms in the first Allen & Unwin 'Studies in Economics' textbook. This series was edited by Charles Carter, who had been a sympathetic but critical reviewer of Shackle's contributions to the theory of choice under uncertainty (see the papers by Carter in Earl 1988). The resulting book sounds excitingly different and relevant, even a quarter century later:

> Production is a complex system of inter-necessary activities, such that the existence of each activity is necessary to that of the system as a whole, which itself ensures the continuance of each individual activity composing it. In such a system resources must be committed to specific technological purposes long in advance of the ultimate sale of goods to the consumer, or durable equipment to the investing businessman. The problems of such a system rest on the durability of the instruments it uses. These are so complex, sensitive and powerful that their huge expense can only be recouped if they can be used for many years. Yet when the decision is taken to invest in them, those years of use are in the future and its conditioning circumstances are unobservable and unknown.
>
> The firm is the essential institutional means, in Western economies, of confronting this problem of uncertainty. Professor Shackle's book is centrally concerned with the nature and mode of the firm as a means of policy formation in the face of uncertainty. It includes also an explanation of the classic maximizing problems in the *absence* of uncertainty, which form the subject-matter of the traditional theory of the firm.
>
> (Shackle 1970: back jacket)

The book is certainly different from standard texts, but it offers only selective coverage of pre-1970 contributions to the theory of the firm that highlighted problems of complexity and uncertainty. Interconnectedness is addressed with reference to Leontief matrices, and the marginalist optimizing analysis is precise and lucid, as is Shackle's introduction to discounted cash-flow analysis. However, the analysis of uncertainty is almost exclusively drawn from Shackle's own potential surprise theory of choice, and there is little on interdependent decision-making.

Given the existing literature at the time, this is an extraordinarily narrow examination of the relationship between uncertainty and business decision-making. Shackle neglected the work of the Carnegie school (Simon 1957; Cyert and March 1963) on using rule-based procedures for coping with uncertainty and complexity. He employed neither the neo-Marshallian analyses of market behaviour and firm growth offered by Andrews (1964) and Penrose (1959), nor Richardson's (1960) work on the significance of market imperfections for helping decision-makers cope with uncertainty and interdependence. These omissions are indeed odd, although they were by no means part of the established wisdom in the economics of the firm. But Shackle had far less excuse than other economists for ignoring such works: he knew Andrews well (both had worked as researchers under Phelps-Brown in Oxford during the late 1930s) and his review of Simon (Shackle 1959) appeared in the same volume of the *Economic Journal* in which Richardson (1959) published his subversive paper on expectations and interdependent decision-making.

Connections between these works and the work of Shackle had already been recognized by Don Lamberton who, with Andrews as a mentor, was working on his doctorate at Oxford around the time that many of these new contributions appeared. Lamberton met Shackle, who was visiting Oxford, over an evening dinner before a student seminar at Nuffield College in 1959; thus began an intermittent flow of correspondence that continued through the rest of Shackle's lifetime. After returning to his native Australia in 1960, Lamberton developed and taught a course based around evolutionary and information-based approaches to the firm, and explored some linkages in his (1965) monograph on profits (which Shackle recommended to Blackwell for publication). However, the most obvious indication of linkages that Shackle could have explored materialized in the now-classic monograph written by Loasby (1976), himself a pupil of Charles Carter. It was many years before textbooks began to appear that offered what Shackle had merely promised (Ricketts 1987; Earl 1995).

At the time that Shackle's textbook appeared, he was not castigated for failing to link his own work with recent knowledge-related contributions to the theory of the firm. Reviewing the book in the *Economic Journal*, Devletoglou (1973) criticized Shackle for not exploring the microfoundations of macroeconomics. However, he seemed inclined to support Shackle's view that a theory of the firm should focus on the problem of doing business calculations in the face of uncertainty and on the role of the entrepreneur.

> If uncertainty were entirely absent, and every individual in perfect knowledge of the situation, there would clearly be no occasion for anything in the nature of responsible management or control of production activity. Even marketing transactions in any realistic sense would not be necessary, and the flow of raw materials and productive services to the consumer would be entirely automatic.
>
> ... the problem of forecasting becomes a significant part of the organisation of the firm – with responsibility for such forecasting and organisation centering on a unique class of producers, i.e., the entrepreneurs.
>
> (Devletoglou 1973: 545–6)

These remarks should be kept in mind when reading the next section, which relates Shackle's vision to the earlier work by Coase (1937) on the nature of the firm.

SHACKLE, MONEY AND COASE

In his writings on macroeconomics Shackle gave considerable attention to money as an institution that facilitates coping with an open-ended choice environment. A persistent theme in this work is that investment spending can dry up if those who make finance available, or those who might undertake capital spending, lose their nerve and decide to avoid commitment. In the event that pessimistic expectations turn out to be justified, assets purchased today may be cheaper tomorrow. When the future can go in several directions, each of which carries different implications, decision-makers will wait and see by holding liquid assets.

Shackle's view of liquidity (1988: 236–7) brings together uncertainty and, in the jargon of modern industrial economics, 'asset-specificity'. General-purpose metal-machining equipment is liquid compared with the highly specialized tooling that Henry Ford's engineers developed for producing the Model-T car, but it is vulnerable compared with money, for circumstances may lead customers away from metal-based products towards ceramics or plastics. By keeping liquid, decision-makers sacrifice opportunities to achieve higher earnings streams; but on the other hand they reduce the risks of capital loss.

Such perspectives on liquidity, which focus on the possibility of surprising discontinuities in the unfolding of economic events causing changes in the market values of particular assets (what Shackle 1974 called 'kaleidic changes'), are independent of the other key element in theories of money – transaction costs. Shackle never uses transaction cost terminology; but it is clear that his theory of liquidity embraces their role, and that he saw costs from using markets as part of the problem of uncertainty. In speaking of a preference for liquidity where people have received income, and where discontinuities and carrying costs are not problematic, he writes of

> the trouble of deciding what to buy, of finding suitable specimens of it, and the prospective trouble of finding for these specimens a buyer when some consumption goods shall eventually be needed. The key word in this sentence is 'finding'. *To find* has a meaning inseparably connected with another, that of *not knowing*. The clue to the meaning and nature of liquidity lies in its avoidance of the trouble arising from not knowing.
>
> (Shackle 1972: 215)

Even without fears of kaleidic changes in long-term relative values, transaction costs militate against holding most physical assets as stores of value. The difficulty in disposing of assets may be expected to increase with their specificity and this is a key reason that an equity shareholding in a company, which is not attached to ownership of any particular item legally owned by that company, will seem relatively liquid in normal times. One can conceive patterns of corporate ownership where shareholders actually owned particular assets and rented them out to firms or received profit dividends in proportion to the fraction of the firm's total assets that they owned, but the transactional barriers to such arrangements are obvious.

Given Shackle's analysis of the role of money, along with his emphasis on uncertainty and, implicitly, transaction costs, it would have been appropriate for him to discuss Coase on the firm in his famous (1967) examination of the development of economic theory from 1926 to 1939 and to develop Coase's ideas in his 1970 text.

Coase (1937) portrays firms as institutions in which resource owners provide services on the basis of loosely specified contracts, with the nature of the services decided by managers as events unfold. Where using markets seems too costly for dealing with changing circumstances, managers decide and direct firm operations. There would be no need to hire managers, and assume the risks that go with contractual ambiguities, if comprehensive contingent claims contracts could easily be devised and implemented along the lines imagined in Arrow–Debreu general equilibrium models. But such contracts cannot be devised in a complex universe where surprise remains a possibility, and where novel products and production processes often arise. Likewise, there would be no need for managers if activities could be arranged seamlessly by a series of short-term contracts without parties having to stop what they were doing in order to negotiate new deals or to sign extensions of contracts that had just expired.

Open-endedness is the characteristic that particularly stands out when we view firms and money as institutional devices for reducing uncertainty. Liquidity provides a freedom to manoeuvre that highly specific assets do not have and, as Foss (1994: 47) notes, it is the flexibility of the firm as a contracting system that forms part of its rationale. For example, it is the flexibility of employment contracts that enables transaction costs to be saved as business conditions change. Unfortunately, Shackle never drew the connection, and he made no reference to Coase's article.

The fact that firms and money would both have no role in the zero transaction cost, closed-choice world of general equilibrium theory did not go unnoticed in Shackle's lifetime. In the mid-1970s both Goodhart (1975: 4) and Loasby (1976: 165–6) commented on this point, while Coase (1991: 231) observed: 'I know of only one part of economics in which transaction costs have been used to explain a major feature of the economic system and that relates to the production and use of money.' It is indeed puzzling that Shackle himself did not recognize the overlap between the theories of money and the firm, and did not give greater attention to Coase. As a postgraduate student at the LSE in 1937, Shackle would have been reading *Economica* (he had published there in 1936) and he had been working on the integration of macroeconomics and the economics of the firm in relation to the causes of trade-cycle downturns (Shackle 1938). He thus should have been ripe for converting to Coase's way of thinking.

SHACKLE, CANTILLON AND SCHUMPETER

When the transaction cost programme took off in the late 1970s it became, via the work of Williamson (1975, 1985), even more focused on the difficulties that specific assets pose in a world of uncertainty. The possibility of unpleasant surprises looms large in Williamson's writings via his focus on opportunism as a barrier to mutually satisfactory dealings. Shackle might have been expected to appreciate this line of thinking given that it implicitly recognized another of his favourite topics – creativity (interpreting what might legally be done within the wording of a contract). But Shackle did not comment on how transaction cost economics related to his own work. Instead, he publicized the early writings of Richard Cantillon (1755) on entrepreneurship (see Shackle 1988, especially ch. 4).

Cantillon viewed the entrepreneur as someone who makes commitments to take delivery of goods at a price known today with a view to selling them in the future at a higher price, which cannot presently be known. This describes the activities of roving merchants in the eighteenth century who bought cottage industry produce in the hope of selling it for a profit in the towns. Cantillon would have had no difficulty in recognizing similar entrepreneurs in the late twentieth century, such as traders from eastern Europe who buy goods at duty-free stores in the Persian Gulf to sell back in their home countries or used-car dealers in New Zealand who purchase heavily depreciated but low-mileage vehicles in Japan for resale to relatively impecunious New Zealanders. Such entrepreneurship is based on alertness to opportunities (the factor most stressed by Austrian writers such as Kirzner 1973), skill in valuing assets in different settings, and bargaining over buying and selling prices.

Given his interest in the creative potential of human imagination and the role of surprise as a force for opening and closing opportunities, it is strange that Shackle should focus on Cantillon, who portrays the entrepreneur as little more than an arbitrageur or, at best, an intermediary who risks being left with unsold stocks that must be sold at knock-down prices. This is a very different vision from that associated with the work of Schumpeter (1934, 1939) and his theory of business dynamics in terms of 'creative destruction'. For Cantillon, the entrepreneur is not the residual claimant to the proceeds of innovation based on creative thinking and skill in engineering, design or marketing. By contrast, for Schumpeter the entrepreneur is proceeding into unfamiliar territory and faces uncertainty on the cost side as well as on the revenue side, for many false trails and disappointments may be encountered before a vision can be turned into reality. This presents a far more heroic image than Cantillon. Schumpeter is talking about enterprise as an activity involving investment and employment, whereas Cantillon would view the paper-shufflers of the 1980s, who bought and sold existing assets, as entrepreneurs. The failure of Shackle to acknowledge Schumpeter's work might be explained by the fact that it appeared around the same time that Shackle was writing his thesis on business cycles (published in 1938 and republished, still without reference to Schumpeter, despite a new introduction, in 1968). However, even in his later work, Shackle barely mentions Schumpeter despite the compatibility between his own kaleidic perspective and Schumpeterian 'creative destruction', and despite the fact that for both authors the clustering of innovations can initiate macroeconomic cycles (see Ford 1994: ch. 6).

STRATEGIC MANAGEMENT AND THE RESOURCE-BASED VIEW OF THE FIRM

His enthusiasm for Cantillon not withstanding, Shackle did write about investment decisions with reference to the opportunity costs faced by managers, and about firms as established entities rather than newly created operations. Even in his early work, Shackle (1938) presented decision-makers as struggling to find a way forward in the face of uncertainty. Decisions taking the firm into new territory increase uncertainty and lead to hesitation and periods of consolidation, particularly if the investment is a crucial experiment involving indivisibilities rather than gradually working up from pilot operations. Despite lacking a Coasian perspective, Shackle was thinking of the individuals or teams who decide which risks to take as the same people who have to take senior decisions concerning the management of current projects.

> Since any conception of the future can be informed only by inference from the immediate and recent past, it is natural that a businessman should feel his way by desisting for a time, before embarking on further addition. An important addition to plant constitutes a change in the basis of his calculation, rendering his inferences as to future conditions and possibilities for his own business more difficult and insecure for the time being. Moreover, a considerable increase in the scale or scope of his operations will make at first a far more than proportional increase in the time and nervous energy which he must devote to mere management, as distinct from the planning of further progress.
>
> (Shackle 1938: 99)

This perspective is at odds with steady-state models of corporate growth that were subsequently proposed by scholars such as Marris (1964), but it provides the basis for Shackle's 'investment bunching' view of macroeconomic cycles. It has much in common with Penrose's (1959) *Theory of the Growth of the Firm*, for it does not suggest that firms have a long-run problem of diseconomies of size even though their growth profiles may exhibit plateaus. The use of the word 'scope' in this context means diversification, as in the modern literature.

Penrose explicitly argues that an increase in the pace of growth, and hence in the size and/or scope of a firm, cannot simply be achieved by hiring more managers, for it will take time for new managers to understand the problems and resources of the firms they join and hence to become effective members of the management team. More generally, the activities that a firm can take on at any moment and perform in a competent manner are constrained by the pool of experience that it can call upon and what it has done in the past. We would not expect IBM to be able to switch quickly into car production, even if the relevant physical assets could readily be bought and sold, for the activities involve very different know-how (also see Richardson 1972). This theme has become a core notion in the 'resource-based' view of the firm (for a survey, see Mahoney and Pandian 1992), and seems to underlie Shackle's writings about the nature of the firm.

> The firm's practical problem is not to start with a clean slate and survey the entire range of technological and market possibilities, for using its abstract total value of resources, that the world presents. At any moment when policy or plan is being formed, the firm is a going concern engaged in a particular skein of activities, equipped with certain plant and staffed by men with certain skills and experience. The question to be answered . . . is how to use these assets.
>
> (Shackle 1970: 29–30)

Recent emphasis on the existing stock of firm resources arises from a recognition that, contrary to the assumptions of neoclassical theory, much knowledge about production functions is not merely expensive but is something that can only be picked up from the experience of working with others who already have know-how but cannot readily articulate it. Firms with different histories will therefore have different production costs of a particular product because their degrees of competence differ. Perceived relative competence may play a major role in determining which activities a management team chooses to internalize. In contrast, the Coase/Williamson view of the firm moves away from production costs and leads to a blinkered focus on the costs of fixing up deals and ensuring that one is not short-changed by opportunistic outsiders or employees (see Foss 1992).

How to use assets is a question that will not go away in a Schumpeterian world where innovation and upgrading of rival products is continually taking place, and making counter-attacks is necessary to keep capacities utilized. Learning by workers and their managers also keeps expanding output potential, as well as making time available for planning and coping with additions to the firm's stock of assets.

But Shackle did not make these themes explicit in his (1970) text; nor did he highlight them elsewhere. It was left to Neil Kay (1984) to fill this gap, integrating Schumpeterian and Shacklean perspectives from a standpoint, which seems to be of the transaction cost variety but which on closer examination turns out to be solidly Penrose-inspired. Kay sees managers as worried by fears of sudden product obsolescence, especially when they are operating in industries where technological change has been a regular feature of the competitive environment. Such managers are aware of their inability to foretell the future, and expect that they will have to deal with unpleasant surprises. Their problem is how far to insure their operations against sudden changes in the rules of the competitive game by taking on activities that use existing resources in conjunction with new assets involving new competencies. In other words, instead of seeking to maximize synergies arising from competence in established markets and technologies, managers may venture into new technologies and markets where at first they will be somewhat out of their depth and vulnerable to competition from those with greater experience in these activities. The advantages of 'sticking to one's knitting' are sacrificed because of the risks of 'having all one's eggs in the one basket' – unless it is judged that a synergy-based strategy offers a better way of weathering the surprises that might arise.

Shackle's impact would no doubt have been greater had he sought to bring the work of scholars such as Penrose and Richardson into his writing about the nature of business activity. This would have led him, like Kay, in the direction of studying how strategic choices regarding diversification and vertical relationships can be used to make uncertainty bearable. However, those who teach strategic management may benefit from studying what Shackle has to say about the business of thinking about the future, which may be summarized as follows.

Once managers have imagined possible sequels to their decisions, the next question is how seriously they should take them. In Shackle's analysis, which has much in common with scenario planning techniques (see Jefferson 1983), the proposed thought-strategy is to look for reasons for disbelief, or for other events that might prevent the imagined outcomes from coming about. This is a strategy that must eventually founder in a complex chain of infinite regress, so uncertainty will remain, and with it the need to judge just how much to sacrifice by guarding against worrying prospects, however vaguely they have been imagined – control and flexibility may both be sought-after in a world of uncertainty but both come at a price. Feelings of pessimism or optimism about the prospects of particular projects seem likely to depend on the range of ideas that managers entertain and their personal systems for assigning degrees of disbelief. This range must be finite if boundaries are placed on possibilities and an expectational basis for action settled upon. What managers imagine will depend on mental elements that they have at their disposal (Shackle 1979: 21). Moreover, these elements need to have an emotional dimension, the ability to arrest attention by virtue of their attractiveness or alarming connotations, for otherwise they are likely to end up being shunted to the back of the decision-maker's mind. If particular elements are missing from their thought-schemes, managers will be blind to threats and opportunities that could arise from them.

ENTREPRENEURSHIP AND INTERNALIZATION

Shackle's failure to include Coase in his own repertoire of elements for constructing economic analysis becomes all the more frustrating if we examine how Coase's work relates to Cantillon and Schumpeter and the resource-based view of the firm. In his article on the nature of the firm, Coase (1937: 5) defines an entrepreneur as 'the person or persons who, in a competitive system, take the place of the price mechanism in the direction of resources'. The Russian market-maker is consistent with Coase's definition as well as with Cantillon's, for otherwise there is no coming together of supply signals from duty-free stores in the Persian Gulf with the latent demand from residents of Moscow. Coase's definition is also consistent with viewing members of a property development firm that subcontract out operations as an 'entrepreneurial team'. The complementary nature of the stages involved in construction projects makes it unlikely that grand schemes will take shape in physical terms unless there is an individual or team to stitch together a diverse collection of contracts and orchestrate the delivery of the services involved (see Sabbagh 1989 for an excellent case study of the construction of Worldwide Plaza in New York). This is precisely the sort of example that Shackle might have been expected to use to illustrate 'inter-necessary' activities in his (1970) textbook while showing how such complementarities can be dealt with in practice.

There are, however, many conceivable institutional devices for dealing with complementarities of this kind. A fundamental gap in Shackle's writing is that, unlike Coase, he never examined how problems of knowledge in business affect the division of business activities among firms. These problems are particularly significant in the case of new products. In many cases, problems of knowledge are such that it is impossible to turn an entrepreneurial vision into reality without managing the many activities that might be contracted in the market. Coase uses the term 'entrepreneur' to describe what we would today call 'business management', coordinating activities that have been internalized within a single legal entity via loosely specified contracts and monitoring the timely delivery of services that have been ordered by inter-firm contracts. (In the Worldwide Plaza case studied by Sabbagh 1989 there is evidence of both kinds of entrepreneurial activity in Coase's sense, for the property developer farmed out the construction coordination task to a construction management company.) Normally the management role is discussed as if the firm under consideration has been in existence for some time and the issues are which activities have been internalized and why managers do not attempt to handle even more. However, it is easy to see scope for market failure that may lead an entrepreneur to create a multi-activity firm in order to exploit the opportunity to fill a market gap or deliver an innovative product.

An entrepreneur may coordinate a variety of related activities because she finds it impossible to find anyone who shares her vision. A classic example is the author who sees a market for her book but continually receives rejection letters from publishers. Here publishers act as intermediaries who refuse to take Cantillon-type risks. Possible solutions to such a market failure are self-publication or paying a vanity publisher some risk premium to handle the production and marketing of the book. The self-publication route need not involve the creation of a Coasian firm, since typesetting and printing can be handled by subcontractors, as can warehousing, order processing and publicity.

For such a venture to succeed, the entrepreneurial writer need not only be justified in her faith in the product, but must also be competent in choosing reliable, cost-effective subcontractors and raising finance to pay for services ahead of sales. (As a related aside it should be noted that the entrepreneurial skill of many publishers includes the ability to judge, based on experience in the industry, how many copies a book may sell and not just how few. Most academics who serve as referees for publishers are prone to underestimate potential sales of books they regard as publishable, even if they themselves are experienced authors. Although each book is to some extent a new product, knowledge of how many copies of somewhat similar books were sold may be invaluable in sizing up the viability of a proposal.)

Pressures to 'do it yourself' will increase if production necessitates new investments characterized by asset specificity. Subcontractors might only be able to complete their contribution to the production and distribution process if they invest in specific capital items (dies and moulds, or training workers in special skills). If they do not share the vision of the entrepreneur it may be difficult for the entrepreneur to realize her vision without paying for such investments on behalf of the subcontractors or paying much higher fees to the subcontractor to insure against the risk that production will be abandoned long before the capital items have generated an acceptable rate of return (compare the passage quoted earlier from the cover of Shackle 1970).

Problems with property rights over knowledge may mean that the product will only reach the market if the entrepreneur produces and distributes it instead of selling to others the right to do so via a licensing or franchise arrangement or by subcontracting these tasks. The entrepreneur may be reluctant to get subcontractors involved, fearing that they may steal the concept or produce a profitable variation on it. The trouble is that before a subcontractor can make a confident estimate of the price at which a particular service can be performed it is necessary to spell out its specification in detail; but once this has been done, the cat, so to speak, is out of the bag. This resembles the Arrow (1971: 74) paradox about failure in markets for information: to know whether information is worth buying, I need to know what information I am going to get, but once this is explained to me I have no need to buy it. The Arrow paradox promotes internalization in cases where the gap in the market simply concerns a failure to supply an existing type of product in a particular territory: it is unlikely that an alert person will be able to capture the bulk of potential profits by selling the information about the market opportunity to an existing supplier who presently focuses on other territories. The latter will be unwilling to pay for information without having a good idea of what the information is, but once alerted in general terms may see no need to pay to get specific details. This is a very acute version of the problem that Lachmann (1976: 59) has noted for entrepreneurs: it is impossible to exploit a gap in the market without running the risk of drawing the attention of other, less alert businesses to its presence.

A final example of how knowledge problems may lead entrepreneurs to engage in 'do it yourself' production and/or distribution centres on problems with articulating a novel vision to subcontractors. According to Silver (1984), pathbreaking projects tend to involve considerable vertical integration. But once their ideas are tried, tested and spread widely, pioneering entrepreneurs may find that their competitors rely more on subcontractors (contrast, Henry Ford's early operations with Japanese followers such as Toyota; cf. Langlois and Robertson 1989). The point here is related to the book example, where the author could not convince conventional publishers that her proposed book could profitably find a market. It is also an inverse of the Arrow problem: the entrepreneur is not worried about opportunistic behaviour by subcontractors, but by the prospect that they will make a mess of things because it is impossible to show them what needs to be done without doing it. Given that even the entrepreneur may have a somewhat incomplete vision of how the new concept is going to work, there may be considerable learning by doing, such as frequent adjustments to specifications as the product is debugged and the production process fine-tuned. Such adjustments may be cheaper to coordinate if activities are internalized, rather than each change needing to be the subject of a fresh contract, which might also entail payments of penalties if existing contracts have to be torn up.

To sum up this section we can say that, given his interest in problems of knowledge associated with multi-stage production and distribution systems, there is much that Shackle might have said on the relationship between entrepreneurship and internalization. These two phenomena go hand in hand – the greater the value of resources required to turn an imagined venture into reality, the more difficult it is to find other parties with whom risks can safely be shared. In the absence of easy access to venture capital, the best way for someone with entrepreneurial capabilities to make things happen is by achieving a position as an influential visionary within an existing firm that has already assembled a formidable pool of resources. Otherwise, one must begin with a small-scale venture and gradually grow one's own firm (as Akio Morita did with Sony) or run the risks associated with trying to sell one's ideas to others via licensing, franchising and so on. Although problems associated with using markets may link the phenomena of entrepreneurship and internalization, it should be noted that people who can see unexploited market opportunities, or who have new visions for products or marketing, may not have the managerial talents to successfully coordinate the activities they internalize.

MAKING SENSE OF SHACKLE'S SCHOLARSHIP

It is unfortunate that Shackle failed to draw obvious connections between his oft-repeated lines of thinking and the central themes of others who, like Shackle, were not prepared to accept the deterministic paradigm. An intriguing question remains: how did he end up being so selective in his use of other scholars' works?

Until historians of economic thought have made a careful study of Shackle's personal library, now deposited at Cambridge University Library, we can only conjecture about his neglect of other writers. Any academic will sometimes fail to use relevant ideas owing to bounded rationality, or fail to cite contributions despite being familiar with them. The risk of this must increase in the case of academics who spend a lot of their time writing rather than reading. Shackle wrote a huge amount but, to judge from Ford (1994: 12–13), he wrote it in a slow methodical manner; and in his reading he returned to classic sources time and again. His habits were definitely the antithesis of modern researchers who scan abstracts for the latest relevant contributions, presuming that anything over five years old is out of date.

It is possible that Shackle did not recognize potential intellectual synergies because his style of academic research was so different from the authors that he failed to cite. In the 1930s Shackle was operating as an armchair theorist and writing in a technical manner, whereas Coase (1991: 234) was following in Marshall's footsteps and anticipating the behaviouralists' strategy of using empirical inquiries to provoke theoretical activity. It is also unclear whether, much later in his career, Shackle would have been happy with Coase's work and its extensions. Much of Coase's analysis lies firmly within the closed neoclassical style of thinking, even though his argument about the rationale of the firm implies a commitment to an open-ended view of economic systems. As Foss (1994: 46–7) has pointed out, the Coasian manager deals with a given set of inputs and outputs in a transaction cost-minimizing manner, and analysis in the 1937 paper is conducted in comparative static terms. A similar tension is evident in the work of Williamson (1975, 1985), perhaps the most influential of Coase's followers (see Foss 1994: 52–7).

It is interesting to note that, as the transaction cost analysis of the firm has taken off, the static elements in Coase's analysis have been taken on board, and neoclassical contributions have had little to say about how loosely specified contracts may be affected by concerns about the possible emergence of new production processes and products. A common area of interest is vertical integration (the make-or-buy decision) and managers are typically portrayed as having a good idea of the kinds of games that subcontractors might engage in, given the extent of asset specificity involved in the production process. Possible technological obsolescence is not a prominent theme in such work, and neither is the possible use of surprise, in Shackle's (1972: 422–6) sense, to rewrite the rules of the game. For Shackle, by contrast, the secret of success is the ability to outflank business rivals by surprising them through imagining and implementing things that they could not conceive. Neoclassical transaction cost economists contrast sharply with Shackle-inspired contributors such as Kay (1984, particularly ch. 5) who, as was noted earlier, focus on ways in which management teams' choices of activities and methods of organization may be shaped by worries about their vulnerability to technological change.

When seeking to understand Shackle's scholarship, it is easy to give insufficient consideration to strategic aspects of his approach to his writing. His extraordinary personal humility and philosophical approach to economics make him appear unlikely to use rhetoric strategically. However, Ford (1994: 482) notes that Shackle was exceedingly resistant to changing his own theories. Ford (1994: 102–4) also reveals some of the diversionary tactics that he used to uphold his position in the face of critics, and argues (Ford 1994: 432) that Shackle 'surely has exaggerated his all-embracing contention' that Keynes did not see the central message of *The General Theory* until 1937. Behind the humble exterior lurked a man with a vision of economics to sell; and his skills as a writer, so frequently remarked upon, had rhetorical uses as well as having the properties of eloquence and lucidity.

To understand his method of writing, I think it is vital to keep in mind the frequency with which he quoted (for example, Shackle 1967: 135) Isaiah Berlin's use of the Archilochus line 'The fox knows many things, the hedgehog knows one big thing' in distinguishing different approaches to science. Shackle appears to have operated as a hedgehog rather than a fox: he had a handful of messages that he wanted to convey about the nature of economics and the human predicament and he sought to get his messages across by citing a select group of authors whose work seemed especially useful towards that end.

Shackle could lavish praise on Cantillon for his early writings on entrepreneurship, not because Shackle was setting out to study entrepreneurship but because he saw employer uncertainty about future revenue streams as central to Keynes's theory of employment in a monetary economy.

> The employer is Cantillon's merchant, who signs contracts to obtain the means of production at known prices in order to sell, when it shall have been produced, a product whose price, when he makes these contracts, he does not know. How then can he know what an extra man's work will be worth to him? He cannot know, or he would have no claim to be called an enterpriser, and that is the point.
>
> (Shackle 1974: 9)

Given his desire to make this point, Shackle could have felt uncomfortable if he had pursued some of the theoretical complementarities considered in this chapter.

Consider once gain the links between the theory of money and the theory of the firm. Enthusiastically embracing Coase's insight about the nature of the firm would have had unfortunate rhetorical connotations for Shackle given his desire to push the line that macroeconomic systems are inherently prone to kaleidic instability. The flexibility provided by money contributes to instability by enabling holders of money not to signal what they will ultimately spend it on and when they will spend it. By contrast, the flexibility that vague employment contracts offers to managerial decision-makers may contribute to the resilience of the economic system, as Loasby (1976: 166) points out. It is in the long-run interests of managers and employees to be flexible and to pull together – rather like a country in a wartime fight for survival, where planned coordination and issuing directives can be a far more effective system for getting things done than would a market-based approach of using new price incentives to encourage people to fix up new deals. As firms become larger and less prone to have all their eggs in the one basket, their managers can think more in terms of the long haul and be less prone to hair-trigger reactions to changes in the state of the news. Where the news is of a change in the pattern of current demand rather than in its total volume, managers who coordinate the use of modern flexible production methods increasingly can be quite insulated to surprises that would be disastrous for enterprises based around specialization to produce a specific design at least cost.

Here lies a paradox: for all his criticism of neoclassical equilibrium theory, Shackle can best convince his readers about the significance of the kaleidic perspective if he sets it out alongside the textbook neoclassical theory of the firm in which relational contracting is conspicuous by its absence, as is strategic diversification, with financial markets ever prodding for short-term profits via their interest with the latest quarterly results. Economic kaleidics has less rhetorical appeal if one's mental stereotype is the Japanese method of corporate organization, with lifetime employment relationships, incestuous cross-ownership patterns, and close ties with banks. Such institutional devices facilitate long-term investment planning, and business can be conducted without perennial worries about take-over raids. If things turn sour, restructuring can be achieved without returning corporate resources to the market and without making workers redundant.

Similar problems would have arisen if Shackle looked towards the management literature for precautionary tactics and institutions that business decision-makers use to make uncertainty less problematic (my words here echo those of McQueen 1994: 43–4). Much of the writing in the management area presents problems for Shackle's Cantillon-inspired vision of the entrepreneur as an agent who heroically shoulders uncertainty. Many policies and tendencies of managers seem decidedly unheroic and are aimed at reducing the riskiness of investments. In addition to the hedging diversification strategies discussed by Kay, consider the following:

1 The use of short-term payback periods in investment appraisal.
2 The suggestion by Cyert and March (1963) that, rather than facing up to uncertainty, managers often select strategies based on 'uncertainty avoidance' or attempts to achieve a 'negotiated environment'.
3 The widespread suggestion in the strategic management literature that firms should only venture into territories if they believe they have a sustainable competitive advantage, such as a product, production process,

supplier system or distribution system that others will find difficult to copy. For example, John Kay (1993) makes a strong case for the competitive role of what he calls 'architecture', a distinctive collection of relational contracts which enables highly flexible responses and effective exchanges of information. More generally, the overriding theme of the resource-based view of the firm is that firms should keep to areas where they have distinctive capabilities.

4 The strategic role of vertical integration as a means of achieving greater control of supply or distribution.

These lines of thought lead to a view of strategic management as an activity aimed at bringing uncertainty within narrow bounds in order to reduce the vulnerability of a firm's asset base to losses (Beckett, forthcoming); they are cases of cautious risk management rather than courageous, all-or-nothing leaps in the dark that involve placing the firm in jeopardy.

CONCLUDING THOUGHTS

Shackle wrote about the business predicament without writing much about entrepreneurship and business institutions along lines that would have been possible on the basis of works available during his lifetime. Towards the end of his career he sought to publicize the writings of Cantillon, but his reasons seem to be based less on an interest in how firms cope with uncertainty than on a desire to highlight the speculative nature of business and scope for macroeconomic instability. Within his writings, however, are fragments that suggest that his view of firms had much in common with some of the most up-to-date writing in the area, for he saw firms as ongoing organizations that comprise pools of resources more suited to some tasks than others.

For all his interest in Cantillon's view of business as a speculative activity, Shackle did not see enterprise simply as the hiring of factors of production to produce a particular set of outputs in a specific way. Unfortunately, he largely left it to others to write an economics of the firm in which knowledge, creativity, uncertainty and prospects for surprise are central themes. Scholars such as Loasby (1976) and Kay (1984) led the way in writing about firms by interweaving Shacklean themes with ideas from industrial economics and strategic management, and by seeking to identify ways in which uncertainty and fears of unpleasant surprises can be prevented from paralysing choosers into inaction.

Shackle's work on the firm has aroused most interest in relation to the problem of choosing between rival investment schemes once conjectures have been formed concerning their possible gain and loss outcomes. However, one can also benefit from reading the transaction cost and resource-based literatures from a Shacklean standpoint. Shackle not only sent a powerful message 'beware of the possibility of discontinuities and the dangers of irreversible commitments'; he also concludes that a firm is limited in what it may be expected to try to do, not merely by its physical assets and past knowledge of using them but also by the particular standpoints from which its decision-makers gather information and view the world. However, some of Shackle's own messages are somewhat tempered by reading his contributions in the light of related literatures. In particular, there is a basic conflict between his vision of the entrepreneur as someone who heroically shoulders risks and his vision of the entrepreneur as someone who may be acutely aware that projects will only be worth embarking upon if the degree of contestability of the market in question can be carefully managed to ensure that business risks fall within acceptable bounds.

REFERENCES

Andrews, P.W.S. (1964) *On Competition in Economic Theory*, London: Macmillan.

Arrow, K.J. (1971) *Essays in the Theory of Risk Bearing*, Chicago: Markham.

Beckett, A. (forthcoming) 'Strategic Management as an Emergent Research Programme', in P.E. Earl (ed.) *Management, Marketing and the Competitive Process*, Aldershot: Edward Elgar.

Boehm, S., Frowen, S.F. and Pheby, J. (eds) (1996) *Economics as the Art of Thought: Essays in Memory of G.L.S. Shackle*, London: Routledge.

Cantillon, R. (1755) *Essay on the Nature of Trade* (English version edited by H. Higgs, 1931, London: Macmillan).

Coase, R.H. (1937) 'The Nature of the Firm', *Economica* 4: 386–405.

——(1991) '1991 Nobel Lecture: The Institutional Structure of Production', in O. Williamson and S. Winter (eds) *The Nature of the Firm: Origins, Evolution, and Development*, Oxford: Oxford University Press.

Cyert, R.M. and March, J.G. (1963) *A Behavioral Theory of the Firm*, Englewood Cliffs, N.J.: Prentice Hall.

Devletoglou, N.E. (1973) 'Review of G.L.S. Shackle's *Expectation, Enterprise and Profit*', *Economic Journal* 83: 545–6.

Earl, P.E. (ed.) (1988) *Behavioural Economics*, Aldershot: Edward Elgar.

——(1995) *Microeconomics for Business and Marketing: Lectures, Cases and Worked Essays*, Aldershot: Edward Elgar.

Ford, J.L. (1994) *G.L.S. Shackle: The Dissenting Economist's Economist*, Aldershot: Edward Elgar.

Foss, N.J. (1992) 'Theories of the Firm: Contractual and Competence Perspectives', *Journal of Evolutionary Economics* 3: 127–40.

——(1994) 'The Two Coasian Traditions', *Review of Political Economy* 6: 37–61.

Goodhart, C.A.E. (1975) *Money, Information and Uncertainty*, London: Macmillan.

Jefferson, M. (1983) 'Economic Uncertainty and Business Decision-making', in J. Wiseman (ed.) *Beyond Positive Economics?*, London: Macmillan.

Kay, J.A. (1993) *Foundations of Corporate Success*, Oxford: Oxford University Press.

Kay, N.M. (1984) *The Emergent Firm*, London: Macmillan.

Kirzner, I. (1973) *Competition and Entrepreneurship*, Chicago: University of Chicago Press.

Lachmann, L. (1976) 'From Mises to Shackle: An Essay', *Journal of Economic Literature* 15: 54–62.

Lamberton, D.M. (1965) *The Theory of Profit*, Oxford: Blackwell.

Langlois, R.N. and Robertson, P.L. (1989) 'Explaining Vertical Integration: Lessons from the American Automobile Industry', *Journal of Economic History* 49: 361–75.

Loasby, B.J. (1976) *Choice, Complexity and Ignorance*, Cambridge: Cambridge University Press.

McQueen, D. (1994) 'On Re-reading Samuelson: A Teacher's Perspective', *Challenge* 37: 39–45.

Mahoney, J.T. and Pandian, J.R. (1992) 'The Resource-based View within the Conversation of Strategic Management', *Strategic Management Journal* 13: 363–80.

Marris, R.L. (1964) *The Economic Theory of 'Managerial' Capitalism*, London: Macmillan.

Penrose, E.T. (1959) *The Theory of the Growth of the Firm*, Oxford: Basil Blackwell.

Richardson, G.B. (1959) 'Equilibrium, Expectations and Information', *Economic Journal* 69: 223–37.

——(1960) *Information and Investment*, Oxford: Oxford University Press.

——(1972) 'The Organization of Industry', *Economic Journal* 82: 883–96.

Ricketts, M. (1987) *The Economics of Business Enterprise: New Approaches to the Firm*, Brighton: Wheatsheaf.

Sabbagh, K. (1989) *Skyscraper: The Making of a Building*, London: Macmillan/ Channel 4.

Schumpeter, J.A. (1934) *Theory of Economic Development*, Oxford: Oxford University Press.

——(1939) *Business Cycles*, New York: McGraw-Hill.

Shackle, G.L.S. (1938) *Expectations, Investment and Income*, Oxford: Oxford University Press (2nd edn 1968).

——(1959) 'Review of H.A. Simon's *Models of Man*', *Economic Journal* 69: 547–9.

——(1967) *The Years of High Theory*, Cambridge: Cambridge University Press.

——(1970) *Expectation, Enterprise and Profit*, London: George Allen & Unwin.

——(1972) *Epistemics and Economics: A Critique of Economic Doctrines*, Cambridge: Cambridge University Press.

——(1974) *Keynesian Kaleidics*, Edinburgh: Edinburgh University Press.

——(1979) *Imagination and the Nature of Choice*, Edinburgh: Edinburgh University Press.

——(1988) *Business, Time and Thought*, London: Macmillan.

——(1989) 'What Did the *General Theory* Do?' in J. Pheby (ed.) *New Directions in Post Keynesian Economics*, Aldershot: Edward Elgar.

Silver, M. (1984) *Enterprise and the Scope of the Firm*, Oxford: Martin Robertson.

Simon, H.A. (1957) *Models of Man*, New York: Wiley.

Williamson, O.E. (1975) *Markets and Hierarchies: Analysis and Antitrust Implications*, New York: Free Press.

——(1985) *The Economic Institutions of Capitalism*, New York: Free Press.

4

HYMAN MINSKY: THE MAKING OF A POST KEYNESIAN

John E. King

The founding father of Post Keynesian economics in the USA, Sidney Weintraub (1914–83), was a distinguished practitioner of orthodox, 'classical' or 'bastard' Keynesianism, who liberated himself from mainstream macroeconomics only after an arduous and protracted intellectual struggle (King 1995). The next generation of Post Keynesian theorists had no such difficulty. Paul Davidson (1930–), for example, was a pupil of Weintraub's and a disciple of Keynes almost from the start, while Alfred Eichner (1937–88) seems never to have taken the neoclassical synthesis at all seriously. The fourth major US Post Keynesian, Hyman Minsky, represents a very interesting intermediate case. Born in 1919, he is closer in age to Weintraub than to either Davidson or Eichner. Yet Minsky was a late developer. He published nothing before the appearance of two important papers in 1957 opened literary floodgates which have yet to close. And his Post Keynesian identity was in doubt up until 1975, when his book *John Maynard Keynes* finally established Minsky as a powerful critic of Keynesian orthodoxy.

Although Minsky has written at some length on his undergraduate years at Chicago, he has been rather reticent concerning his subsequent intellectual development (Minsky 1985, 1992). This issue has been the source of some disagreement, with Randall Wray (1992) pointing to recognizable Post Keynesian themes in some of Minsky's earliest works, while Marc Lavoie (1995) has identified a significant neoclassical element in other articles from the same period.

Just how Minskyian the early Minsky actually was, is the first question I attempt to answer in this chapter. I argue that there is merit in the interpretations of both Wray and Lavoie, and hence some inconsistency in Minsky's early thought. The second issue, dealt with more briefly, concerns the nature and causes of his change of mind. I suggest that real-world developments, practical experience and mature reflection all contributed to the emergence of Minsky as a fully fledged Post Keynesian in the 1970s.

MINSKY'S VISION

Minsky's original interest in economics was a direct result of his political and social commitments. He joined the youth wing of the American Socialist Party while still a secondary school student, and later attended a lecture course on the economics of socialism put on for the Socialist Party by one of his teachers at the University of Chicago, Oskar Lange. Minsky took a pioneering math–major/economics–minor degree at Chicago, where the economics department was not the conservative monolith that it would soon become. In addition to Lange, there were centrists like Jacob Viner and 'wet' conservatives like Frank Knight and Henry Simons. At this time Simons took a strong (if critical) interest in democratic socialism, and his focus on debt deflation and proposals for 100 per cent money were broadly consistent with the *General Theory*. Lange encouraged Minsky to move to Harvard, where Joseph Schumpeter was his first PhD supervisor until his death in 1950, at which time he was succeeded in this role by Wassily Leontief. At Harvard, Minsky also came under the influence of Alvin Hansen. 'The positive influence of Hyman Minsky may be viewed,' he wrote recently, 'as a struggle through the years to reconcile Lange and Simons and to integrate this reconciliation with the deep insights of Schumpeter and the pragmatism of Hansen' (Minsky 1992: 335; cf. Minsky 1985, Papadimitriou 1992).[1]

Thus Minsky's vision of the capitalist system was formed very early on, under the influence of Chicago and then Harvard. It emerges very sharply in his published work. Capitalism, for Minsky, is all about finance. Flows of funds are what really matter, and the representative capitalist is first and foremost a manager of money. This 'Wall Street' view of the economic process has always been the most fundamental, and also the most distinctive, aspect of Minsky's thought, and it owes a great deal to Simons (Dymski and Pollin 1992). His debt to Schumpeter is apparent in the second crucial part of his vision. Capitalism is dynamic, creative, innovative, but it is also inherently unstable. According to Minsky, endogenous cyclical fluctuations originating in the financial sector are the essence of capitalist economies. The most important single year of the twentieth century is 1929, and the most pertinent question that an economist can ask is 'Can "It" Happen Again?' (Minsky 1982).

It follows that Minsky has never taken much interest in the analysis of production or the concept of an economic surplus as the difference between outputs and inputs. He simply sees no merit in the rival vision of capitalism as a system of commodity flows and the performance of human labour. He is a theorist of the short period, who has no time for the concept of a steady state and regards only *cyclical* growth as deserving of analytical attention. Moreover, despite his socialist upbringing and his deep respect for Lange, Minsky has not been attracted by claims that the class struggle is central to the economics of capitalism, or that distributional conflicts determine the character and pace of economic development. It is financial markets, not labour unions, that are important to the vision of Minsky.

This underpins the unqualified hostility to Sraffian theory that Minsky (1990: 363) expresses with great forthrightness:

> At the arid level of Sraffa, the Keynesian view that effective demand reflects financial and monetary variables has no meaning, for there is no monetary or financial system in Sraffa. At the concrete level of Keynes, the technical conditions of production, which are the essential constructs of Sraffa, are dominated by profit expectations and financing conditions.

It also explains his indifference to much of the Cambridge Post Keynesian tradition, which has concentrated on issues that leave him unmoved: Minsky refuses to place income distribution, steady-state growth theory or the capital controversies at the heart of his version of Post Keynesian economics. And it accounts for his unease with the analysis of Sidney Weintraub who, Minsky felt, exaggerated the power of trade unions, the theoretical significance of distributional battles, and the practical importance of a tax-based incomes policy, all at the expense of the financial variables and the cyclical instability which he regarded as fundamental.[2]

As he wrote to Weintraub, while justifying the critical remarks in his review of Davidson's (1972) *Money and the Real World*:

> I thought I commended Paul highly in the review article and I thought I was very favorable to his book, commending it to all and arguing that students must be made aware of the serious issues it raises. However, I do have a serious substantive quarrel with his approach, which is the approach adopted by Joan Robinson and Kregel among others. They insist upon defining as a base for their argument a steady growth process and elucidating the circumstances under which this process can be maintained. They also conclude more or less in passing that the maintenance of steady growth is difficult if not impossible under capitalist processes.
>
> My perspective is that once you define the financial institutions of capitalism in any precise form then the normal path of the economy is intractably cyclical and the problems [*sic*] of macroeconomic theory is to spell out the properties of the cyclical process. Thus much of what is very valid in Paul's analysis is diminished in significance because of his basic approach. It follows from the fact that decisions are made within the context of cyclical expectations that these ideas and constructs which depend upon the marginal physical productivity of capital assets for either the determination of investment or the distribution of income (capital share) are irrelevant to the economic processes. Thus the inadequacy of production function based economics can only be demonstrated by this shift in vision as to the normal functioning

> properties of the economy. In addition with a cyclical perspective uncertainty becomes operational in the sense that myopic hindsight determines the current state of Keynesian/Robinsonian Animal Spirits: without a cyclical perspective uncertainty is more or less of an empty bag.
> (Minsky to Weintraub, 19 November 1974: Sidney Weintraub Papers, Special Collections Department, Duke University Libraries, Durham, North Carolina, Box 3 Folder 3)

To what extent is this perspective evident in the early work of Minsky?

EARLY WRITINGS

Minsky was already in his thirty-eighth year when he commenced his career as a publishing economist with major papers in two leading journals. The first appeared in the *Quarterly Journal of Economics*, with the title 'Central Banking and Money Market Changes'. It deals with contemporary financial innovations and the difficulties that they presented for central bank control of the monetary system. Minsky argues that profit-seeking behaviour in a period of high and rising interest rates had induced two profound institutional changes – the growth of the federal funds market and the increasing importance of non-financial corporations in the financing of government bond houses. The first made a given volume of reserves more efficient in supporting deposits and the second, by freeing bank resources to finance other activities, was equivalent to an increase in reserves. As a result, the relationship between the rate of interest and the velocity of circulation had shifted outwards. Monetary policy became less effective and the overall liquidity of the economy decreased, since the ratio of (risky) private debt to (risk-free) government debt was increasing steadily. This posed the danger of a financial crisis, in which the insolvency or temporary illiquidity of a major non-bank institution might have a chain reaction on others. Thus a shock from the financial sector could induce a deep depression in the real economy. Minsky concluded that the central bank cannot realistically aim to stabilize the economy, since instability is a necessary feature of a dynamic capitalism. What the central bank can, and must, do is act as lender of last resort to the money market as a whole (not merely to the commercial banks), and thus protect the financial system from crisis (Minsky 1957a).

In the second paper, published by the *American Economic Review* with the title 'Monetary Systems and Accelerator Models', Minsky models the relations between finance and the real economy in much greater detail. His starting-point is a problem that had exercised the minds of many orthodox Keynesian macroeconomists from Samuelson (1939) to Hicks (1950) – how to obtain a credible theory of cyclical growth from the canonical multiplier–accelerator model, which more easily produces explosive growth or bottomless contraction. Minsky's solution is to introduce finance into the model, making the acceleration coefficient dependent upon money market conditions and the balance sheets of firms. Investment must be financed either by running down firms' cash balances, or by issuing more equity, or by increasing business debt.

Minsky discusses four possible monetary regimes. In the first, with both the money supply (*M*) and the velocity of circulation (*V*) held constant, any excess of *ex ante* investment over *ex ante* saving leads to the rationing of saving among potential investors through a rise in the rate of interest.

A second regime allows *V* to vary, with *M* remaining constant. If *V* is subject to a maximum value, this imposes a ceiling on money income at 'that level at which all of the available money supply is required for transactions' (Minsky 1957b: 867). This is a monetary ceiling, and is independent of both the full employment of labour and full capacity working in the capital-goods industries.

For the third regime, Minsky holds *V* constant, and allows *M* to vary. There is a strong flavour of endogenous money here: 'we assume that commercial banks create money by lending to business firms. The maximum realized increase in the money supply is equal to the difference between *ex ante* investment and *ex ante* saving' (Minsky 1957b: 870). If the money supply is infinitely elastic (Minsky the horizontalist!) there is a possibility of explosive growth in real output, constrained only by the increase in Kaleckian borrowers' risk associated with the consequent rise in debt/equity ratios. If, however, the growth of *M* is limited (for example, by a fractional reserve banking system), investment will be restrained by the money market, though not appreciably so in the early stages of a boom when banks still have excess reserves.

In the fourth regime, both *M* and *V* are variable. Once again there is no constraint upon the growth of output (assuming $V>1$), except for the increase in business debt relative to equity.

Minsky concludes by drawing some implications for policy. If the goal is steady growth and a constant price level, something very close to a monetarist 'golden rule' is called for. Steady growth requires a money supply that increases at a geometric rate; a too rapidly growing money supply results in rapid price inflation while a too slowly growing money supply results in a downturn of income (Minsky 1957b: 882). To offset the inhibiting effect on investment of rising debt–equity ratios, the central bank should design its interest rate policy to keep $V>1$, while fiscal policy must provide budget deficits so as to increase private sector assets without thereby raising the level of business debt: 'government deficit financing, even during a period of sustained growth and similarly rising prices, may be desirable in order to maintain the conditions for further growth' (Minsky 1957b: 883).

Many characteristically Minskyian themes can be seen in these two articles – the Wall Street vision of capitalism, the significance of financial innovation, the endogeneity of the money supply, the dangers of financial instability, the need for big government and for a lender of last resort. All this lends support to the contention of Wray (1992) that there is a powerful continuity in Minsky's thinking. But there are also strong neoclassical undertones. These are most obvious in the loanable funds approach to the theory of interest rates, which dominates the *American Economic Review* paper. As Lavoie (1995) notes, this is a pre-Keynesian construct which Minsky derives from Bertil Ohlin and the Stockholm school. It entails (though Minsky apparently did not realize it) acceptance of a Wicksellian conception of a long-period natural rate of interest determined by capital productivity and thrift. For Minsky, investment does not generate the saving required to finance it, as it does for Keynes and the Post Keynesians. On the contrary, investment is constricted by saving.[3] In effect it is crowded out (although Minsky does not use the term) by increasing interest rates, even when there is unemployment and there exists excess capacity in the capital goods sector. There is even worse to come: 'Symmetrically, if *ex ante* saving is greater than *ex ante* investment then an increase in investment is forced so that all of the available finance is absorbed by real investment' (Minsky 1957b: 866). A clearer statement of the pre-Keynesian view of the relationship between saving and investment would be difficult to imagine.

Thus it is not surprising that Minsky invokes the Pigou effect in his *American Economic Review* article (Minsky 1957b: 868), and subsequently in an application of his model to growth in less developed countries (Minsky 1959a: 155) and in the 'Linear Model of Cyclical Growth', which he published in the *Review of Economics and Statistics* (Minsky 1959b: 134). Admittedly Minsky (1959b: 144) uses what he terms the 'Tobin–Pigou effect' in a rather unorthodox way, citing the wartime growth in the ratio of household real wealth to income as a major cause of the post-war boom which also rendered most unlikely a financial crisis in the foreseeable future. Public confidence in the financial system formed an important component of the theory of cost-push or 'sellers' inflation', that Minsky presented to the Joint Economic Committee of Congress in September 1959, together with the increase in trade union power and the market strength of large corporations. In these circumstances monetary policy would be ineffective, he argued, since tight money and high interest rates would lead only to a sharp increase in velocity, with the consequent danger of financial instability as firms adjusted their portfolios in order to finance their expenditures (Minsky 1959c: 2215). Significantly, he did not propose an incomes policy, tax-based or otherwise, as a remedy for inflation. Instead Minsky (1959c: 2207–8) called for measures to make the US economy more competitive, including a commitment to free trade and the elimination of entry barriers established by unions and professional bodies.

Minsky's monograph, *Financial Crisis, Financial Systems, and the Performance of the Economy*, published by the Commission on Money and Credit in 1964, was in fact written four years earlier (Minsky 1964a: 173). In substance a book-length elaboration of his 1957 *American Economic Review* paper, this study contains a much more comprehensive statement of the financial instability hypothesis than he had provided in earlier work, together with a mass of supporting evidence and a pioneering attempt to simulate the financial repercussions of a severe recession in the real economy. If a boom results from increased investment, Minsky argues, in the absence of inflation in equity and real estate prices, debt/asset ratios will increase and financial instability will grow. A 'normal' cyclical peak in the real economy, imposed by supply constraints, may have such powerful financial effects that it generates a deep depression, as in 1929. In practice there was no serious threat of a financial crisis in the early 1960s, Minsky concluded, because the large budget deficits which were a feature of even mild recessions pumped large quantities of riskless government assets into the financial system, and welfare payments allowed the unemployed to maintain their consumption expenditure. But if debt/equity ratios continued to rise, and the speculative element in asset prices grew, the probability of a financial crisis would also increase. Minsky repeated his earlier policy prescriptions – a lender of last resort and regulating role for the central bank, together with a secular increase in the national debt and in the level of government transfer payments (Minsky 1964a: 179–84).

The principal themes of the early Minsky can be briefly summarized. First, the multiplier–accelerator framework is a good basis for a dynamic macroeconomic theory, and can yield a plausible model of cyclical growth so long as it incorporates financial variables to account for the ceiling (or upper turning point) of the cycle. Second, the financial system is innately unstable. Each upswing contains the financial seeds of its own destruction, and these are often compounded by the processes of financial innovation generated by profit-seeking agents in the money markets. Third, institutional behaviour is critical and institutional change must be allowed for in any realistic economic analysis. Fourth, government intervention is essential if the instability of the capitalist economy is to be contained and another Great Depression – the 'It' in the titles of Minsky (1963c; 1982) – is to be avoided. These arguments are advanced with great confidence, and with relatively few references to the work of others. Minsky gives credit where he thinks that it is due,[4] but he shows little interest in the history of ideas, or in past or contemporary controversies. In particular, and in marked contrast to Weintraub and Davidson, he makes no effort whatsoever in this early work to justify his own ideas by representing them as a legitimate interpretation of Keynes. This was to come later. But one could almost infer from reading the early Minsky that he had never read the *Treatise* or the *General Theory*.

A 'CLASSICAL KEYNESIAN'?

In my (King 1995) assessment of Sidney Weintraub's early career, I specified six aspects of Post Keynesian economics – rejection of the IS-LM interpretation of the *General Theory*; opposition to the Walrasian or general equilibrium approach to Keynes adopted by Patinkin; repudiation of the marginal productivity theory of distribution on the grounds that its incoherence had been demonstrated during the capital controversies; replacement of marginalist price theory by some version of mark-up pricing; an endogenous view of money; and a methodological commitment to realism, and to policy relevance, in theory construction. The young Weintraub took a 'bastard Keynesian' position on each and every one of these issues.

Applying these criteria to Minsky's early work, the verdict is less clear-cut. There is no explicitly IS-LM model in Minsky's writings, nor any reference to Walrasian theory or to Patinkin. But there does not need to be, given his endorsement of the Pigou effect and his (pre-Keynesian) loanable funds theory of the rate of interest. Minsky never writes an aggregate production function, or refers to marginal productivity in his analysis of interest, but these neoclassical concepts are implicit in the *American Economic Review* article and elsewhere. Thus it comes as no surprise when he cites Solow's 1956 growth model with approval, praises Denison's growth accounting framework or expresses total indifference towards Joan Robinson's critique of orthodox capital theory (Minsky 1961a: 498; cf. Fazzari 1992: 4). Minsky has nothing (and, *a fortiori*, nothing critical) to say about marginalist price theory.

On the question of endogenous money the position is more than a little unclear. There is no shortage of references to endogenous money in his early writings, which are derived from Minsky's emphasis on financial innovation as a means of circumventing tight monetary policies. He can even be interpreted as a horizontalist: 'As a result [of financial innovation] during a strong boom, interest rates will not rise very much for the supply of financing is, in fact, very elastic' (Minsky 1957a: 185). Even an infinitely elastic money supply curve does not strike Minsky as at all absurd (Minsky 1957b: 871–5). There is, however, no hint of endogenous money in the 1960 monograph. Very much the reverse:

> The amount of money in existence is not determined by the public; it is determined within the monetary system. Given the reserves and the reserve ratio, the amount of money and also the value of the earning assets owned by the monetary system are in principle determined. The reserves and reserve ratio are both determined within the monetary system. Hence in a very significant way it is not true that the monetary system adjusts to the behavior of the economy; what happens is that within wide limits the economy adjusts to the behavior of the monetary system.
>
> (Minsky 1964a: 190; cf. Minsky 1961b: 139–40)

Here Minsky is, very explicitly, a verticalist: 'within an economy money is an indestructible asset; there is nothing that can be done (ignoring the silly case of the physical destruction of currency or coin) by a household or a business firm to change the quantity of money' (Minsky 1964a: 190). It is significant, too, that Minsky's (1964a: 280, 374) objections to Milton Friedman are, at this early stage, moderate in tone and technical in substance; they do not involve the endogeneity of the money supply.

There are hints at endogeneity in Minsky's later critique of Friedman and Schwartz (Minsky 1963a: 68–9), but they are not central to his anti-monetarism as they were, for example, to Nicholas Kaldor (1970). In an application of the financial instability hypothesis to the theory of long waves, he writes that 'what changes do occur in the money supply may very well be induced by the behavior of the economy, witness the (excess reserves) of commercial banks in the 1930s' (Minsky 1964b: 326). Then, discussing the problems facing the financial system in the state of California, Minsky asserts that the money supply is exogenously determined for a nation, but endogenous for a region within a nation: 'That is, the line of causation within a region of a national economy is more from income to money than from money to income, whereas many economists argue that the line of causation for the country is from money to income' (Minsky 1965: 21; cf. Minsky 1964b: 7). By the mid-1960s, Minsky's position on the endogeneity of money can only be described as unstable.

Only with respect to his method, in fact, would the early Minsky clearly qualify as a Post Keynesian. His most mathematically demanding papers always focused on the institutional characteristics of contemporary capitalism, and invariably carried a powerful policy message. Theory must incorporate 'attitudes, expectations, beliefs, ways of doing things as well as the legal and organisational structure', he told the Joint Economic Committee. 'Each time the relevant institutions undergo a significant change, it is risky to extrapolate relations derived from observations of the past' (Minsky 1959c: 2209).

Methodology apart, it would have been very difficult to recognize in Minsky, circa 1964, the future Post Keynesian. He made no significant allusion to Keynes or to conflicting interpretations of his work, still less to the notion that 'classical Keynesianism' might involve a serious mis-reading of the *General Theory.* He set out his financial instability hypothesis, but in a form that lacks two vital ingredients: the two-price level model of investment, and the Kaleckian theory of aggregate profits. There are glimpses of the former in the 1960 monograph (Minsky 1964a: 213), and in his critique of Friedman and Schwartz (Minsky 1963a: 69–70), but it is no sooner advanced than withdrawn in favour of the capital-stock adjustment principle (Minsky 1963b: 412). As for the profit theory of Kalecki, I have been unable to find the slightest trace of it in any of Minsky's early work. There is no hint that in aggregate, in a closed economy, capitalists' receipts are determined by their (investment and consumption) expenditures, plus the difference between government expenditure and taxation. This Kaleckian version of the theory of effective demand is important in its own right. Its use also enabled Minsky subsequently to plug a major gap in his analysis of the determinants of corporate debt, for which incomings are no less important than borrowings and the size of the budget deficit is crucial.

This, however, lay well in the future. Only two characteristics – both of them very important, it is true – serve to distinguish Minsky at this stage from the mainstream proponents of 'bastard Keynesian' with whom he still had much in common. Money matters; more so for Minsky than even for Friedman and Schwartz. And he totally lacks the complacency engendered by liberal versions of the neoclassical synthesis, which made a recurrence of 'It' appear totally impossible. If Minsky was a classical Keynesian in 1964, he was already something of a deviant.

HOW MINSKY CHANGED, AND WHY

In a brief autobiographical article for the *Biographical Dictionary of Dissenting Economists*, Minsky (1992: 356) lists his seven principal theoretical achievements. The first is his interpretation of Keynes as supplying both an investment theory of the trade cycle and a financial theory of investment, the latter based on the distinction between the price levels of assets and of current output. Second is the financial instability hypothesis and the associated debt deflation approach to economic crises. There follow: the importance that Minsky attached to central banks as lenders of last resort; the cash flow analysis of financial relations, with special emphasis placed on Kalecki's theory of profits; the necessity for big government; the significance of financial innovation; and the 'tiers approach' to the balance of payments. As I have indicated, some of these themes are evident in Minsky's early work. All but the last can be found in his book *John Maynard Keynes*, which was completed by 1972 but not published until 1975, although the first reference I can find to the Kaleckian theory of profits is in Minsky (1977). In a sense this was the crucial missing piece in the Minskyian puzzle, since it provided him with a means for analysing aggregate cash flows *into* firms that was as convincing as his earlier modelling of their liabilities and financial commitments. This, in turn, enabled him to liberate himself from the loanable funds theory where, to paraphrase James Meade (1975: 82), the dog called 'saving' wags its tail called 'investment'. By 1977, Minsky was quite clear that investment was the dog, and saving the tail.

There is no evidence of any blinding light on Minsky's Damascus road. In 1994 he told Randall Wray that his transition to a Minskyian view of the world had taken place over a long period, and had not been completed until the mid- or late 1970s. Although he must have read Kalecki very early on (at the insistence of Oskar Lange), Kalecki's theory of the trade cycle had not impressed Minsky at the time, and the relevance of Kaleckian ideas did not become apparent to Minsky until the 1970s.[5] Minsky had earlier recalled (Papadimitriou 1992: 22) Kaldor's visit to Berkeley in 1959 as a major influence on the development of his ideas, although there was presumably a substantial time-lag between stimulus and response.

Minsky has always regarded himself as an economist of the real world, ready to modify his formal analysis in the face of empirical evidence. He attributes his first article (Minsky 1957a) to observations made during a summer spent on Wall Street,[6] although the 'near-miss' of 1966, in which a Federal Reserve-inspired credit crunch almost led to a major financial crisis, probably served more to confirm Minsky in his opinions than significantly to change them (Minsky 1976). Much more important, on his own account, was his twenty-three-year spell as a director of the Mark Twain Banks in St Louis, which convinced him that the two-price theory of investment, unlike conventional interest-rate models, explained how the loan officers of banks and corporate treasurers actually behaved.[7]

To judge by the footnotes in *John Maynard Keynes*, Minsky was largely uninfluenced by the work of other US Post Keynesians, although (as already noted) a certain paucity of citations is one of his trademarks. Reaction against the late 1960s upsurge of monetarist ideas may well have been a more important impulse. During his 1969–70 sabbatical in Cambridge, Minsky came into personal contact not only with Robinson, Kahn and Kaldor, but also with the young Jan Kregel, whose influence he has acknowledged (Papadimitriou 1992: 23).

I suspect, however, that to a very large extent Minsky found his own way, increasingly appreciating the logical gaps in his earlier versions of the financial instability hypothesis and turning quite naturally to Keynes, and then to Kalecki, to fill them. Indeed, Minsky remains very much his own man, deeply influential but also somewhat remote from the Post Keynesian mainstream. He was a founding member of the editorial board of the *Journal of Post Keynesian Economics* (with many others), but does not publish there and has never been closely associated with other prominent Post Keynesians. Minsky is not given to joint authorship. There is no Minsky school, and few obvious Minsky disciples – Steven Fazzari, Randall Wray, perhaps Charles Kindleberger (as far as the financial instability hypothesis is concerned), and possibly a few radical monetary theorists like Gary Dymski and Robert Pollin.

There remains the distinct possibility that Minsky may be reclaimed by economic orthodoxy in its current, seductive New Keynesian guise, in which asymmetric information gives rise to credit rationing and prevents interest rates from playing their traditional role of equilibrating the supply and demand for loans. In New Keynesian theory the financial condition of the firm significantly affects its ability to proceed with investment projects, and the neoclassical forces which create and sustain a powerful tendency to full employment are radically weakened. Minsky is sometimes interpreted as being much closer to New Keynesian ideas than is, for example, Paul Davidson (Fazzari 1992; cf. Davidson 1994), although Minsky himself denies this.[8] Alternatively, he may yet honour the intellectual cheque that he signed in 1960 and explore the 'real system which generates real income and employment' (Minsky 1964a: 176) as the dual to the financial system to whose analysis he has devoted so much of his professional life. A Minsky–Sraffa synthesis would really lay down the gauntlet to those who believe that (neo)classical economics comes into its own in the long run.[9, 10]

NOTES

1 John Henry suggests that the influence on Minsky of Lange, by far the most neoclassical of socialist economists, may well have been greater than I , or Minsky himself, allow.

2 Mike Howard reminds me that this was a much more contentious position to take in the strike-prone, inflationary 1970s than it appears to be in the de-unionized, low-inflation 1990s.

3 Basil Moore's (1994) monetary criticism of the multiplier is analogous to this. Also see Cottrell (1994).

4 To Alexander, Allen, Baumol, Duesenberry, Goodwin, Harrod, Hicks and Samuelson on cycle theory; to Ellis, Gurley and Shaw, Mints and Simons on monetary questions; and to Kalecki (one reference only, on the principle of increasing risk), Ohlin, Pigou, Solow and Tobin on other macroeconomic issues.

5 Personal communication from Randall Wray, October 1994. For a general appraisal of Post Keynesian reactions to Kalecki in the United States, see King (1996).

6 Personal communication from Hyman Minsky, 15 May 1995.

7 *Ibid.*

8 Minsky claims that his ideas are no closer to neoclassicism than Davidson's. The difference is that he is *personally* closer to leading orthodox economists, some of whom are among his favourite ex-students (personal communication, 15 May 1995).

9 Although Minsky no longer regards the distinction between real and financial domains as at all useful (*ibid.*), his relative neglect of real variables remains a significant weakness.

10 I am grateful to John Henry, Mike Howard, Marc Lavoie, Hyman Minsky and Steve Pressman for comments on an earlier draft. The usual disclaimer applies, forcibly.

REFERENCES

Cottrell, A. (1994) 'Endogenous Money and the Multiplier', *Journal of Post Keynesian Economics* 17,1: 111–20.

Davidson, P. (1972) *Money and the Real World*, London: Macmillan.

——(1994) *Post Keynesian Macroeconomic Theory*, Aldershot: Edward Elgar.

Dymski, G. and Pollin, R. (1992) 'Hyman Minsky as Hedgehog: The Power of the Wall Street Paradigm', in S. Fazzari and D.B. Papadimitriou (eds) *Financial Conditions and Macroeconomic Performance: Essays in Honor of Hyman P. Minsky*, Armonk, N.Y.: Sharpe, 27-61.

Fazzari, S. (1992) 'Introduction: Conversations with Hyman Minsky', in S. Fazzari and D.B. Papadimitriou (eds) *Financial Conditions and Macroeconomic Performance: Essays in Honor of Hyman P. Minsky*, Armonk, N.Y.: Sharpe.

Hicks, J. R. (1950) *A Contribution to the Theory of the Trade Cycle*, Oxford: Clarendon Press.

Kaldor, N. (1970) 'The New Monetarism', *Lloyds Bank Review* 97: 1–18.

King, J. E. (1995) 'Sidney Weintraub: The Genesis of an Economic Heretic', *Journal of Post Keynesian Economics* 18,1: 65–88.

——(1996) 'Kalecki and the Americans', in J. E. King (ed.), *An Alternative Macroeconomic Theory: The Kaleckian Model and Post Keynesian Economics*, Boston: Kluwer.

Lavoie, M. (1995) 'Loanable Funds, Endogenous Money, and Minsky's Financial Fragility Hypothesis', Perth: Curtin University of Technology, mimeo.

Meade, J. E. (1975) 'The Keynesian Revolution', in M. Keynes (ed.) *Essays on John Maynard Keynes*, Cambridge: Cambridge University Press.

Minsky, H. P. (1957a) 'Central Banking and Money Market Changes', *Quarterly Journal of Economics* 71,2: 171–87.

——(1957b) 'Monetary Systems and Accelerator Models', *American Economic Review* 47,6: 859–83.

——(1959a) 'Indicators of the Developmental Status of an Economy', *Economic Development and Cultural Change* 7,2: 151–72.

——(1959b) 'A Linear Model of Cyclical Growth', *Review of Economics and Statistics* 41,2: 133–44.

——(1959c) 'Summary Statement', in Joint Economic Committee, 86th Congress of the United States, 1st session, *Hearings, Part 7, the Effects of Monopolistic and Quasi-Monopolistic Practices*. Washington, D.C.: USGPO.

——(1961a) 'Review of J. Robinson, *Collected Economic Papers, Volume 1*', *Journal of Political Economy* 69,5: 487–8.

——(1961b) 'Review of J. G. Gurley and E. S. Shaw, *Money in a Theory of Finance*', *Journal of Finance* 16,1: 138–40.

——(1963a) 'Comment' [on M. Friedman and A. Schwartz, 'Money and Business Cycles'], *Review of Economics and Statistics* 45,1: 64–72.

——(1963b) 'Discussion', *American Economic Review* 53,2: 411–12.

——(1963c) 'Can "It" Happen Again?', in D. Carson (ed.) *Banking and Monetary Studies*, Homewood, Ill.: Irwin.

——(1964a) 'Financial Crisis, Financial Systems, and the Performance of the Economy', in Commission on Money and Credit, *Private Capital Markets*, Englewood Cliffs, N.J.: Prentice Hall.

——(1964b) 'Longer Waves in Financial Relations: Financial Factors in the More Severe Depressions', *American Economic Review* 54,2: 324–35.

——(1965) 'Overview', in H. P. Minsky (ed.) *California Banking in a Growing Economy*, Berkeley: Institute of Business and Economic Research.

——(1975) *John Maynard Keynes*, New York: Columbia University Press.

——(1976) 'How Standard is Standard Economics?', *Society* 14,3: 24–9.

——(1977) 'The Financial Instability Hypothesis: An Interpretation of Keynes and an Alternative to "Standard" Theory', *Nebraska Journal of Economics and Business* 16,1: 5–16.

——(1982) *Can 'It' Happen Again? Essays on Instability and Finance*, Armonk, N.Y.: Sharpe.

——(1985) 'Beginnings', *Banca Nazionale del Lavoro Quarterly Review* 154: 211–21.

——(1990) 'Sraffa and Keynes: Effective Demand in the Long Run', in K. Bharadwaj and B. Schefold (eds) *Essays on Piero Sraffa*, London: Unwin Hyman.

——(1992) 'Hyman P. Minsky (born 1919)', in P. Arestis and M. Sawyer (eds) *A Biographical Dictionary of Dissenting Economists*, Aldershot: Edward Elgar.

Moore, B. J. (1994) 'The Demise of the Keynesian Multiplier: A Reply to Cottrell', *Journal of Post Keynesian Economics* 17, 1: 121–33.

Papadimitriou, D. B. (1992) 'Minsky on Himself', in S. Fazzari and D.B. Papadimitriou (eds) *Financial Conditions and Macroeconomic Performance: Essays in Honor of Hyman P. Minsky*, Armonk, N.Y.: Sharpe.

Samuelson, P. A. (1939) 'Interactions between the Multiplier Analysis and the Principle of Acceleration', *Review of Economics and Statistics* 21,2: 75–8.

Wray, L. R. (1992) 'Minsky's Financial Instability Hypothesis and the Endogeneity of Money', in S. Fazzari and D.B. Papadimitriou (eds) *Financial Conditions and Macroeconomic Performance: Essays in Honor of Hyman P. Minsky*, Armonk, N.Y.: Sharpe.

5

MONOPOLY CAPITAL REVISITED

Allin Cottrell

The object of this chapter is to reassess Baran and Sweezy's *Monopoly Capital* three decades after its original publication.[1] For a time in the 1960s *Monopoly Capital* enjoyed the status of an economic Bible for the New Left, and was more widely read than Marx's *Capital*. Today, however, the book is discussed infrequently. How, I wish to ask, have the arguments of Baran and Sweezy fared in the light of the subsequent empirical record, and how do they stand up to theoretical scrutiny? I begin with a brief account of how this work came to be written.

The gestation of *Monopoly Capital* – for Sweezy at any rate – can be traced back to Sweezy's experiences as a graduate student at the LSE in 1932–3. There he was first exposed, via Harold Laski and, even more so, via the ferment of ideas among a highly international group of graduate students in the social sciences, to Marxist ideas. Marxism made sense of the cataclysmic events of the early 1930s: 'What up to then had seemed a senseless chaos of inexplicable disasters now appeared as the logical, indeed the inevitable, consequence of the normal functioning of capitalism and imperialism' (Sweezy 1981: 13). Like many others in this period, Sweezy (1981: 13) concluded that 'the way out of the crisis was through revolution and socialism, a course that the Russian Bolsheviks were pioneering and in which they needed all the support like-minded people in the rest of the world could give them'.

On his return to the USA in 1933, Sweezy found that the deepening Depression had opened the way for a discussion of Marxism in American academic circles. It was in this context that Sweezy's lifelong mission first emerged. As he tells it, '[t]hat mission was to do what I could to make Marxism an integral and respected part of the intellectual life of the country, or, put in other terms, to take part in establishing a serious and authentic North American brand of Marxism' (Sweezy 1981: 13). Sweezy's personal contribution to this development can be traced in a long series of influential works, beginning with *The Theory of Capitalist Development* (1942) – long the pre-eminent English-language account of Marxian economics – and proceeding through *Socialism* (1949), *The Present as History* (1953), *Monopoly Capital* (Baran and Sweezy 1968), *Introduction to Socialism* (1968, with Leo Huberman), as well as many other books on the current state of US capitalism and the international and historical aspects of both capitalism and socialism.[2]

Sweezy's stature as an expositor and promoter of Marxist economics is surely self-evident. In the hostile climate of the post-war West, prior to the ideological upheavals of the later 1960s, only Maurice Dobb played a comparable role. In what follows, however, I shall be more concerned with Sweezy's distinctive contribution to Marxist theory – his modifications of, rather than his exposition of, classical Marxism. *Monopoly Capital* represented a challenge to orthodox Marxism as well as to the society of which it was a critique. As Brewer (1980: 133) remarks, from *The Theory of Capitalist Development*, to Baran's (1957) *Political Economy of Growth*, to *Monopoly Capital*, 'there is a consistent development, starting very close to classical Marxism, but evolving into something distinctively different'. Our task here is to consider the merits of this 'distinctively different' Marxism – with the benefit, of course, of thirty years' hindsight.

Broadly speaking, the critique of capitalism offered by Marxism is twofold. First, while capitalism is historically progressive up to a point, beyond that point it is wasteful and irrational because it fails to exploit fully the capacity of humanity to better its condition. Second, capitalism is a deeply unjust system, resting on the exploitation of labour, and generating poverty and insecurity alongside vast and obscene concentrations of private wealth. These themes of Marx's *Capital* are also present in *Monopoly Capital*, although they are given a somewhat different inflection. There is less emphasis in the latter book on the poverty and insecurity of the working class in leading capitalist economies, the brunt of capitalistic inequality being borne, in Baran and Sweezy's view, by the working classes in those countries on the receiving end of imperialism. Also – and this is the point on which I will focus here – there is a different account of capitalism's tendency to waste resources. Marx stressed waste due to the 'anarchy of competition', and also the waste of labour due to its undervaluation via the wages system. In Baran and Sweezy the emphasis is on stagnation due to a shortage of effective demand under monopoly capitalism, and on secondary wastage contained in the 'sales effort' by which the system attempts (ultimately, unsuccessfully) to stave off such stagnation. The stagnation mechanism posited by Baran and Sweezy is addressed in the next section.

THE MECHANISM OF STAGNATION IN *MONOPOLY CAPITAL*

The basic thesis of Baran and Sweezy is well known. As capitalism moves from its competitive phase into its monopoly phase, the 'laws of motion' of the system are subject to qualitative change. Marx's 'tendency for the rate of profit to fall' – valid, if at all, only under competitive capitalism – is replaced by a new 'law of rising surplus'. First, oligopolistic firms effectively abolish price competition and collude to realize a close approximation to the theoretical monopoly price. This does not, however, mean the end of all competition; indeed competition 'takes new forms and rages on with ever-increasing intensity' (Baran and Sweezy 1968: 76). Prominent among the intensified forms of competition is cost-cutting via increasing productivity (Baran and Sweezy 1968: 76-80). This accelerated tendency to pursue lower costs via technical innovation may seem to warrant viewing monopoly capitalism as a rational and progressive system, but unfortunately cost reduction increases profits rather than benefiting society as a whole. The maintenance of monopoly pricing means that 'under monopoly capitalism, declining costs imply continuously widening profit margins. And continuously widening profit margins, in turn, imply aggregate profits which rise not only absolutely but as a share of national product. If we provisionally equate aggregate profits with society's economic surplus, we can formulate as a law of monopoly capitalism that the surplus tends to rise both absolutely and relatively as the system develops' (Baran and Sweezy 1968: 80).

The stagnation tendency arises from this law in conjunction with the dwindling propensities to consume and invest on the part of the capitalist class as a whole in the monopoly phase. Following Lintner (1956), Baran and Sweezy argue that under conditions of rising profits capitalist consumption tends to fall as a proportion of total profit due to a lag of dividend payments behind profit growth. This means that 'the investment-seeking part of surplus tends to rise as a proportion of total income' (Baran and Sweezy 1968: 89).[3] The whole surplus will therefore be 'absorbed' only if the ratio of investment to GDP rises continuously. But this is 'nonsensical from an economic standpoint', since it means that 'a larger and larger volume of producer goods would have to be turned out for the sole purpose of producing a still larger and larger volume of producer goods in the future' (Baran and Sweezy 1968: 89). Not only are monopoly capitalist firms disinclined to participate in such a 'snowballing expansion program'; they are in fact *less* inclined toward new investment by the development of new methods and products than are competitive firms. While cost-cutting innovation is important in monopolistic competition, the degree to which it gives rise to net investment is limited by the desire and ability of monopolists to avoid spoiling their markets by excessive growth of capacity and to avoid the devaluation of their existing capital stock (Baran and Sweezy 1968: 100–3).[4]

This combination of factors is seen as generating stagnation via an argument of Kaleckian derivation. Keynes's version of the argument, more familiar to most macroeconomists, may be used as a heuristic aid. According to Keynes individuals are free to choose the *proportion* of their incomes that they wish to save; but total saving is determined at macro level by total investment expenditure. There must then be a mechanism for reconciling the aggregate of individual saving *plans* with total savings. Reconciliation is achieved via variation in aggregate income and employment, desired savings being an increasing function of aggregate income. One famous consequence of this is the paradox of thrift. Suppose individuals decide to save a higher proportion of income, but there is no parallel increase in the inducement to invest. With investment constant, *total* savings must also remain constant. An excess of intended savings over intended investment means a shortfall of intended expenditure in relation to output, and output falls. Therefore income falls too, and people end up saving the same amount as before, only now it is a larger fraction of a smaller income.

In Kalecki's (1971: ch.7) variant, profit *margins* (over cost of production) are determined at the micro level by the 'degree of monopoly', but *total* profit is determined at the macro level by the sum of capitalists' expenditures (plus the budget deficit and the trade surplus, minus worker savings, if any). Again, there must be a mechanism for reconciling these two factors, and again it is variation in total income. If an increase in the degree of monopoly raises profit margins,[5] but there is no increase in the total of capitalists' expenditures (consumption and investment), total income falls. As with the paradox of thrift, the capitalists end up making the same *total* profit as before, but now in the form of a larger fraction of a smaller total sales revenue. Just as a rising propensity to save will tend to induce stagnation in Keynes's system (absent a corresponding increase in the inducement to invest), so a rising degree of monopoly will tend to induce stagnation in the Kaleckian system (absent a corresponding increase in the capitalists' propensity to consume, or to accumulate). This is the basic mechanism envisaged by Baran and Sweezy.

We shall return to examine the details of this argument, but first we consider very broadly the degree to which it is supported by the historical record.

A FIRST LOOK AT THE LEDGER

In his own twenty-five-year assessment of *Monopoly Capital*, Sweezy (1992: 16) stated that his argument 'holds up pretty well when judged in the light of all the developments and changes that have taken place in this eventful quarter century'.[6] This view has a certain plausibility. Baran and Sweezy's central thesis – that advanced capitalist economies have an inherent tendency toward stagnation as the growth of labour productivity outstrips the rate of growth of effective demand – looks quite good in light of the so-called jobless recovery of the early 1990s in the US economy, and, even more so, in light of the persistent mass unemployment plaguing western Europe for a decade or more. In contrast, Brewer's (1980: 138) critical comment that Baran and Sweezy 'should have realised' that the post-war boom showed that 'monopoly capitalism is not incompatible with growth' now appears rather dated. And the tables also seem to have turned on Brewer's remark that Baran and Sweezy concentrated too much on the USA, at a time when western Europe and Japan were expanding faster.

Baran and Sweezy also argued that insofar as state expenditure could offset the tendency of monopoly capitalism towards stagnation (albeit partially and temporarily), structural features of US society made military spending uniquely acceptable (to the ruling class). Chapters 6 and 7 held, against the liberal Keynesians, that it would be extraordinarily difficult to substitute 'welfare state' expenditures for military spending. This claim would appear to be borne out by the failure of a substantial 'peace dividend' to emerge following the cold war.

Certain correct predictions, however, do not validate the specific theory that led Baran and Sweezy to make those predictions. The predictions thus might have come out right, but for the wrong reasons. To investigate this possibility, we begin by confronting the mechanism of stagnation in *Monopoly Capital* with some anomalous empirical observations. This will lead us into a critical assessment of the theory.

SOME AWKWARD FACTS

First, and most generally, there is the question of the monopolization of the economy. Baran and Sweezy seem committed to the proposition that the degree of monopoly should continue to increase under monopoly capitalism (see also Sweezy 1984: 44). It is clear that a *reduction* in the degree of monopoly would be quite inconsistent with their theoretical scheme. Yet this seems to have occurred. William Shepherd (1982: 613), employing a fourfold categorization of industries into 'pure monopolies', 'dominant firms', 'tight oligopolies' and 'effectively competitive' markets, argues that over the 1958–80 period 'the scope of competition increased substantially ... virtually throughout the economy'. Summarizing his study, Shepherd (1982: 624) states that 'tight oligopoly covers nearly one-fifth of the economy, down by half from 1958. Pure monopoly and dominant firms have shrunk to about 5 per cent of the economy (compared to 8 per cent in 1958 and 11 per cent in 1939), while effectively competitive markets now account for over three-fourths of national income – up from 56 per cent in 1958 and 52 per cent in 1939'.

Shepherd's effectively competitive markets are by no means all textbook examples of perfect competition, but they are markets where the top four firms produce less than 40 per cent of output and entry barriers are low. Carlton and Perloff (1990: ch. 7), citing work by Golbe and White, produce figures consistent with Shepherd's findings. Between 1970 and 1984 the share of non-farm, private sector employment accounted for by the largest 25, 50 and 100 firms fell from 10 to 7 per cent, 19 to 15 per cent, and 25 to 21 per cent, respectively. The share of total assets of all non-financial corporations accounted for by the biggest 25, 50 and 100 firms also fell, from 17 to 13 per cent, 29 to 27 per cent, and 38 to 34 per cent, respectively.

To explain the trend toward greater competition and reduced monopolization, Shepherd cites anti-trust laws, increased competition from imports, and deregulation. More tentatively, he suggests that technological change may have reduced the minimum viable size of operations in some industries. Insofar as the reduction in the degree of monopoly in the US economy is an effect of policy (anti-trust, deregulation, lowering of tariff barriers), one may be tempted to say that this represents an 'exogenous' intrusion into the system, which the authors of *Monopoly Capital* could not reasonably have been expected to predict. But this sort of response is problematic. It is inconsistent with the general Marxian approach which typically regards the state as serving the interests of the ruling class. This is a point that Baran and Sweezy themselves make in the course of explaining why the label '*State* Monopoly Capitalism' is misleading:

> [T]erms like 'State capitalism' and 'State monopoly capitalism' almost inevitably carry the connotation that the State is somehow an independent social force, coordinate with private business, and that the functioning of the system is determined not only by the cooperation of these two forces but also by their antagonisms and conflicts. This seems to us a seriously misleading view – in reality, what appear to be conflicts between business and government are reflections of conflict within the ruling class – and we think it desirable to avoid terminology which tends to give it currency.
>
> (Baran and Sweezy 1968: 75–6)

From this perspective, if the state helped to reduce the degree of monopoly this would have to be seen as reflecting a changed balance of forces among the factions of the ruling class, such that the defenders of monopoly are no longer dominant. Howard and King (1990: 86) remind us that Sweezy 'criticized Hilferding and Lenin for mistakenly generalizing, in their notion of "finance capital", from a specific, brief phase of banker dominance over industry to characterize twentieth-century capitalism as a whole'. Could it be that Baran and Sweezy similarly failed to realize that the high-water mark of monopolization of the US economy had passed even as they were writing?[7]

Second, I wish to draw attention to some observations that present problems for the core of the Baran and Sweezy argument – the law of rising surplus and the thesis of a diminishing propensity to consume out of profits. Table 5.1 and Figures 5.1 to 5.3 are relevant here. Many of Baran and Sweezy's formulations would lead one to expect a progressive increase in the growth rate of labour productivity, as competition is progressively displaced from prices onto cost reduction (Baran and Sweezy 1968: ch. 3). As Figure 5.1 and the first column of Table 5.1 show, this has not been the case. While productivity growth has recovered somewhat over recent years, the overall trend for the post-war period is clearly downward. Figure 5.2 and the second column of Table 5.1 show the behaviour of the share of after-tax corporate profits in total income. Again the trend is clearly downward; indeed, the decade averages in Table 5.1 show a monotonic decline. Finally, Figure 5.3 and the third column of Table 5.1 show trends in the ratio of aggregate consumption to income. Baran and Sweezy claim that the profit share tends to rise, and that the propensity to consume out of profits tends to fall. This implies a fall in the ratio of consumption to income. But while this ratio has fluctuated, there is no downward trend. In fact, since the mid-1960s the consumption share has shown a trend increase.

Admittedly, one could object to using these measures against the theory of *Monopoly Capital*. For one thing, the surplus which Baran and Sweezy claim tends to rise under monopoly capitalism is not identical with (being much broader than) corporate profits.[8] But their theory would not lead one to expect a negative correlation between the trend of the surplus share and the trend of the profit share in aggregate income.

Further insight into this issue can be obtained by examining Baran and Sweezy's reaction to a comment made by Nicholas Kaldor. Kaldor (1957) had broadly anticipated the stagnationist argument of *Monopoly Capital* and suggested that it would likely be attractive to Marxist economists; but he claimed that the prediction of a rising profit share in total income was counterfactual. Baran and Sweezy (1968: 83) remark that while Kaldor 'apparently does not reject the theory which he attributes to Marxist economists', nonetheless 'he asserts, in effect, that no matter how sound the theory, it is refuted by the statistical record'. This, they go on to say, 'is an unsatisfactory way to leave the matter. There must be something wrong with either the theory or the statistics.' From their point of view, of course, it is the statistics that are at fault. Besides distinguishing profits from the surplus, Baran and Sweezy (1968: 84) argue that the process which Kaldor outlines as an implication of the Marxist view – the share of profit 'rising beyond the point where it covers investment needs and the consumption of capitalists' – is inherently self-limiting and 'cannot appear in the statistics as an actual continuing increase of profits as a share of total income'.

Why not? Baran and Sweezy (1968: 84) make reference to the basic Keynesian idea that 'profits which are neither invested nor consumed are no profits at all'. But, as we saw above, in the Keynesian paradox of thrift there is no problem with raising the *ratio* of savings (or profits) to income: only the absolute amount of savings is limited by investment. So Kaldor's point is not so easily dismissed. In order to sustain the case that a Keynesian–Kaleckian

Table 5.1 Decade averages for some relevant data

Period	*Productivity growth (%)*	*Profits/GDP (%)*	*Consumption/GDP (%)*
1947–56	3.17	14.58	65.44
1957–66	3.08	11.30	63.97
1967–76	1.98	9.82	63.54
1977–86	0.96	7.94	64.95
1987–92	1.20	6.10	67.70

Sources: Survey of Current Business for productivity growth and Profits/GDP; NIPA tape for consumption/GDP.

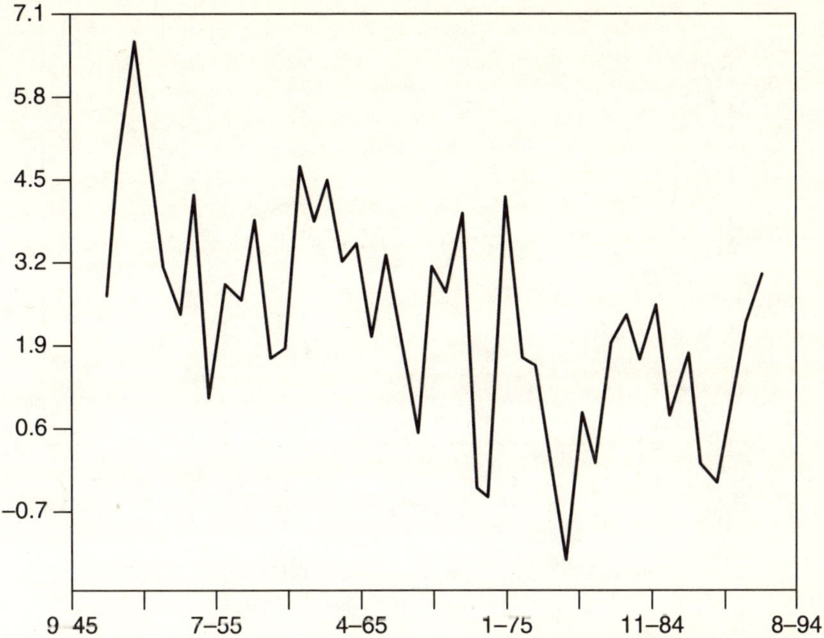

Figure 5.1 Change in output per hour (four-quarter span), 1948–92
Source: Department of Commerce, BCI data files

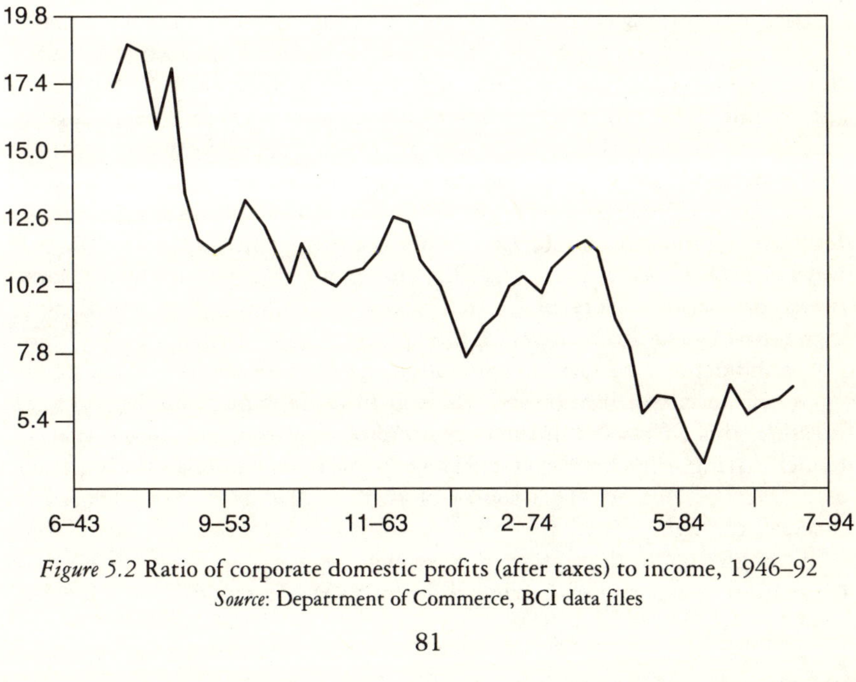

Figure 5.2 Ratio of corporate domestic profits (after taxes) to income, 1946–92
Source: Department of Commerce, BCI data files

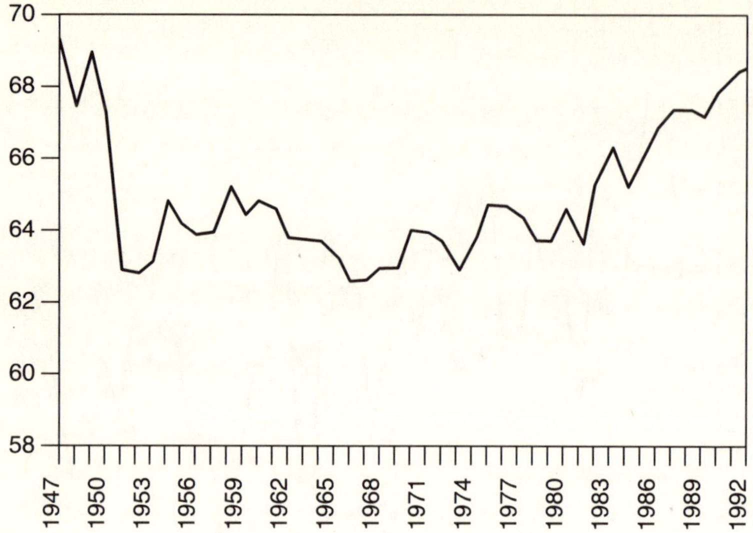

Figure 5.3 Ratio of consumption to GDP, 1947–92
Source: NIPA tape

limitation applies not just to the *amount* of profit but also to the profit *share*, one needs to also argue that the profit share is an increasing function of the rate of capacity utilization. If this is so, then an increase in the *ex ante* profit share, by depressing total output and lowering the degree of capacity utilization, may prove abortive in raising the measured, *ex post* profit share.

Baran and Sweezy (1968: 91–5) proceed to supply such an argument based on standard break-even analysis. Their basic idea is that fixed costs constitute a large part of the total costs for large-scale capitalist enterprises. An increase in the volume of output, associated with an increase in the degree of capacity utilization, 'spreads' these fixed costs, and hence reduces the average cost per unit of output. For a given output price, therefore, greater capacity utilization will generate a higher profit margin. While this analysis makes sense in its own terms, its relationship to Marxian theory is entirely unclear. In *The Theory of Capitalist Development* Sweezy (1942: ch. 9) wrote approvingly of Marx's overaccumulation theory of the business cycle, according to which rapid accumulation leads to relatively full employment, and thereby tends to raise wages and depress the rate of exploitation and the rate of profit. Since a high degree of capacity utilization and relatively full employment surely tend to go together, this effect cuts in the opposite direction from break-even analysis (which distinguishes between fixed and variable costs, but takes the wage rate as a given parameter). This source of theoretical tension gets ignored in *Monopoly Capital*.

A rough and ready empirical assessment of the hypothesis of positive covariation of capacity utilization and profit share is reported in Table 5.2,

Table 5.2 Regressions of the profit share on capacity utilization

	Model A	*Model B*
constant	– 4.248	0.157
	(– 1.133)	(0.124)
trend	– 0.046	
	(– 8.591)	
caputil	0.182	0.001
	(4.105)	(0.058)
profshare(-1)		0.966
		(37.319)
R^2	0.549	0.947
DW	0.084	
Q(26-0)	814.550	26.668
p-value of *Q*	0.000	0.427

Source: *Survey of Current Business*
Note: Dependent variable, profshare = share of after-tax corporate profits in total income. OLS estimation using quarterly data, 1967: 2 to 1993: 3; *t*-ratios in parentheses.

using data from the period 1967–93. Model A offers a straightforward regression of the profit share (profshare) on capacity utilization (caputil) and a time-trend. At first glance this model appears to show a significant positive association as postulated by Baran and Sweezy on the basis of break-even analysis, but the severe first-order autocorrelation indicated by the Durbin–Watson statistic of 0.084 vitiates hypothesis testing. Model B, which overcomes the autocorrelation problem by including the lagged value of the dependent variable,[9] shows *no* marginal explanatory power for the degree of capacity utilization in accounting for the profit share.

My tentative conclusion here is that the presumed relationship between profit share and capacity utilization does not provide a firm basis for rejecting Kaldor's critique, and does not provide a basis for dismissing as irrelevant the data in Table 5.1. That is, if there were powerful forces *tending* to raise the profit share, as Baran and Sweezy contend, we should expect this to be registered in the form of an actual rise in the profit share, something we do not see.

CAPITAL VERSUS *MONOPOLY CAPITAL*

As Baran and Sweezy say in response to Kaldor, there must be something wrong with either the theory or the statistics. Perhaps it is the theory after all.

Baran and Sweezy must be given full credit for attempting to come to grips with the concrete reality of post-war US capitalism using Marxian concepts, rather than simply repeating the formulas of the master as some of their 'fundamentalist' critics have been wont to do. In the course of their investigations, Baran and Sweezy reached the conclusion that some Marxian concepts had to be revised in light of a century of capitalist development since Marx wrote *Capital*. Naturally, there can be nothing objectionable about this a priori.

But it is not dogmatism to suggest that the revisions proposed by Baran and Sweezy are open to criticism, and that some of their departures from classical Marxism may be retrograde.

In the most general terms, one might say that Baran and Sweezy are vulnerable to the charge that they over-emphasized the structure of product markets (as well as possibly mistaking its trend), to the relative exclusion of the capital–labour relationship and the Marxian conception of the economy as a metabolism of social labour time. Consider in this light the 'law of rising surplus' (LRS) as formulated in *Monopoly Capital*.

The proposition that the mass and rate of surplus value both have a tendency to increase over the course of capitalist development is not something new with Baran and Sweezy. Marx himself made such statements;[10] but he does not see it as inconsistent with his 'law of the tendency for the rate of profit to fall' (TRPF). If the organic composition of capital is on the increase, a rising share of surplus value in total income is quite compatible with a fall in the rate of profit on capital stock. It therefore seems odd that Baran and Sweezy (1968: 80f.) should claim that the LRS has to be *substituted* for the TRPF under monopoly capitalism.

If the LRS is in fact part of classical Marxism, the 'spin' which it is given by Baran and Sweezy is nonetheless new – for they see it as a specific result of combining cost-cutting innovation (this is in Marx, of course) with *monopoly pricing*. One is perilously close here to the notion that profits are made in the sphere of circulation, via unequal exchange, a conception that Marx dismembered very effectively in Volume 1, chapter 5 of *Capital*. In Volume III, where Marx does offer some comments on monopoly, he makes it clear that monopoly pricing results in a redistribution of surplus value among capitalists. Monopolists are able to garner a larger share of the total surplus value than would have gone to them under the equalization of the rate of profit, at the expense of smaller and more competitive capitals. On this analysis, one would expect that the effect of a generalization of monopoly would not be the *generalization* of monopoly profit but rather its *cancelling out*. (There is clearly a fallacy of composition in the idea that every capitalist can be the beneficiary of a redistribution of surplus value.) The problem here, it should be noted, is not unique to *Monopoly Capital*; Kalecki and Steindl (1952) also share the assumption that an increase in the degree of monopoly will tend to raise the profit share.[11]

From a classical Marxian standpoint, what really matters is the monopoly of the means of production on the part of the capitalist class as a whole (and the consequent compulsion of propertyless workers to sell their labour power for a wage), rather than the degree of product-market concentration. According to this view, there are two sources of increased profits – absolute surplus value (resulting from lengthening the working day and/or cutting the consumption standards of workers) and relative surplus value (resulting from the cheapening of the workers' means of consumption via technical progress). If an increase in the degree of product-market monopoly is to have a bearing on the matter, it must be via the promotion of either absolute or relative surplus value. Implicitly, Baran and Sweezy seem to be saying that monopoly promotes relative surplus value, but exactly how is this supposed to work?

Is it that in the competitive past, the benefits of cost-cutting innovations were unproblematically passed on to the consumer in the form of lower prices, while under monopoly they are retained in the form of higher corporate profits? This idea seems naive. Clearly, Marx did not believe that the benefits of increased labour productivity were passed on to the working-class consumer under the competitive capitalism of his day. The whole point of his theory of relative surplus value was that a cheapening of the workers' means of consumption would lead to a corresponding cut in money wages, and hence an increase in the rate of surplus value, rather than a rise in the real commodity wage (although if the productivity gains are large enough, a rise in the rate of surplus value is compatible with some degree of increase in the real wage). The division of the spoils will presumably depend on the relative bargaining strength of capital and labour, which will be influenced by the level of unemployment as well as the degree of organization of the conflicting parties. The degree of seller concentration among the capitalists may have *some* role to play in the latter regard, but there is no warrant for the idea that this factor could be the decisive one. Surely no valid conclusions can be reached by considering seller concentration in isolation from the labour market and the wage-determination process. The ability of workers to appropriate some part of the gains resulting from increases in labour productivity has varied from time to time and place to place; but it would be difficult to maintain that it has tended to decrease over the post-war (and presumably monopolistic) period.

Baran and Sweezy (1968: 84) do offer some brief remarks on the question of wage determination, by way of fending off a possible objection – namely 'that labor unions are now strong enough to capture for their members increments in profits resulting from the combination of declining costs and monopoly pricing'. But this seems out of focus: the real objection is that workers were not necessarily any *more* able to capture the gains flowing from increased productivity in an earlier phase of capitalist development. Anyway, Baran and Sweezy's (1968: 85) response is that labour unions cannot substantially influence the overall distribution of income between wages and profits (rather than simply improving the relative position of the unionized workers) because 'under monopoly capitalism employers can and do pass on higher labor costs in the form of higher prices'.

Two comments are in order here. First, the fact that capitalist firms are able to answer higher wages with higher prices (and vice versa, presumably) does not of itself license any general conclusion regarding the overall result of that process. The existence of a wage–price spiral is consistent with a rising, falling or constant profit share. Baran and Sweezy just assume that the monopolization of product markets confers a decisive advantage on the capitalists, while the competing monopolization represented by labour unions is powerless to affect the outcome. Second, if one seeks a general understanding of this process, it is necessary to enquire into the conditions for a wage–price spiral. Seller concentration in itself is not sufficient; clearly it also takes an accommodating monetary policy. But while the absence of any substantial discussion of the capital–labour relation in *Monopoly Capital* has been remarked upon by many critics, equally noteworthy is the absence of any reference to monetary matters.

If they had examined this point further, presumably Baran and Sweezy would have come to the conclusion that modern central banks are in collusion with monopoly capitalists to maintain the profits of the latter. This conclusion may not seem remarkable from a Marxian viewpoint, but there is something else to consider: in a curious inversion of the standard Keynesian ideas, an accommodating monetary policy would have to be seen, from the perspective of *Monopoly Capital*, as a factor contributing to stagnation and unemployment. Monetary accommodation, by permitting capitalists to raise their prices in response to any increases in money wages – and hence to maintain their generalized monopoly profits – 'validates' the tendency for the growth of effective demand to fall behind the growth of productive capacity. (Remember that in Baran and Sweezy's analysis stagnation of effective demand is basically an effect of monopoly profit.) Tight monetary policy, conversely, would presumably limit the ability of monopolists to maintain their excessive profit margins, hence boosting aggregate demand. This conclusion seems hard to accept. If it does indeed follow from the basic logic of *Monopoly Capital*, this might be taken as additional grounds for questioning that logic.

CONCLUSION

The awkward facts noted earlier pose a more serious problem for the theory of *Monopoly Capital* than they pose for classical Marxism. The trend fall in the profit share of income over the post-war period is a problem for both theories, although not necessarily an insurmountable one. The rise in the ratio of consumption to total income since the 1960s and the falling growth rate of labour productivity are specific problems for the Baran and Sweezy approach; classical Marxism has no strong commitment on these matters. And while the fall in the degree of monopoly (indicated by Shepherd's work) would not have been expected on the basis of classical Marxism, it is clearly a more serious anomaly for Baran and Sweezy, whose insistence on a high and increasing degree of monopoly was a key feature of their analysis of post-war capitalism.

This is certainly not to say that a 'correct' alternative to the Baran and Sweezy analysis can be found in the pages of *Capital*. It is only to say that a more adequate Marxian analysis would have a somewhat different emphasis and would build on Marx's insights (and, yes, revise his concepts) in a somewhat different way. If stagnation cannot be explained by *Monopoly Capital*'s combination of a monopoly-induced rise in profit margins and a diminishing propensity to consume out of profits, perhaps it is worth reconsidering Marx's tendency for the rate of profit to fall. Could it be that the slow pace of capital accumulation is a result of sagging, rather than excessive, profitability? This is not the place to develop an alternative to *Monopoly Capital*, but I should point out that some colleagues and I (Cockshott, Cottrell and Michaelson 1995) have offered some empirical results tending to support this thesis for the UK.

If I have seemed critical of certain aspects of Sweezy's economics, I should emphasize, in closing, his courage and tenacity in maintaining his Marxist convictions, and his vision of a rational non-exploitative social order – whether or not these ideas were fashionable. I have drawn attention to that which is distinctive in Baran and Sweezy's theory within the field of Marxian economics; but in relation to the dominant political and intellectual culture of the USA it is Sweezy's continued adherence to Marxism that is most remarkable. What are we to make of this in the mid-1990s?

The primary force of the Marxian critique of capitalism, whatever specific form it takes, derives from the claim that there is a better alternative – a system based on social ownership of the means of production, where cooperation replaces market competition, and planning in the public interest replaces the pursuit of private profit. Today, one is forced to ask whether the demise of Soviet socialism demonstrates that the Marxist alternative is chimerical. Many Western Marxists (Sweezy included) in the post-war period held that the Soviet Union was *not* a socialist society, and that the system built under Stalin was a travesty. Yet the collapse of that system, rather than removing an obstacle (in the form of a false example) to the propagation of true socialism, has reduced many erstwhile socialists to silence. Paul Sweezy has bucked this trend. Intellectual courage, or mere stubborn persistence in error? Many may say the latter; but there are those of us who believe it is the former.

NOTES

1 Although *Monopoly Capital* was first published in 1966, Sweezy tells us in the preface that the text was essentially complete at the time of Baran's death in 1964.

2 For further biographical details, see Hillard (1985a), Sweezy (1987), Lebowitz (1990); for bibliographical details, see Hillard (1985b).

3 Sweezy's mentor Schumpeter comes in for criticism in this context. While Schumpeter had suggested that the modern businessman is less driven by the motive of accumulation, and more prone to consume the surplus, than his predecessors, Baran and Sweezy (1968: 54) argue that 'the real capitalist today is not the individual businessman but the corporation' and that 'there can be no doubt that the making and accumulation of profits hold as dominant a position today as they ever did'.

4 Lange (1939: 111–14) argues that this second point means that a socialist economy is capable of generating faster technological improvement than a monopolistic capitalist economy.

5 We shall find cause to question this assumption below.

6 Sweezy's only substantial misgiving is that he and Baran failed to predict the burgeoning, and increasingly prominent, role of the financial sector in subsequent decades, the 1980s in particular.

7 Fine (1988) suggests that Sweezy may have generalized unduly on the basis of his early investigation of monopoly in the British coal industry (Sweezy 1938), thus supporting the claim of Weeks (1981) that the authors of *Monopoly Capital* may have 'projected the monopolies of the past onto the modern world'.

8 For a discussion of the concept of 'surplus' employed in *Monopoly Capital*, see the essays in Davis (1992).

9 The Ljung-Box Q statistic quoted in Table 5.2 provides a test for autocorrelation that is valid in the presence of a lagged dependent variable (as the Durbin-Watson statistic is not). The p-value of 0.427 for Model B says that we may accept the null hypothesis of no autocorrelation in this case.

10 Again, this is not incompatible with a fall in the measured share of corporate profits in national income – if the proportion of total surplus value appearing as profit, as opposed to, say, expenditure on unproductive labour, is decreasing at a sufficient rate. However, as remarked above, there is no obvious theoretical reason for expecting such a negative correlation.

11 As a distinguished expositor of Marx, Sweezy is clearly familiar with Marx's writings on monopoly profit as a redistribution of surplus value. Indeed, Sweezy (1981: appendix B) has written specifically on the relationship between his own views and those set out in Volume III of *Capital*. I do not, however, think that Sweezy has succeeded in clarifying this relationship.

REFERENCES

Baran, P.A. (1957) *The Political Economy of Growth*, New York: Monthly Review Press.

Baran, P.A. and Sweezy, P.M. (1968) *Monopoly Capital: An Essay on the American Economic and Social Order*, Harmondsworth: Pelican. (Original publication, New York: Monthly Review Press, 1966.)

Brewer, A. (1980) *Marxist Theories of Imperialism: A Critical Survey*, London: Routledge & Kegan Paul.

Carlton, D.W. and Perloff, J.M. (1990) *Modern Industrial Organization*, New York: Harper Collins.

Cockshott, W.P., Cottrell, A. and Michaelson, G.J. (1995) 'Testing Marx: Some New Results from UK Data', *Capital and Class* 55: 103–29.

Davis, J.B. (ed.) (1992) *The Economic Surplus in Advanced Economies*, Aldershot: Elgar.

Fine, B. (1988) 'The British Coal Industry's Contribution to the Political Economy of Paul Sweezy', *History of Political Economy* 20,2: 235–50.

Hillard, M. (1985a) 'Harry Magdoff and Paul Sweezy: Biographical Notes', in S. Resnick and R. Wolff (eds) *Rethinking Marxism: Struggles in Marxist Theory*, Brooklyn: Autonomedia.

—— (1985b) 'Harry Magdoff and Paul Sweezy: Selected Bibliographies,' in S. Resnick and R. Wolff (eds) *Rethinking Marxism: Struggles in Marxist Theory*, Brooklyn: Autonomedia.

Howard, M.C. and King, J.E. (1990) 'Marxian Economists and the Great Depression', *History of Political Economy* 22,1: 81–100.

Kaldor, N. (1957) 'A Model of Economic Growth', *Economic Journal* 67,4: 591–624.

Kalecki, M. (1971) *Selected Essays on the Dynamics of the Capitalist Economy*, Cambridge: Cambridge University Press.

Lange, O. (1939) *On the Economic Theory of Socialism*, Minneapolis: University of Minnesota Press.

Lebowitz, M.A. (1990) 'Paul M. Sweezy', in M. Berg (ed.) *Political Economy in the Twentieth Century*, Savage, Md.: Barnes & Noble, 131–61.

Lintner, J. (1956) 'Distribution of Incomes of Corporations among Dividends, Retained Earnings and Taxes', *American Economic Review* 46,2: 97–113.

Shepherd, W.G. (1982) 'Causes of Increased Competition in the U.S. Economy, 1939–1980', *Review of Economics and Statistics*, 64,4: 613–26.

Steindl, J. (1952) *Maturity and Stagnation in American Capitalism*, Oxford: Oxford University Press.

Sweezy, P.M. (1938) *Monopoly and Competition in the English Coal Trade, 1550–1850*, Cambridge, Mass.: Harvard University Press.

——(1942) *The Theory of Capitalist Development*, New York: Oxford University Press.

——(1949) *Socialism*, New York: Monthly Review Press.

——(1953) *The Present as History*, New York: Monthly Review Press.

——(1981) *Four Lectures on Marxism*, New York: Monthly Review Press.

——(1984) 'Some Problems in the Theory of Capital Accumulation', in J.B. Foster and H. Szlajfer (eds) *The Faltering Economy: The Problem of Accumulation under Monopoly Capitalism*, New York: Monthly Review Press.

——(1987) 'Interview with Paul M. Sweezy', *Monthly Review* 38,11: 1–28.

——(1992) 'Monopoly Capital After 25 Years', in J.B. Davis (ed.) *The Economic Surplus in Advanced Economies*, Aldershot: Edward Elgar.

Sweezy, P.M. and Huberman, L. (1968) *Introduction to Socialism*, New York: Monthly Review Press.

Weeks, J. (1981) *Capital and Exploitation*, Princeton: Princeton University Press.

Part III

COMPARATIVE APPROACHES TO POLITICAL ECONOMY

6

PRICES, EXPECTATION AND INVESTMENT

A critical assessment of Keynes's marginal efficiency of capital

Claudio Sardoni

Investment plays a crucial role in *The General Theory*. Given the propensity to consume, 'the equilibrium level of employment ... will depend on the amount of current investment' (Keynes 1936: 27). But firms as a whole will not necessarily push their investment to a level associated with the full utilization of existing capacity and the full employment of labour.

Chapter 11 of *The General Theory* sets out to demonstrate why investment does not necessarily increase until full employment is reached. While Keynes's treatment of investment in a market economy is much richer in chapter 12 of the *General Theory*, where the notion of uncertainty takes centre stage, this paper concentrates on the treatment of investment in chapter 11 and tries to point out some problems with this analysis. More precisely, I argue that the decreasing marginal efficiency of capital is based on an analytical construct which cannot demonstrate the possibility of underemployment equilibria. I also argue that an alternative explanation for the decreasing expected profitability of investment can be found by setting analysis of firms' decision making in a framework which is explicitly different from pure competition. This more satisfactory analysis of the investment demand function also provides more solid foundations for Keynes's general theory.

The first important criticism of Keynes's analysis of investment was made by Kalecki in his 1936 review of *The General Theory*. This critique, and Kalecki's own approach to investment, bears remarkable similarities to the famous article by Kahn (1931) on home investment. Both Kahn and Kalecki employed a dynamic sequential approach when analysing investment. Kahn's 1931 article greatly influenced Keynes; yet Keynes failed to perceive the importance of what Kahn suggested concerning the investment process.

Keynes may have been right that the sequential approach was inadequate for his own analytical purposes. However, a more careful consideration of Kahn's arguments could have saved him from some of the logical flaws, pointed out by Kalecki, which undercut the notion of the decreasing marginal efficiency of capital. In particular, following Kahn could have helped Keynes to draw a clearer distinction between *ex ante* and *ex post* factors in his analysis of the investment process.

Within this context, the notion of decreasing expected profitability of investment can be provided with more solid analytical foundations by paying greater attention to the issue of market forms than Keynes did in *The General Theory*. Keynes, as is well known, argued that his results were general and held regardless of the assumed degree of competition. Had Keynes explicitly assumed a market form different from pure competition, his idea that the expected profitability of investment is a decreasing function of investment would have been given a more convincing justification than the one offered in chapter 11. As Sraffa (1926) pointed out, the ability of a firm to expand productive capacity in the long period is limited by demand. Had Keynes followed Sraffa here, he could have provided a more convincing explanation as to why aggregate investment is not necessarily pushed to its full employment level.

The next three sections outline the views of Kahn, Keynes and Kalecki concerning investment. Then I suggest an alternative explanation for the decreasing expected profitability of investment. The last section draws some conclusions.

KAHN: PRICES, REAL WAGES, PROFITS AND INDUCEMENT TO INVEST

Kahn exerted an enormous influence on Keynes, both through his work and through their long-standing friendship. Keynes, on his part, never hesitated to acknowledge his intellectual indebtedness to Kahn. In 1931, Kahn published his article on home investment with the objective of analysing the effect of an increase in public investment on the aggregate level of employment. This article is most famous for the introduction of the multiplier, a notion that was then modified[1] by Keynes to become one of the central innovations in *The General Theory*. But the article is also important for the analytical relations that Kahn established between changes in investment, prices and profits. Some of these relations were taken up by Keynes and introduced into *The General Theory*.

Dealing with the effect of an increase in public investment on the output and price of consumer goods, Kahn (1931: 177) followed a 'common-sense' approach, arguing that the price level and the output of consumer goods were determined by conditions of supply and demand. Since he assumed moderately increasing short-period supply curves for consumer goods (Kahn 1931: 186), a rise in demand for consumer goods (due to an increase in employment caused by a larger public investment) brings about an increase in their price level along with an increase in their output. The assumption of increasing supply prices was accompanied by the assumption that money wages were constant (Kahn 1931: 175), so greater demand also causes a decrease in the real wage rate and *an increase in profits*.

Throughout most of his article Kahn ignored the effects that a rise in profits has on private investment; only in the last two pages did he deal with this problem.

> An increase in output, and of the margin of profit that goes with it, *cannot, taken by themselves, fail both to increase the attractiveness and to facilitate the process of investment at home* .... If there were no opposing forces in operation, it might easily happen that, in spite of the rise in the rate of interest, the ordinary processes of home investment would be promoted rather than retarded by a policy of public works.
>
> (Kahn 1931: 197; emphasis added)

This holds on the assumption that government spending leaves the general state of confidence unaltered. Changes in the state of confidence could affect investment in either direction, but Kahn tended to believe that the state of confidence would be positively affected: 'There is strong justification for concluding on *a priori* grounds that the inauguration of an active economic policy would promote confidence rather than upset it' (Kahn 1931: 197).[2]

Kahn did not examine the effects of increased investment on the prices of capital goods, but it seems obvious that greater investment should cause prices to rise also in the capital-goods sector. Since Kahn never argued to the contrary, it is natural to assume that supply curves of capital goods are also upward sloping, so that an increase in public investment brings about a general price rise. Kahn's analysis can thus be generalized and expressed in the following terms. An increase in public investment, or more generally any increase in aggregate investment, leads to an expansion of output and a rise in the general price level; if money wages do not vary (or they increase less than prices), there is a decrease in real wages and an increase in profits which will affect private investment decisions positively.

Kahn here employed a sequential analytical approach: changes in investment, output, prices, and their interactions are considered by looking at the economic process over time as the system moves from one stage to another. Once investment changes, a cumulative process starts whereby past investment affects current investment decisions through its effect on prices, profits and, possibly, the state of confidence. Kahn examined the multiplier process in this way, analysing the growth of employment through successive periods.

This sequential approach differs from that of Keynes: *The General Theory* does not analyse the effects of investment over time. Kahn himself noted that Keynes had no interest in the dynamic process by which the economy heads towards its equilibrium positions; and he referred, with approval, to those who criticized Keynes on this point. In his fifth lecture on the making of *The General Theory*, Kahn (1984: 119–68) mentions the criticism by Robertson and Pigou regarding this aspect of Keynes's theory. Quoting a passage from Pigou (1950),[3] Kahn observed:

> Pigou devoted the final passage of his partial renunciation of his bitter and sarcastic review-article on the *General Theory* to an account – *for the*

> *most part highly acceptable to Keynesians* – of the same fundamental factors which I am identifying as determining the position of the economy.
>
> (Kahn 1984: 125; emphasis added)[4]

Despite this methodological difference, Keynes did use some of Kahn's analytical blocks to build his general theory. The general price level in *The General Theory* is determined in essentially the same way that it is determined in a single industry by Kahn. At the single industry level, price depends on the supply function and the level of output and 'there is no reason to modify this conclusion when we pass to industry as a whole' (Keynes 1936: 294). As to the shape of supply curves, Keynes assumed that short-period decreasing returns prevailed, so that supply curves were upward sloping. Even in 1939, Keynes held this position and relied on the authority of Kahn to defend it.[5] Finally, with given money wages, an increase in output for Keynes was also accompanied by a fall in real wages and an increase in profits. Keynes developed this point in chapters 2 (pp. 17–18) and 20 (pp. 281–6) of *The General Theory.* In particular, he related changes in income distribution to the elasticity of output and to changes in effective demand.[6] Let us now look at how Keynes used the above relations.

KEYNES'S THEORY OF INVESTMENT IN CHAPTER 11 OF *THE GENERAL THEORY*

Chapter 11 of *The General Theory* sets out to formulate a demand schedule for investment. This demand schedule had to demonstrate why aggregate investment is not necessarily pushed to its full-employment level. The determination of the equilibrium level of investment is based on an investment demand schedule relating the rate of aggregate investment to the marginal efficiency of capital, the latter being defined as 'the relation between the prospective yield of a capital-asset and its supply price or replacement cost' (Keynes 1936: 135). The rate of investment will be pushed to the point on this function where the marginal efficiency of capital (ϵ) is equal to the rate of interest (i).

If we ignore the effects of changes in investment and income on the rate of interest, a stable equilibrium level of investment lower than its full-employment level can be found only if the investment demand schedule is downward sloping; that is, *only if the marginal efficiency of capital is a decreasing function of investment itself.* With a given rate of interest, a constant marginal efficiency of capital would imply either that aggregate investment is pushed to its full-employment level (when $\epsilon \geq i$) or that firms as a whole do not invest at all ($\epsilon < i$).

Keynes held that the marginal efficiency of capital was in fact a decreasing function of the level of investment:

> If there is an increased investment in any given type of capital during any period of time, the marginal efficiency of that type of capital will diminish

> as the investment is increased, partly because the prospective yield will fall as the supply of that type of capital is increased, and partly because, as a rule, pressure on the facilities for producing that type of capital will cause its supply price to increase; the second of these factors being usually the more important in producing equilibrium in the short run, but the longer the period in view the more does the first factor take its place.
>
> (Keynes 1936: 136)

Individual functions are then aggregated to obtain the aggregate investment demand schedule. In symbols, if we denote the supply prices of investment goods by p, and the expected yields by E (long-term expectations), we have

$$\epsilon = f(p, E)$$

$$\frac{d\epsilon}{dp} < 0, \quad \frac{d\epsilon}{dE} > 0$$

with p and E, in turn, functions of the level of investment

$$\frac{dp}{dI} > 0, \quad \frac{dE}{dI} < 0.$$

The supply price of investment goods will rise with the level of investment and expected yields will decrease as capital becomes less scarce thanks to investment.

Investment is a function of the marginal efficiency and the rate of interest,

$$I = g(\epsilon, i)$$

with

$$\frac{dI}{d\epsilon} > 0, \quad \frac{dI}{di} < 0.$$

The volume of investment so determined is associated with a certain level of aggregate output, which is not necessarily its full-employment level, and with a certain general price level. An increase in investment leads to an increase in output, an increase in prices and, with a given money wage rate, greater profits.

The analytical relations employed by Keynes to construct his investment function clearly derive from those that Kahn used in 1931, but they differ in one significant respect. Since Keynes was essentially interested in decisions made at one point in time, rather than in the analysis of sequential processes, his analysis is based on the expected values for the variables, rather than on their current values. Keynes repeatedly stressed that the marginal efficiency of capital had to be interpreted as a variable whose value depended on *expected* values.[7] In any current period entrepreneurs decide to carry out a certain volume of investment because they *expect* that more investment would have a lower rate of return than the current interest rate. In other words, entrepreneurs decide on a certain level of investment I because they expect that a further increase in investment would cause a rise in prices and a fall in yields such as to push ϵ below i.

Both the prices of capital goods and yields enter into the function of the marginal efficiency of capital as expected variables. That this is the case for the prices of capital goods emerges from the fact that Keynes referred to their supply prices rather than to their current prices. The supply price of a capital good is defined as the price 'which would just induce a manufacturer to produce an additional unit' of such capital good and not the price at which it can be currently bought in the market (Keynes 1936: 135). As to yields, it is even more obvious that they are expected values, because they are returns to capital assets not yet operating.

Although concentrating on expectations, Keynes failed to take into account the positive effect that an increase in profits, determined by an increase in investment, will have on entrepreneur expectations and investment decisions, something that Kahn had previously pointed out.

KALECKI'S CRITIQUE OF THE MARGINAL EFFICIENCY OF CAPITAL

The decreasing marginal efficiency of capital can be examined from two different viewpoints – by looking at the underlying assumptions that capital goods prices rise as investment increases and that returns to capital decrease as it becomes less scarce, or by considering how Keynes related the actual behaviour of these variables to the formation of expectations by entrepreneurs. I focus here on the second issue, and do not raise questions concerning the actual behaviour of returns in either the short or the long period.[8]

In considering this topic, the obvious reference is Kalecki's criticism of the investment theory of Keynes. In a review of *The General Theory*, published in Polish in 1936 (now in Kalecki 1990: 223–32), Kalecki criticized the analysis of investment in chapter 11 by rejecting the idea that individual entrepreneurs can form expectations of the type hypothesized by Keynes.

Accepting the assumption of short-period decreasing returns.[9] Kalecki first questioned the ability of single entrepreneurs to foresee the effect of their own investment on the supply prices of capital goods. He argued that a single entrepreneur makes investment decisions by referring to the current market prices of capital goods; these are taken as given because entrepreneurs cannot foresee the *ex post* effect on prices that is produced by a change in the *aggregate* demand for investment.

In this context, given an expected rate of return higher than the rate of interest, every single entrepreneur would invest as much as possible. Therefore, Keynes's analysis

> does not say anything about the sphere of investment *decisions* of the entrepreneur, who makes his calculations in 'disequilibrium' on the basis of *existing* market prices of investment goods. It shows only that, if the expected profitability, calculated on the basis of this price level, is not equal to the rate of interest, a change in the level of investment will occur.
>
> (Kalecki 1990: 230)

If the expected rate of return on investment is higher than the rate of interest, any single firm should try to invest as much as possible. However, this does not mean that the investment process at the aggregate level can proceed indefinitely, as it is necessary to take into account the *ex post* effects of individual investment decisions. Kalecki then carried out this analysis. Entrepreneurs, *ex post*, realize that the prices of capital goods have increased, so that the investment process will stop because the marginal efficiency of capital falls and comes to equal the rate of interest.

> This will transform the existing situation into one in which expected profitability is *equal* to the rate of interest. Using the terminology of Swedish economists, one can say that Keynes's theory determines only the *ex post* level of investment but it does not say anything about its *ex ante* level.
>
> (Kalecki 1990: 230)

Having reached this conclusion, Kalecki went on to argue that the *ex post* level of investment so determined cannot be considered a stable equilibrium level. At this point Kalecki denied the validity of assuming that expected yields are a decreasing function of investment. The general price rise caused by the increase in investment causes expectations to change. Since the current situation is likely to affect long-term expectations, increased profits engendered by the price rise make entrepreneurs more optimistic and

> a difference between the marginal efficiency of investment and the rate of interest will rise again. 'Equilibrium', then, is not reached, and the growth of investment will still persist (we are dealing here, as may easily be seen, with a cumulative Wicksellian process).
>
> (Kalecki 1990: 231)

The point here is similar to the one made by Kahn in 1931 – an increase in aggregate demand brings about an increase in aggregate profits and this, in turn, affects expectations and investment decisions in a positive way.

Kalecki criticized Keynes for assuming decreasing expected yields to investment and emphasized that the increase in prices and profits affects expectations positively, so that they become an increasing function of investment. But Keynes can also be criticized from another point of view. Even if it is accepted that a decreased scarcity of capital implies lower returns, it is not legitimate to argue that single entrepreneurs can anticipate what is an *ex post* aggregate outcome resulting from decisions made by entrepreneurs as a whole to increase their stocks of capital. In other words, the effects of capital becoming less scarce cannot be felt by single entrepreneurs at the time when as a whole they are making investment decisions that will actually make capital become less scarce. Single entrepreneurs cannot anticipate future decreasing yields for the same reasons that they cannot anticipate increasing prices of capital goods.

Kalecki's review of *The General Theory* was written in Polish and therefore Keynes was not aware of it.[10] However, one year later, Kalecki (1936–7: 83–4) made the same criticism in an article published in English, which Keynes read and commented upon. The correspondence between Keynes and Kalecki on this article shows that Keynes failed to understand Kalecki, and failed to pick up on the positive relation between increased profits and investment outlined by Kahn.

Keynes objected to Kalecki:

> you seem to be assuming not merely that the current rise of prices will have a disproportionate effect on expectations as to future prices, but that future prices will be expected to rise in exactly the same proportion. Surely this is an extravagant over-emphasis of the effect of the immediate situation on long-term expectations? It appears to me that it is only if future prices are expected to rise *in the same proportion* as present prices that you have established the result that equilibrium is not reached and investment continues to rise.
>
> (Keynes 1983: 793)

And Kalecki replied:

> I think that my statement ... is independent of *how much* expectations improve under the influence of the present rise of prices. I state ... only that the increase of prices of investment goods which equates the marginal efficiency based on the initial state of expectations to the rate of interest, does not create an 'equilibrium', for at the same time expectations improve to some extent and thus investment increases further.
>
> (in Keynes 1983: 795)[11]

Even though future prices are expected to rise less than current prices, long-term expectations are affected and investment changes (it increases); so the initial equilibrium determined by the increase in current prices of capital goods is not stable.

It is easy to see similarities between the observations of Kahn and the observations of Kalecki on the relationship between the price level and investment decisions. Both pointed out that an increase in prices is likely to increase investment because higher prices imply higher profits. Both carried out their reasoning by using a sequential model. In particular, Kalecki concluded his criticism of Keynes by holding that a satisfactory analysis of the investment process cannot fail to consider the sequential process in time by which current actual phenomena (produced by past expectations) affect current expectations of the future:

> Thus it is difficult to consider Keynes's solution of the investment problem to be satisfactory. *The reason for this failure lies in an approach which is basically static to a matter which is by its nature dynamic*. Keynes takes as given the state of the expectations of returns, and from this he derives a certain definite level of investment, overlooking the effects that investment will in turn have on expectations. It is here that one can glimpse the road one must follow in order to build a realistic theory of investment.
>
> (Kalecki 1990: 231; emphasis added)

Kalecki's criticism of Keynes's theory of investment, based on the marginal efficiency of capital, was accepted and developed by Joan Robinson and by Asimakopulos. Robinson held that

> Kalecki asked the pertinent question: If there are schemes which promise a rate of profit greater than the rate of interest, would not each individual enterprise be willing and anxious to carry out an indefinitely large amount of investment? It was no use to reply that a faster rate of investment would raise the cost of capital goods and so reduce the prospective rate of profit; for the rise in costs would come about as a result of actual investment, *ex post*, while the marginal efficiency of capital concerns investment plans *ex ante*.
>
> (Robinson 1965: 96)

Similarly, in summarizing the criticisms of Keynes's marginal efficiency of capital, Asimakopulos has stated:

> Not only is the marginal efficiency of capital based on this mixture of *ex ante* and *ex post* factors, it is selective in its inclusion of the latter in order to produce a single downward sloping curve. Expected returns depend largely on the amount of existing capital equipment, its degree of utilization, state of technology, and prices and wages recently experienced. They are therefore affected by the present level of investment, but no indication of this is given in the standard treatment of Keynes's investment demand schedule. The impact of a higher rate of investment on prices of capital goods is included, but not its effect on expected profits. This latter factor must also be introduced to obtain a clearer picture of the various elements in Keynes's model and their interactions.
>
> (Asimakopulos 1971: 384; see also Asimakopulos 1991: 70–7)

In constructing his investment demand schedule Keynes mixed together *ex ante* and *ex post* factors in an unjustified manner – assuming an ability of entrepreneurs to foresee future events which is not justified in the type of economy to which he referred. The *ex ante* and *ex post* factors must be disentangled. It is not legitimate to assume that single entrepreneurs can foresee the effect of collective investment decisions on prices; the effect of the price rise will manifest itself only after time has elapsed, and *only then* will the investment process stop. Moreover, Keynes can be criticized for being 'selective': while he took into consideration the negative effect on expected yields of a lower degree of scarcity of capital, he ignored the positive effect on expectations produced by higher prices and profits.

AN ALTERNATIVE EXPLANATION FOR DECREASING EXPECTED PROFITABILITY OF INVESTMENT

The downward sloping investment demand function based on the notion of a decreasing marginal efficiency of capital cannot be regarded as acceptable, but the problem of finding a justification for such a function remains. This issue is important because the existence of a downward sloping investment demand function is a necessary condition for the existence of an underemployment equilibrium. Moreover, the justification for this function must be compatible with the fact that the analysis refers to entrepreneurs' *ex ante* decisions. If this cannot be accomplished, the only viable alternative would be a sequential approach in which the investment process is halted before the economy reaches full employment by intervening *ex post* factors that entrepreneurs did not expect when they made their decisions.

One alternative explanation for the downward sloping investment demand function (see Pasinetti 1974: 36–7 and Davidson 1994: 56–62) is based on the hypothesis that there exist investment projects with varying expected returns. Entrepreneurs rank the projects in the descending order with respect to their expected profitability. In this framework, entrepreneurs adopt only those projects whose expected profitability is larger than, or equal to, the current rate of interest. Therefore, the volume of investment is an inverse function of the rate of interest. This line of reasoning is not subject to the type of criticisms leveled at Keynes by Kalecki, but neither does it offer a completely satisfactory explanation of investment decisions.

In particular, the explication above does not explain why an entrepreneur should adopt less profitable investment projects in order to expand capacity. It would be more rational for the entrepreneur to adopt only the project with the highest expected profitability and expand by buying more units of that project.[12] Firms with projects whose expected profitability is higher than the given rate of interest would keep on investing. They would stop investing only when they realize, *ex post*, that the rise in the prices of capital goods has made the expected return from their projects lower than the rate of interest. Thus, this approach also cannot provide a satisfactory justification for decreasing individual investment demand functions.[13]

To understand why individual firms do not expand their capacity indefinitely we must take a different route; in particular, we need to reconsider the issue of the market form in which firms are assumed to operate. Keynes himself did not pay much attention to this issue, as he thought that his general results were independent of the assumed market form.[14] However, it is quite evident that, throughout the book, he implicitly assumed perfect competition[15] or, more correctly, pure competition[16] – a market form in which there are no significant monopolistic elements and individual producers cannot affect the prices at which their goods are sold.

This choice can be explained in 'tactical' terms – Keynes wanted to choose the most favourable terrain for his adversaries and to avoid the objection that his general results were contingent on the assumption of market imperfections.[17] But Keynes also had no sympathy for the 'imperfect competition revolution'; he regarded the formal intricacies of the assumption of imperfect competition as 'esoteric abracadabra' (Keynes 1983: 831).

However, in order to find more solid foundations for his theory of investment, Keynes did not have to take account of all the implications and intricacies of imperfect competition. It would have been sufficient for him to pay more attention to Sraffa who, in starting the debate on imperfect competition, observed:

> Business men, who regard themselves as being subject to competitive conditions, would consider absurd the assertion that the limit to their production is to be found in the internal conditions of production in their firm, which do not permit of the production of a greater quantity without an increase in cost. The chief obstacle against which they have to contend when they want gradually to increase their production does not lie in the cost of production – which, indeed, generally favours them in that direction – but *in the difficulty of selling the larger quantity of goods* without reducing the price, or without having to face increased marketing expenses.
>
> (Sraffa 1926: 543; emphasis added)

Sraffa was concerned only with the long period; therefore the limits to the expansion of firm production are limits to the expansion of their size and, hence, to their investment.

For Sraffa, investment is limited by the fact that demand for goods is limited. If firms did not take account of these limits, they would be subject to decreasing profitability. Obviously, there are similarities between Sraffa's observation that in the long period the expansion of firms is limited by demand, and Keynes's point that in the short period firm production is limited by demand. For Keynes, aggregate demand is limited because market economies do not behave as is postulated by neoclassical economics – Say's Law does not hold. For Sraffa demand is limited because firms do not operate in markets that have the characteristics postulated by neoclassical economics.[18]

Sraffa rejected the hypothesis of perfect competition, and he rejected neoclassical economics, on the grounds that theory should be closer to the actual behaviour of markets. Keynes likewise stressed the need for a theory to explain the 'world in which we live'. Had Keynes given Sraffa's article more serious attention, and had he pointed out that, both in the short and in the long period, demand is the crucial factor governing firm production and investment decisions, he would have provided more solid foundations to his decreasing investment demand schedule. In considering how firms form their expectations of future returns to investment, Keynes took account of the role of expected demand (see Keynes 1936: 147), but his case would have been much stronger had he referred to firms operating outside a competitive framework. While it must be assumed that a purely competitive firm faces a perfectly elastic demand for its goods, it need not be so when we look at firms operating in the 'world in which we live', which is hardly a world of perfect or pure competition. Firms in the actual economy know that the demand for their goods is limited, and they do not expand their productive capacity indefinitely.

CONCLUSIONS

A major weakness of the theory of investment found in chapter 11 of *The General Theory* is its inability to disentangle *ex ante* and *ex post* factors. Moreover, Keynes did not contemplate the possibility that entrepreneurs could incorporate into their expectations aggregate outcomes which would affect investment positively. Entrepreneurs are assumed to foresee the negative aggregate outcomes of their individual decisions, but they are assumed not to take account of the positive effect of an increase in investment – the rise in profits brought about by the rise in prices while the money wage rate remains constant.[19]

For Keynes, the rise in prices does not have positive effects on investment, whereas for Kahn and Kalecki rising prices induce entrepreneurs to invest. Only by ignoring the effect of higher profits on investment could Keynes obtain the result he desired – a downward sloping investment demand schedule. If the positive effects on profits and expectations of the price rise brought about by an initial increase in investment were taken into account, the marginal efficiency of capital would no longer necessarily be decreasing and it might be impossible to determine an equilibrium level of investment below full employment.[20]

The sequential, dynamic approach suggested by Kahn and developed by Kalecki avoids the confusion between *ex ante* and *ex post* factors determining investment. The analysis of processes from a sequential point of view is based on the distinction between expected and realized values of the relevant variables. In this context, *past actual* investment leads to an increase in *current* profits which, in turn, causes a positive change in *current expectations* about the future and, hence, in *current investment decisions*. In his analysis of investment, Myrdal (one of the most important representatives of the Swedish *ex ante–ex post* approach to macroeconomics) introduced the notion 'yield of real capital', which is quite similar to Keynes's marginal efficiency of capital but is characterized by a rigorous distinction between expected and actual values.[21]

Keynes, however, was reluctant to follow the *ex ante–ex post* approach because he thought it contained serious conceptual difficulties. In a 1937 letter to Ohlin, Keynes (1973: 184–5) wrote:

> the *ex post* and *ex ante* device cannot be precisely stated without very cumbrous devices. I used to speak of the period between expectation and result as 'funnels of process', but the fact that the funnels are all of different lengths and overlap one another meant that at any given time there was no aggregate realized result capable of being compared with some aggregate expectation at some earlier date.
>
> (Keynes 1973: 185) [22]

If the analytical concern is the determination of an equilibrium which can be characterized by the existence of unemployment, it is necessary to be able to compare aggregate results with aggregate expectations at a certain time. This is not possible in a sequential analysis unless strong simplifying assumptions on the length of periods are made.[23]

The sequential dynamic approach to analysing investment cannot be considered inherently superior to the approach of Keynes.[24] Which method is best depends upon the objective of the analysis. It is true, however, that the sequential approach has the merit of providing a clearer distinction between decisions and actual results, which is also important for Keynes's equilibrium approach. It is important to show that, given the level of investment, the economy can reach an underemployment equilibrium; but it is also important to provide a satisfactory explanation as to why the investment decisions made at a point in time might not give rise to full employment.

To some extent, Keynes himself came to recognize that he should have paid more attention to the way in which *ex ante* decisions are made. In a 1937 lecture, he stated:

> *Ex ante* decisions may be decided by trial and error or by judicious foresight, or (as in fact) by both. I should have distinguished more sharply between a theory based on *ex ante* effective demand, however arrived at, and a psychological chapter indicating *how* the business world reaches its *ex ante* decisions.
>
> (Keynes 1973: 183)

Had Keynes drawn this sharper distinction, he would have probably avoided the flaws in his analysis of the marginal efficiency of capital that have been discussed; a more careful analysis of how decisions are made would have allowed Keynes to better explain why the level of investment at any point in time tends to be below its full employment level. It is in this sense that Kahn and Kalecki could have 'taught' something to Keynes.

Furthermore, a more precise and rigorous distinction between investment decisions and actual investment would have allowed Keynes to put more stress on the central importance of investment in the determination of output and employment. Pasinetti (1974: 43–4), in pointing out methodological similarities between Keynes and Ricardo and methodological differences between Keynes and the general equilibrium approach, showed how investment is the logical *prius* in the explanation of the level of income for Keynes. Once the rate of interest is determined in the money market, it is investment that 'rules the roost'. Given the level of investment, and the propensity to consume, there exists a unique equilibrium level of income. Changes in investment bring about changes in income, the latter will in turn affect the rate of interest and, hence, feedback on investment itself; but this feedback effect can be ignored as it is of secondary importance with respect to the effect taken into consideration in the one-way causal chain from I to Y.

A precise distinction between investment decisions and actual investment gives greater analytical strength to Keynes's methodological approach. With such a distinction, actual investment in any period *must* be taken as given as it has been decided in a previous time; the effects that it has on output, prices and the interest rate will affect investment decisions only in later periods. The feedback effect of the interest rate on investment is to be ignored not only because it is of secondary importance but because the concern for it belongs to the analysis of a different period and, hence, of a different equilibrium position. In this way the break between the Keynesian approach and the general equilibrium approach (which is typical of IS-LM presentations of *The General Theory*) becomes even clearer.

The problem of finding an adequate analytical justification for why, at any point in time, firms do not tend to expand indefinitely – and, hence, why we have an aggregate level of investment which is below its full-employment level – can be solved by taking a further step toward the construction of an economic theory for the 'world in which we live'. If a market environment different from perfect or pure competition is explicitly assumed, it is not difficult to explain why firms do not expand indefinitely – investment is limited by demand.[25]

NOTES

1 Kahn was concerned with the direct effects of investment on employment and introduced the notion of an *employment multiplier*, which Keynes (1936: 113–31) transformed into an *income multiplier*.

2 Kahn considered the possibility that confidence would decline, but he was quite sceptical that entrepreneurs would react negatively to an expansionary policy (Kahn 1931: 197–8). Also see Kahn (1984: 91–104), concerning the effects of government policy on the state of confidence.

3 'Keynes' method could then tell us, not merely what employment, investment and so on tend to be at the two dates, but what they actually will be. But it could not tell us what happens to employment, investment and so on while the system is in *course of movement* from one of these equilibrium positions to the other; what they

will be on the intervening days or months or years of this disequilibrium .... These are very serious limitations – limitations of which it is specially proper to remind ourselves when attempts are made to apply Keynes' apparatus to the solution of practical problems' (Pigou 1950: 64).

4 On Kahn's dynamic approach see Goodwin (1994).

5 'Even if one concedes that the course of the short-period marginal cost curve is downwards in its early reaches, Mr. Kahn's assumption that it eventually turns upwards is, on general commonsense grounds, surely beyond reasonable question; and that this happens, moreover, on a part of the curve which is highly relevant for practical purposes. Certainly it would require more convincing evidence than yet exists to persuade me to give up this presumption' (Keynes 1939: 47).

6 '... [I]f the output of the industry is perfectly inelastic, the whole of the increased effective demand (in terms of wage-units) is expected to accrue to the entrepreneur as profit', and 'if the elasticity of output is unity, no part of the increased effective demand is expected to accrue as profit, the whole of it being absorbed by the elements entering into marginal prime cost' (Keynes 1936: 283). For intermediate values of the elasticity, the increased effective demand would accrue to profits only partially.

7 'The most important confusion concerning the meaning and significance of the marginal efficiency of capital has ensued on the failure to see that it depends on the *prospective* yield of capital, and not merely on its current yield .... The mistake of regarding the marginal efficiency of capital primarily in terms of the *current* yield of capital equipment, which would be correct only in the static state where there is no changing future to influence the present, has had the result of breaking the theoretical link between to-day and tomorrow' (Keynes 1936: 141, 145).

8 For Keynes, prices actually increase because he assumed short-period decreasing returns (increasing short-period supply curves). On the other hand, returns to capital decrease as the volume of investment increases because Keynes believed that the returns to capital depend on its scarcity. For a detailed discussion of Keynes's position on returns in the short period, see Sardoni (1994); on Keynes's concept of capital, see Kregel (1976b: 47–9).

9 In his review, Kalecki retained the hypothesis of increasing marginal costs. He dropped this hypothesis later on (see Kalecki 1938).

10 It was translated into English by Targetti and Kinda-Hass (1982).

11 On the correspondence between Keynes and Kalecki on this topic, see also Asimakopulos (1990: 55–9).

12 It is possible, of course, to hypothesize special cases in which a single firm cannot adopt the most profitable project more than once. These special cases, however, could hardly represent the basis for a general theory of investment.

13 However, it can offer a justification for an *aggregate* investment function which, at any point in time, is a decreasing function of the rate of interest. In this respect, it is sufficient to hypothesize that the most efficient projects that are available to different firms have a different expected profitability which may depend on technological factors as well as on differing attitudes to uncertainty among firms. In this case, for any given rate of interest, there are a number of firms in all, or some, industries that decide to invest while others do not invest at all. The firms that invest are those whose most efficient available investment project has a higher expected profitability than the current rate of interest; all firms whose most efficient available investment project is expected to yield less than the rate of interest will refrain from investing. As the rate of interest varies so does the number of firms that decide to realize their investment projects. Therefore the aggregate volume of investment is an inverse function of the rate of interest.

Changes in the rate of interest give rise to changes in the volume of aggregate investment as well as to changes in the sectoral composition of the economy if projects of differing profitability are randomly distributed through industries.

14 As is well known, in *The General Theory* Keynes (1936: 245) took the degree of competition as a given, a choice leading one to think that market form was not crucial for determining the levels of employment and national income.

15 Keynes accepted the inverse correlation between real wages and level of employment (the first postulate of classical economics), and noted (Keynes 1936: 5) that this inverse correlation holds only when competition is perfect.

16 The notion of pure competition (Chamberlin 1962: 6) is preferable to that of perfect competition as the latter also implies perfect knowledge, which is hardly compatible with Keynes's notion of uncertainty.

17 On Keynes's tactics, see Harcourt and Sardoni (1994).

18 The two points 'in which the theory of competition differs radically from the actual state of things which is most general are: first, the idea that the competing producer cannot deliberately affect the market prices, and that he may therefore regard it as constant whatever the quantity of goods which he individually may throw on the market; second, the idea that each competing producer necessarily produces normally in circumstances of individual increasing costs' (Sraffa 1926: 542–3).

19 In *The General Theory*, Keynes (1936: 301) also contemplated the possibility that money wages start increasing before full employment is reached, and that this could offset the increase in profits due to higher prices. However, he (1936: 302) regarded such a possibility as theoretically irrelevant. In fact, cases of increases in wages before full employment 'do not readily lend themselves to theoretical generalisations'.

20 It could be possible to have an increasing marginal efficiency of capital function. In this situation not even a rate of interest, which is an increasing funtion of I, could stop investment before it has reached its full employment level, I^*. If, for any value of I to the left of I^*, it is $di/dI < d\epsilon/dI$ no level of investment less than I^* could be a stable equilibrium level of investment.

21 'Any calculation of a yield must evidently be related to a *point of time* at which the calculation is made and not to a *period of time* for which the yield is reckoned .... It is the latter method of calculation, based on discounted anticipations, i.e. the *expected profitability* of an undertaking, which, of course, is decisive for entrepreneurs' programs, not the profitability actually experienced during a past period. The latter profitability in principle has importance in the calculations only indirectly as evidence of future profitability .... But that does not mean that the two concepts should not be kept separate in theory .... We must be careful not to mix up a causal relationship with a logical identity' (Myrdal 1939: 54–5).

22 On Keynes on *ex ante* and *ex post*, see Kregel (1976a: 223–5).

23 On the conceptual difficulties of period analysis, see Myrdal (1939: 43–5).

24 As Goodwin (1994: 73) seems to argue by referring to the multiplier: 'The Kahn process was a dynamic path or trajectory towards higher or lower levels, if nothing else happened on the way .... Keynes simplified and made more comprehensible Kahn's discovery but, at the same time, he impoverished it.'

25 I wish to thank M. Amendola, V. Chick, M. Dardi, G. C. Harcourt, M. Lippi, L. L. Pasinetti, A. Roncaglia, M. Tonveronachi and R. L. Wray for their helpful comments on earlier versions of this chapter. The usual disclaimers apply. This chapter is part of the work of a research group on non-competitive market forms and economic dynamics funded by the Italian Ministry for Universities and Scientific Research.

REFERENCES

Asimakopulos, A. (1971) 'The Determination of Investment in Keynes's Model', *Canadian Journal of Economics* 4: 382–8.

——(1990) 'Kalecki and Keynes: Their Correspondence', *History of Political Economy* 22: 50–63.

——(1991) *Keynes's General Theory and Accumulation*, Cambridge: Cambridge University Press.

Chamberlin, E. H. (1962) *The Theory of Monopolistic Competition*, 8th edn, Cambridge: Harvard University Press.

Davidson, P. (1994) *Post Keynesian Macroeconomic Theory*, Aldershot: Edward Elgar.

Goodwin, R. M. (1994) 'Kahn and Economic Dynamics', *Cambridge Journal of Economics* 18: 73–6.

Harcourt, G. C. and Sardoni, C. (1994) 'Keynes's Vision: Method Analysis and "Tactics" ', in J.B. Davis (ed.) *The State of Interpretation of Keynes*, Boston: Kluwer Academic Publishers.

Kahn, R. F. (1931) 'The Relation of Home Investment to Unemployment', *Economic Journal* 41: 173–98.

——(1984) *The Making of Keynes' General Theory*, Cambridge: Cambridge University Press.

Kalecki, M. (1936–7) 'A Theory of the Business Cycle', *Review of Economic Studies* 4: 77–97.

——(1938) 'The Determinants of Distribution of National Income', *Econometrica* 6: 67–112.

——(1990) *Collected Writings*, Vol. I, Oxford: Clarendon Press.

Keynes, J. M. (1936) *The General Theory of Employment, Interest and Money*, London: Macmillan.

——(1939) 'Relative Movements of Real Wages and Output', *Economic Journal* 49: 34–51.

——(1973) *Collected Writings*, Vol. XIV, London: Macmillan.

——(1983) *Collected Writings*, Vol. XII, London: Macmillan.

Kregel, J. A. (1976a) 'Economic Methodology in the Face of Uncertainty: The Modelling Methods of Keynes and the Post-Keynesians', *Economic Journal* 86: 209–25.

——(1976b) *Theory of Capital*, London: Macmillan.

Myrdal, G. (1939) *Monetary Equilibrium*, London: Hodge.

Pasinetti, L. L. (1974) *Growth and Income Distribution*, Cambridge: Cambridge University Press.

Pigou, A. C. (1950) *Keynes's 'General Theory': A Retrospective View*, London: Macmillan.

Robinson, J. (1965) 'Kalecki and Keynes', in J. Robinson, *Collected Economic Papers*, Vol. III, Oxford: Blackwell.

Sardoni, C. (1994) '*The General Theory* and the Critique of Decreasing Returns', *Journal of the History of Economic Thought* 16: 61–85.

Sraffa, P. (1926) 'The Laws of Returns Under Competitive Conditions', *Economic Journal* 36: 535–50.

Targetti, F. and Kinda-Hass, B. (1982) 'Kalecki's Review of Keynes' *General Theory*', *Australian Economic Papers* 21: 244–60.

7

SOME CRITICAL OBSERVATIONS ON POST-KEYNESIAN MACROECONOMICS

Gary Mongiovi

In this chapter I want to draw attention to some problematic aspects of post-Keynesian macroeconomic analysis. I do not intend to offer a comprehensive critique, which would require more space than is available to me here, but merely to point out in a general way, with a view to provoking discussion, what I regard as the main deficiencies of this approach.[1] These deficiencies stem from a single cause, the failure of the post-Keynesian tradition to pay adequate attention to the theory of value and distribution.

The following remarks should perhaps be prefaced by the observation that post-Keynesian economics is not a unified theoretical framework, but a body of methodological views and analytical propositions grounded in a particular interpretation of Keynes's theory of employment. This interpretation assigns central roles to the discussion of uncertainty and expectations in chapter 12 of *The General Theory* (1936) and to the remarks of Keynes (1937a) on the finance motive for holding money. These elements of Keynes's argument, however, appear to be defensive manoeuvres. They were intended to compensate for theoretical vulnerabilities that are present because Keynes was unable fully to detach himself from his Marshallian roots; in particular, because Keynes incorporated into his analysis two key features of the marginalist theory of distribution – a downward-sloping investment demand curve, and the notion that in equilibrium the real wage must coincide with the marginal product of labour.

What is innovative and essential in the theory of effective demand is the proposition that it is the level of aggregate income, rather than the interest rate, that adjusts to bring saving and investment into equality. The soundness of this proposition depends *not* upon the presence of uncertainty or upon the properties of the liquidity preference function, but upon the fact that the Sraffa-based critique of orthodox capital theory has demonstrated that the factor substitution mechanisms that underlie the marginalist theory of distribution are without foundation (Sraffa 1960; Garegnani 1970). Far from being a 'barren controversy', as Davidson (1994: 138) contends, the capital theory debates are crucial to validating the results of Keynes. The first order of business for Keynesians should be to ground the theory of effective demand in an analysis of distribution that is compatible with its results; such an analysis can be found in the writings of the old classical economists and Marx; that is, in the surplus approach that Sraffa sought to revive and reconstruct in *Production of Commodities by Means of Commodities*.

Gerald Shove once said that Keynes never spent the twenty minutes necessary to understand the theory of value. What Shove may have meant was that if Keynes had paid more attention to the theory of value he might have been better able to see why his contemporaries had difficulty understanding his new theory. The post-Keynesian literature, following the lead of Keynes, has not paid enough attention to the theory of value and distribution. As a result, there is no unified body of post-Keynesian theory; instead there exists only a fragmented set of propositions – some insightful, some misleading – that have done very little to strengthen the scientific foundations of Keynes's economics.

Most post-Keynesians would contend that the litmus test of a theory's Keynesian pedigree is its rejection of the following four concepts:

1 the IS-LM model as an interpretation of *The General Theory*;
2 Say's Law;
3 the neutrality of money; and
4 the ergodicity of economic processes.

THE IS-LM MODEL

The IS-LM model is indeed wrong, not because it ignores expectations or distorts Keynes's message, but because it is grounded in a defective theory of distribution. All of the elements of the IS-LM model can in fact be found in *The General Theory*, especially in chapter 18 where Keynes (1936: 245) pauses to 'gather together the threads of [his] argument'. It is significant also that Keynes himself had 'next to nothing to say by way of criticism' about the article in which Hicks (1937) introduced the IS-LM device (Keynes 1971–89, Vol. XIV: 79).[2] The fact that Hicks (1980–1) recanted the IS-LM interpretation reflects the evolution of his own thinking, but has little bearing on whether the model captures what Keynes wrote in 1936; it certainly does not represent a vindication of the post-Keynesian interpretation, which would have to be grounded in textual evidence.[3]

The essential defect of the IS-LM model is that one of its basic components, the downward-sloping investment demand function, is grounded in a demand for capital function that has been discredited by the Cambridge critique. That same demand function is present in *The General Theory* and constitutes its Achilles heel. Not coincidentally, it is precisely this element of Keynes's argument that made possible the IS-LM interpretation. The problem is not that the IS-LM model is a distortion of Keynes's argument, but that this model, which is a reasonably accurate depiction of what Keynes wrote, incorporates the same defective elements of the marginalist theory of distribution that are found in *The General Theory*. What is required to rehabilitate the theory of effective demand is to undermine the marginalist theory of distribution; this is equivalent to dismantling the basis for the IS curve. We could then discard those aspects of Keynes's argument that are grounded in marginalist theory. The effective demand mechanism, which is not anchored to any particular theory of distribution, would not only remain intact but would thereby finally be rendered capable of determining the level of employment independently of the endowment of labour.

Some writers, such as Pasinetti (1974: 42–4) and Chick (1983: 118–22), have noted that Keynes's derivation of a downward-sloping investment curve is not grounded directly in the marginal productivity of capital. Keynes posited a ranking of investment projects in declining order of their internal rate of return; as the interest rate falls, more projects become worthwhile, and the aggregate level of investment demand increases. But this argument is hardly persuasive, as it rests on the supposition that relative prices, and hence the ranking of projects, will not change with variations in the interest rate (cf. Petri 1993). Nor does it make sense for Keynes to rank investment projects in order of profitability if his purpose is to explain unemployment as an equilibrium phenomenon, since in equilibrium all invested capital should earn the same rate of return – as he acknowledges himself in chapter 17 of *The General Theory*. If a thing looks like a duck, walks like a duck and quacks like a duck, then, for all practical purposes, it ought to be considered a duck. Keynes incorporated into his theory a device that resembles, in all practical respects, the conventional marginalist investment function; it is this device that undermines his results and that must be discarded if his results are to be salvaged.[4]

SAY'S LAW

Say's Law is a red herring. It asserts that any level of aggregate production will generate a matching level of aggregate spending. This proposition is found in the classical literature, beginning with Smith and including James Mill and Ricardo. The classical writers who accepted it offered no persuasive justification for it, and in fact appear to have adopted it as an axiom solely to compensate for their lack of a theory of aggregate output and employment. Say's Law was never understood to imply a tendency toward the full employment of labour. It simply enabled the classicals to evade the problem of explaining the level of aggregate output: if any level of output will be sustained by aggregate spending, the social product could safely be regarded as parametric when explaining prices and the profit rate. But if a suitable theory of output – such as the theory of effective demand – had been available to the classicals, they could easily have dispensed with Say's Law.[5]

Nor is Say's Law an element of marginalist theory. In marginalism, it is *not* the case that any level of aggregate output is sustainable. Only one level of output will be supported by aggregate spending – that is the full employment level of output.[6] Marginalist theory, moreover, contains a fully articulated mechanism that claims to establish this outcome; that mechanism is the adjustment of the forces of supply and demand – the marginalist theory of value and distribution. It is the latter that needs to be discredited in order to validate Keynes's idea of an underemployment equilibrium. Say's Law, which has nothing to do either with the presumed tendency toward full employment or with the marginalist explanation of aggregate output and employment, is irrelevant to the theory of employment; and the attention that some post-Keynesian writers (e.g. Chick 1983; Davidson 1994) have devoted to it is therefore misplaced.

THE NEUTRALITY OF MONEY[7]

In the post-Keynesian literature, two properties which Keynes attributed to money in chapter 17 of *The General Theory* – zero elasticity of production and zero elasticity of substitution – account for unemployment (Chick 1983; Davidson 1980, 1994; Minsky 1975). But Keynes certainly knew that credit money is pervasive (cf. Keynes 1930) and that therefore the elasticity of production of money is *not* zero. Davidson (1980), however, interprets the first of these properties as referring, not to the parametric treatment of money, but to the technical aspects of the process by which money comes into existence. This interpretation starts from the valid premise that the production of money does not require the expenditure of labour or the diversion of resources from other production processes. Thus when individuals desire to increase their holdings of money relative to their demand for commodities, the resources released from the production of these commodities are not absorbed by the process that increases the quantity of available money. But this does not rescue Keynes from the exogenous money assumption. Davidson overlooks the fact that the argument by which Keynes derives the zero elasticity of production property rests precisely on the inability of the quantity of money to increase when the own rate of money exceeds that of other commodities. He also overlooks the fact that when Keynes discusses money and the rate of interest, an increase in the demand for money manifests itself primarily in the sale of 'bonds' (i.e. other financial assets) rather than through a diversion of expenditure from produced commodities.

With respect to the idea that money has a near-zero elasticity of substitution, there exist a large number of highly liquid assets that are capable of (partially) displacing money in the portfolios of agents. Keynes's theory of interest itself requires that agents substitute interest-bearing assets for money (or vice versa) in response to changes in bond prices. Thus, if the demand for money function is to have any elasticity at all with respect to the interest rate, there must be substitutability between money and other assets.

Chapter 17 does not advance Keynes's argument, and the post-Keynesian emphasis on these 'essential properties of money' again obscures the fundamental issue, which concerns not money but the theory of distribution. If money is what accounts for unemployment, it follows that in a non-monetary economy the postulates of marginalist theory hold and such an economy would tend toward full employment.[8] This diagnosis is off the mark. The reswitching controversy undermines the marginalist theory of distribution, and hence its theory of employment, regardless of whether the economy utilizes money or not; the critique applies equally to a barter economy.

I am not arguing that money is neutral. The question is: how is it non-neutral? One way in which it might be non-neutral is through the effect of the money rate of interest on distribution. Pivetti (1985; cf. also Panico 1985), developing a remark made by Sraffa (1960: 33), has argued that the rate of interest fixed by the monetary authorities regulates the rate of return on industrial capital. Starting from the idea that interest payments enter into commodity prices as an element of cost, and abstracting from barriers to the movement of capital, Pivetti suggests that competition operates to make the overall rate of profit r^* equal to the sum of the long-term money rate of interest plus a historically rigid normal net rate of return r_n. Prices then will be given by the solution to $p = pA(1 + r^*) + wl$, where A is an input coefficient matrix, l is a row vector of labour input requirements, w is the money wage rate, p is a row vector of prices in money terms, and $r^* = (i + r_n)$. If r_n is presumed to be constant over long stretches of time, an increase of i by the monetary authorities will entail an increase in money prices, and with a given money wage a decline in the real wage, and hence an increase in the gross profit rate r^*.

Pivetti's model starts from the familiar stylized fact that central banks are able to regulate interest rates but cannot generally fix the money supply; the model is therefore consistent with the endogeneity of money, an important post-Keynesian theme. In the model, money is not neutral at all: the monetary authorities, by setting the interest rate, influence the distribution of income, and this of course has consequences for the composition, level and growth rate of aggregate output, and for employment. One might question the supposition that the underlying normal net rate of return, r_n, is somehow left untouched by a change in the long-term interest rate; for a change in the interest rate will trigger reactions not only by capitalists trying to preserve their former net rate of return, but also by workers trying to preserve their real wage. Depending on the circumstances r_n (and r^*) may end up higher or lower than before the change in i. Moreover the model is meant to explain the normal long-period distribution pattern, and therefore requires that the interest rate fixed by the monetary authorities be permanent or lasting in some meaningful sense; but it is unclear what meaning can be given to a lasting change in the interest rate when the monetary authorities typically alter interest rates at frequent intervals (Nell 1988). And since interest rates are established through the operation of the bond market, there are questions also about the ability of the monetary authorities to sustain the target rate of interest at a level that is not compatible with public assessment of the appropriate value of bonds (which of course depends in part upon the profitability, net of interest, of private capital). Finally, in the case of an open economy, the level of interest rates in other countries can limit the ability of the monetary authorities to set and maintain a particular rate of interest.

If the forces that regulate distribution in a market economy are too complex to be fully captured by Pivetti's model, his approach nevertheless helps to clarify some aspects of the distributional role of finance. The question, again, is not *whether* money is non-neutral, but *how* it is non-neutral. What one says about money depends, or should depend, on what one thinks about the theory of value and distribution. Much of the post-Keynesian literature, in contrast to the model just described, is murky or ungrounded as regards value and distribution, and so it must fall back on arguments about the pervasiveness of uncertainty in money economies. These arguments are not in themselves wrong; but aside from stating the obvious, they do not carry us very far. As Pivetti's analysis indicates, the non-neutrality of money does not rest upon these phenomena. There is no apparent incompatibility between the non-neutrality of money and the competitive tendency toward a uniform rate of return. Non-neutrality is indeed incompatible with the marginalist theory of distribution; but it need not be inconsistent with classical and Marxian approaches to distribution.

ERGODICITY AND EQUILIBRIUM

There is in the post-Keynesian literature a profound antagonism toward attempts to explain economic phenomena in terms of equilibrating forces. This antagonism has led to the emergence of counterproductive tensions between proponents of the classical surplus approach and post-Keynesian writers. In a recent outbreak of hostilities, Minsky has gone so far as to suggest that on fundamental matters there is no real difference between the classical surplus theories and mainstream economics. Like 'orthodox neoclassical economists', Minsky (1990: 370–1) writes, surplus theorists 'work within a framework set up to demonstrate that markets achieve and sustain an equilibrium', whereas actual economies are characterized by 'endogenous instabilities' that preclude gravitation to a position of central tendency. Thus, he concludes, surplus theorists must 'stand mute when problems of the path of the economy through time are addressed'. There can be no doubt that the themes emphasized by post-Keynesians – uncertainty, expectations, disequilibrium, economic dynamics – are of paramount importance. What is at issue is how best to incorporate these phenomena into a coherent explanation of social processes. Post-Keynesians reject the notion that market activity is coordinated by persistent and systematic gravitational forces. The difficulty is that once the existence of a systematic coordinating principle is denied, social science becomes unable to say anything definite about the consequences of a given change in circumstances.

Post-Keynesians contend that questions about the gravitational properties of a market economy are irrelevant because spontaneous changes in expectations will prevent these properties from manifesting themselves. After Keynes, Shackle (1968: 289–90) remarks:

> Problems of 'the price of a cup of tea' ... no longer counted for much against the problem of unemployment arising ... from the failure of the incentive to invest, which failure itself was due to the sudden oppression of business minds by the world's incalculable uncertainties. There was no longer equilibrium in fact, and there could no longer be equilibrium in theory.[9]

In fact, the problem of what determines 'the price of a cup of tea' is hardly irrelevant. For if tea happens to be a basic good, in the sense of Sraffa, then the forces that regulate its price are intimately connected with the distribution of income, and therefore will have important repercussions on output, employment and accumulation. Expectations cannot explain why the price of (let us say) a new automobile is £9,000, while that of a cup of tea is 50 pence, rather than the other way round. If the ratio of the prices of the two goods is accidental, or determined by institutions, why then must it strike any reasonable person as absurd to contemplate the possibility of their prices being reversed? The answer to this question lies in the fact that prices do have a generally recognized objective basis: they depend in some systematic way on cost of production, which in turn depends on the distribution of income between labour and capital. Of course observed prices are influenced by expectations, uncertainties and speculation. But transitory fluctuations in price have traditionally been interpreted as deviations, caused by accidental forces, of the commodity's market price from its long-period centre of gravitation; and post-Keynesian theory offers no refutation of this interpretation.

The world does not need to be 'tranquil', as Joan Robinson and the post-Keynesians insist, for the method of long-period gravitation to be useful. It need only be characterized by regularities governed by mechanisms like those outlined by the classical economists, Marx and Sraffa (and, I might add, Keynes); and the data that regulate prices and distribution must not change too abruptly or too rapidly. No one outside the New Classical school claims that the economy is always, or usually, *or ever*, in equilibrium. The claim is that (a) market forces push relative prices toward their long-period values, and (b) this process tends to equalize profit rates when there are no impediments to the movement of capital.

Uncertainty, technical change, coordination failure and similar phenomena contribute to the complexity of economic life. Post-Keynesians, to their credit, have made it difficult for economists to ignore such analytically difficult issues. But it is the very complexity of these issues that makes indispensable the anchor of a long-period theory of distribution which clarifies the dominant coordinating forces that operate in a market economy. Disequilibrium processes can be understood only by reference to the gravitational forces they disrupt.

NOTES

1 See Chick (1995) for a sympathetic overview of the post-Keynesian framework.

2 It is worth noting that although Joan Robinson coined the term 'bastard Keynesians' in a 1962 review of a book by Harry Johnson, the intense opposition to the IS-LM model that one finds in the post-Keynesian literature first became noticeable in the early 1970s, only after monetarists had appropriated the IS-LM model to undermine the rationale for Keynesian demand management policies. If the IS-LM model were a blatant misinterpretation of *The General Theory*, it is curious that Robinson and Richard Kahn, Keynes's closest collaborators, failed for over thirty years to notice the distortion. Sidney Weintraub's earlier objections to IS-LM were mild in tone, and were directed mainly at the liquidity side of the model. His suggestions (1958: 156) for modification were intended 'to strengthen the liquidity approach, and not to supplant it'.

3 This is not to deny that some elements of Keynes's thinking are not captured by the IS-LM model. There can be no doubt that Keynes viewed expectations and uncertainty as important aspects of social and economic affairs. But in *The General Theory*, Keynes confines his discussion of these matters largely to chapter 12, and indeed in chapter 5 he notes (a) that it is usually safe to ignore short-term expectations, and (b) that in explaining the equilibrium level of output it will be convenient to take the state of long-term expectations as parametric. It is only in subsequent defensive clarifications of his theory (1937b,c) – after he began to encounter mainstream criticism – that he placed expectations and uncertainty at the centre of his argument.

4 It is unclear why some post-Keynesian authors want to preserve Keynes's investment analysis. Not only is it indefensible on theoretical grounds, but it seems to be incompatible with real-world investment behaviour. In addition, it does not appear to matter one way or the other for the arguments about uncertainty and expectations that form the basis of much of the post-Keynesian literature on investment. If investment depends mainly upon expectations, why should the interest rate be brought into the picture at all?

5 Marx, whose approach to the theory of value and distribution is substantially the same as Ricardo's, rejected Say's Law. See Mongiovi (1990) for a more detailed discussion of Say's Law.

6 It is no accident that, in their major works, Marshall and Walras never mention Say's Law; not only is the Law of Markets unnecessary to their theoretical systems, but within those theoretical systems the Law is false.

7 See Mongiovi and Rühl (1993: 88–92) for a more thorough critique of post-Keynesian monetary theory.

8 Cf. Davidson (1994: 95): 'It is the existence of these two elasticity properties [of money as discussed in chapter 17 of *The General Theory*] that creates the possibility of underemployment equilibrium . . .'. Also relevant are Keynes's notes on 'The Distinction between a Co-operative Economy and an Entrepreneur Economy' (Keynes 1971–89, Vol. XXIX: 76–87), which indeed support the post-Keynesian reading, and precisely on that account, have been the cause of much misunderstanding about the nature of Keynes's contribution.

9 The difficulty that arises here is that if Keynes's theory can be reduced to a set of propositions about the impact of uncertainty and changing expectations on investment and liquidity preference, then his explanation of unemployment amounts to a variation on the orthodox theory he proposed to discard. Long before publication of *The General Theory*, changes in the state of business confidence had been understood to cause unemployment and economic crises by knocking the system out of equilibrium. The novelty introduced by Keynes lies in having shown, albeit imperfectly, that unemployment is a normal feature of a market economy, in the sense that the mechanisms which regulate and coordinate the system do not generate a tendency toward full employment. What is revolutionary about Keynes's theory is its assertion that massive persistent unemployment can occur as the *outcome* of the coordination process. Post-Keynesians seem to want to have it both ways: they want to deny the relevance of equilibrium analysis while at the same time they want to characterize Keynes's theory as determining an underemployment equilibrium (cf. Davidson 1994).

REFERENCES

Chick, V. (1983) *Macroeconomics after Keynes*, Cambridge, Mass.: MIT Press.

—— (1995) 'Is there a Case for Post Keynesian Economics?', *Scottish Journal of Political Economy* 42: 20–36.

Davidson, P. (1980) 'The Dual-Faceted Nature of the Keynesian Revolution: Money and Money Wages in Unemployment and Production Flow Prices', *Journal of Post Keynesian Economics* 2: 291–307.

Davidson, P. (1994) *Post Keynesian Macroeconomic Theory*, Aldershot: Edward Elgar.

Garegnani, P. (1970) 'Heterogeneous Capital, the Production Function and the Theory of Distribution', *Review of Economic Studies* 37: 407–36.

Hicks, J.R. (1937) 'Mr. Keynes and the "Classics": A Suggested Interpretation', *Econometrica* 5: 147–59.

—— (1980–1) 'IS-LM: An Explanation', *Journal of Post Keynesian Economics* 3: 139–54.

Keynes, J.M. (1930) *A Treatise on Money: The Pure Theory of Money*, London: Macmillan.

—— (1936) *The General Theory of Employment, Interest and Money*, London: Macmillan.

—— (1937a) 'Alternative Theories of the Rate of Interest', *Economic Journal* 47: 141–52.

—— (1937b) 'The "Ex Ante" Theory of the Rate of Interest', *Economic Journal* 47: 663–9.

—— (1937c) 'The General Theory of Employment', *Quarterly Journal of Economics* 51: 209–23.

—— (1971–89) *The Collected Writings of John Maynard Keynes*, Vols I–XXX, London: Macmillan.

Minsky, H. (1975) *John Maynard Keynes*, New York: Columbia University Press.

—— (1990) 'Sraffa and Keynes: Effective Demand in the Long Run', in K. Bharadwaj and B. Schefold (eds) *Essays on Piero Sraffa*, London: Unwin Hyman.

Mongiovi, G. (1990) 'Notes on Say's Law, Classical Economics and the Theory of Effective Demand', *Contributions to Political Economy* 9: 69–82.

Mongiovi, G. and Rühl, C. (1993) 'Monetary Theory after Sraffa', in G. Mongiovi and C. Rühl (eds) *Macroeconomic Theory: Diversity and Convergence*, Aldershot: Edward Elgar.

Nell, E.J. (1988) 'Does the Rate of Interest Determine the Rate of Profit?', *Political Economy: Studies in the Surplus Approach* 4: 263–8.

Panico, C. (1985) 'Market Forces and the Relation between the Rates of Interest and Profits', *Contributions to Political Economy* 4: 37–60.

Pasinetti, L.L. (1974) *Growth and Income Distribution*, Cambridge: Cambridge University Press.

Petri, F. (1993) 'Critical Notes on Kalecki's Theory of Investment', in G. Mongiovi and C. Rühl (eds) *Macroeconomic Theory: Diversity and Convergence*, Aldershot: Edward Elgar.

Pivetti, M. (1985) 'On the Monetary Explanation of Distribution', *Political Economy: Studies in the Surplus Approach* 1: 73–103.

Shackle, G.L.S. (1968) *The Years of High Theory*, Cambridge: Cambridge University Press.

Sraffa, P. (1960) *Production of Commodities by Means of Commodities*, Cambridge: Cambridge University Press.

Weintraub, S. (1958) *An Approach to the Theory of Income Distribution*, Philadelphia: Chilton.

8

IN DEFENCE OF POST KEYNESIAN ECONOMICS

A response to Mongiovi

Paul Davidson

'In economics you cannot *convict* your opponent of error – you can only *convince* him of it. And, even if you are right, you cannot convince him ... if his head is already so filled with contrary notions that he cannot catch the clues to your thought'. These words were part of an early draft of *The General Theory*. They correctly describe the reaction of Post Keynesians in responding to the criticism that Mongiovi has developed from his unquestioning faith in classical theory. Mongiovi's head is already so filled with neo-Ricardian, classical notions that he has failed to grasp any of the clues embedded in the writings of Keynes or other Post Keynesian economists.

Mongiovi declares that deficiencies in the Post Keynesian tradition stem from their 'failure' to pay adequate attention to the theory of value and distribution. It is not clear from his remarks whether he believes that *The General Theory* is deficient or the interpretation of *The General Theory* by Post Keynesians is the problem. Since I believe that Post Keynesian theory is an accurate representation of Keynes, I shall interpret Mongiovi as attacking Keynes by alleging an inadequate attention to the classical (neo-Ricardian) theory of value and distribution.

In what follows I set forth Mongiovi's major accusations against *The General Theory*. I shall then demonstrate that Mongiovi is not correct either in his interpretation of Keynes or in his argument that Keynes and the Post Keynesians pay inadequate attention to the value and distribution aspects of real-world market-oriented monetary economies.

CRITICISMS OF KEYNES

The criticism that Mongiovi levels at Keynes can be divided into two categories. A first category involves how the (alleged) inadequacies of Keynes's microeconomic theory of value and distribution lead him to wrong statements. A second category explains how Keynes's monetary analysis is not compatible with the real world. From this Mongiovi concludes that Keynes's analysis of the causes of unemployment is wrong-headed.

Keynes's microfoundations in *The General Theory*

Mongiovi (1996: 111) refers to the statement, allegedly made by Gerald Shove, that 'Keynes never spent the twenty minutes necessary to understand the theory of value' as proof that Keynes never 'paid enough attention to the theory of value and distribution'. The failure of Keynes to genuflect at the altar of the classical theory of value and distribution, Mongiovi claims, leads Keynes to use an incorrect marginalist theory of distribution, thereby invalidating his work and that of the Post Keynesians who adopt Keynes's microfoundations. Reliance on Keynes's alleged incorrect microeconomic foundations results in two vital errors, according to Mongiovi:

1 Keynes requires a downward sloping investment demand curve. The reswitching controversy 'undermines' the possibility of such a curve, as well as the marginalist theory of distribution and unemployment. Since Keynes relied on this marginalist distribution theory, his explanation of unemployment must be wrong.
2 Keynes misinterprets Say's Law as requiring that the economy automatically converges on a full employment equilibrium. In reality, 'Say's Law was never understood to imply a tendency toward the full employment of labour' (Mongiovi 1996: 112).

Keynes's faulty monetary theory

According to Mongiovi, Keynes's theory of money involves three additional errors:

1 Keynes was in error when he stressed that uncertainty was the primary cause of a non-neutral money. Neo-Ricardian theory is superior to this faulty view and can explain the existence of non-neutral money on the basis of the distribution of income, even in the absence of uncertainty.
2 Keynes was in error for arguing that the elasticity of production of money was zero, for where 'credit money is pervasive ... the elasticity of production of money is *not* zero'; and Keynes was in error when claiming a zero elasticity of substitution for money, for 'there must be substitutability between money and other assets' (Mongiovi 1996: 113).
3 Keynes and Post Keynesians are in error when they emphasize non-ergodic uncertainties as the cause of unemployment in a monetary economy. Emphasis on non-ergodicity precludes an analysis in terms of long-period positions that the economy gravitates towards.

In any long-run classical theory, Mongiovi claims, there can be no uncertainties since there must exist observable persistent patterns or regularities, which Mongiovi characterizes as 'long-run centres of gravity'. This gravitational centre is the 'indispensable ... anchor of a long-period theory of distribution which clarifies the dominant coordinating forces that operate in a market economy . . . . [Keynesian] disequilibrium processes can be understood only by reference to the gravitational forces they disrupt' (Mongiovi 1996: 116–17). In other words, Mongiovi is claiming that, at best, Keynes's theory of unemployment is just a theory of short-run deviations from the classical full employment equilibrium centre of gravity.

A DEFENCE OF KEYNES'S VALUE AND DISTRIBUTION THEORY

In correspondence with Robertson, Keynes (1973: 513) accepted an aggregate supply function that is directly derived from the classical theory of supply flows of profit-oriented business enterprises. His disagreement with classical theory had nothing to do with production analysis. The problem was that when classical economists accepted Say's Law they produced a model where the aggregate demand curve was the same as (coincident with) the classical aggregate supply curve *for all levels of employment* (Keynes 1936: 26). If this presumed coincidence of aggregate demand and aggregate supply at all employment levels 'is not the true law relating the aggregate demand and supply functions, there is a vitally important chapter of economic theory which remains to be written and without which all discussions concerning the volume of aggregate employment are futile' (Keynes 1936: 26).

In a money-using entrepreneurial economy, Keynes insisted, some determinants of the aggregate demand function differed from those of a classical aggregate supply function. Since this distinction was overlooked by classical theory, Keynes felt obliged to explain why this difference between the aggregate demand function and the aggregate supply function would occur – even if one accepted the classical supply theory of profit-oriented enterprises. *The General Theory* sought to explain why the classical theory of demand was not applicable to a monetary economy. Accordingly, 'virtually the whole . . . book . . . is directed to discovering what determines D' (Keynes 1973: 513).

This emphasis on determining aggregate demand may be what Mongiovi means when he complains that Keynes did not pay adequate attention to the income distribution and value theory embedded in the aggregate supply function. However, Weintraub's (1957) pathbreaking article on Keynes's aggregate supply function[1] (which was later elaborated on in an entire book which Weintraub (1958) devoted to the theory of distribution) demonstrated that *The General Theory* had a full-blown theory of distribution and prices.

Drawing from an early draft of *The General Theory* (Keynes 1979: 73–102), Keynes (1973: 408–11) published an article entitled 'A Monetary Theory of Production'. In this paper Keynes indicated that, in an entrepreneur economy, money was never neutral in either the short run or the long run. In this money-using entrepreneur economy, workers are hired via money-wage contracts while nominal contracts are used to organize *all* production flows sold in the market-place (see Davidson and Smolensky 1964; Davidson 1972). For

Keynes, therefore, explaining the existence of nominal contracts to organize production, exchange, value and distribution became the essence of his *General Theory*. When Mongiovi complains that Keynes did not pay attention to value and distribution theory he really laments that Keynes concentrated on a distribution theory for a money-contracting entrepreneur economy and did not narrowly focus on the special case taken up by classical theory, which attempts to explain distribution and relative values for a non-monetary economy. The crux of Keynes's revolution is that the classical analysis is inapplicable to an economy that uses money and nominal contracts to organize production flows.

If Mongiovi disagrees with Keynes's claim that the classical value and distribution theory is a special case, which is not applicable to the monetary economy in which we live, then the onus is upon Mongiovi to explain how and why classical theory applies to a money-using market economy while Keynes's theory does not. As we shall see, neo-Ricardians cannot provide such an explanation.

Does Keynes require a downward sloping investment demand curve?

Mongiovi is simply confused when he argues that Keynes's Marshallian demand curve for capital goods must be downward sloping. Chapter 11 of *The General Theory* indicates that the reason for demanding capital goods is $\Sigma Q_r d_r$, the expected series of discounted perspective yields associated with any piece of capital where d_r is the value of £1 deferred r years, and Q_r is the quasi-rent from an asset at time r. For Keynes, this '$\Sigma Q_r d_r$ is the demand price of the investment' (1936: 137). As a good Marshallian, Keynes noted that the complete set of demand prices associated with every unit of a capital goods makes up the demand curve for a specific capital good, while the marginal costs of production make up the schedule of Marshallian short-period flow supply prices. Accordingly, Keynes (1936: 137) noted that 'investment will be carried to the point where $\Sigma Q_r d_r$ [the demand price] becomes equal to the supply price of investment'.

Although I usually draw the chapter 11 demand curve as downward sloping (e.g. Davidson 1994: 57–61), there is nothing that prohibits a horizontal schedule. In fact, Minsky (1975: 111–16) has argued that micro-demand curves for specific types of capital goods might be horizontal.

In his chapters on units and on the marginal efficiency of capital, Keynes (1936: 37–9, 138) argued that it is not possible to aggregate a non-homogeneous group of commodities (e.g. capital goods) to obtain an aggregate physical quantity measure for use in an aggregate demand curve for investment goods. To aggregate across heterogeneous units, Keynes (1936: 41) insisted, one can use only 'two fundamental units of quantity, namely quantities of money-values and quantities of employment. The first of these is strictly homogeneous.' Accordingly, when discussing aggregate investment spending for any given interest rate, Keynes adds up the equilibrium sums that would be spent on each type of specific capital good at alternative interest rates.

The resulting aggregate investment spending at alternative interest rates is *not* a demand curve in the Marshallian sense of a schedule of demand prices. It is a statistical cumulative frequency distribution that statisticians call an ogive (see Davidson 1994: 62–6). This statistical ogive is Keynes's marginal efficiency of capital (MEC) schedule; it shows the cumulative distribution of all investment spending that is expected to earn a return equal to or more than the marginal return on the last (equilibrium) unit purchased at any given interest rate. Because Keynes, unfortunately, notes that we could also call this schedule 'the investment demand schedule', Mongiovi makes the semantic confusion between an ogive and a Marshallian demand price curve by mistaking the former for the latter.

Keynes's MEC ogive is designed to show the cumulated funds spent on investment whose expected rates of return are more than or equal to any given rate of return. As long as different units of any homogeneous capital good are expected to earn different rates of return, a downward sloping ogive can be constructed. Mongiovi (1996: 112) admits the ogive basis for Keynes's downward sloping MEC schedule when he notes that the curve is 'not grounded directly in the marginal productivity of capital ... [instead it depends on] a ranking of investment projects in declining order of the internal rate of return'. Nevertheless, Mongiovi argues that the possibility of reswitching jeopardizes the existence of any downward sloping MEC ogive – as if reswitching *per se* can prevent a cumulative frequency distribution from being constructed that ranks investments in declining order of their expected internal rate of return for any given set of expectations. As long as the analyst develops an ogive as a 'more than' cumulative frequency distribution, the shape of the ogive must be (by construction) downward sloping. It does not matter if reswitching occurs or not. As long as entrepreneurs can conceive of additional capital goods projects that are expected to earn a lower, or even a negative return, then a downward sloping 'more than' ogive can be constructed.

Consequently, Mongiovi's alternative argument against the downward sloping MEC schedule, namely that 'in equilibrium all invested capital should earn the same rate of return', is irrelevant. If entrepreneurs can conceive of one or more investment projects that are expected to earn less than the equilibrium return, then ranking 'investment projects in declining order of their internal rate of return' is possible. And although projects that are expected to earn less than the equilibrium rate are not undertaken, they still exist in the MEC schedule sense.

In the limiting case, where all additional units of each capital good are expected to earn the same quasi-rents in each period throughout their useful lives, the MEC ogive will still be downward sloping, for as Keynes (1936: 187n.) explained, if

> an extensive increase in the demand for capital-goods cannot be immediately met by an increase in the total stock [perhaps because of diminishing returns or full capacity utilization in the capital-goods producing industry], it will have to be held in check for the time being by a rise in the supply price of capital-goods sufficient to keep the marginal efficiency of capital in equilibrium with the rate of interest without there being any material change in the scale of investment; meanwhile (as always) the factors of production adapted for the output of capital-goods will be used in producing those capital-goods of which the marginal efficiency is greatest in the new conditions.

In other words, as long as the capital-goods producing industry has a finite capacity, or at least significantly rising costs of production, there will be some additional projects whose rate of return will be lower as the result of the higher cost of trying to bring them on line in the current period.

In sum, the downward sloping MEC ogive takes into account the heterogeneity of units of capital, the possibility of diminishing returns, and capacity constraints in various capital-goods producing industries. Keynes does not require a downward sloping Marshallian demand-price curve for any type of capital goods. His analysis supports the construction of a downward sloping MEC ogive for any economic system that has either heterogeneous capital goods, and/or some capital goods producing capacity restrictions.

Mongiovi would sweep all of these real-world characteristics under the table. The theory that he advocates assumes that an infinite number of potentially homogeneous units of capital goods can be obtained, without any diminishing returns or capacity constraints, at constant returns to scale.

What Say's Law says

Mongiovi (1996: 112) contends that Keynes did not recognize that Say's Law 'asserts that any level of aggregate production will generate a matching level of aggregate spending .... Say's Law was never understood to imply a tendency towards the full employment of labour.' Unfortunately, this criticism is misplaced. Keynes's description of the use of Say's Law by classical theory is technically identical with Mongiovi's interpretation of Say's Law. Keynes stated that Say's Law requires that the aggregate demand curve and the aggregate supply curve

> are equal for *all* values of N, i.e., for all values of output and employment ... the classical theory assumes, in other words, that aggregate demand price (or proceeds) always accommodates itself to aggregate supply price; so that whatever the value of N may be, the proceeds D assumes a value equal to the aggregate supply price Z which corresponds to N. That is to say, effective demand, instead of having a unique equilibrium value, is an *infinite range of values all equally admissible*; and *the amount of employment is*

indeterminate except in so far as the marginal disutility of labour sets an upper limit.

(Keynes 1936: 26; second and third italics added)

Keynes agrees with Mongiovi that the classical theory lacks a determinate theory of output and employment. To fill this void, Keynes developed a general theory of output and employment which demonstrated that a money-using market economy could possess a unique unemployment equilibrium.[2]

A DEFENCE OF KEYNES'S MONETARY THEORY

Mongiovi (1996: 113) recognizes that 'the two properties which Keynes attributed to money in chapter 17 of *The General Theory* – zero elasticity of production and zero elasticity of substitution' are 'essential' to Keynes's determinate theory of employment. But Mongiovi argues that 'Keynes certainly knew that credit money is pervasive ... and that therefore the elasticity of production of money is *not* zero'. Thus Mongiovi implies that this 'essential' elasticity property identified by Keynes is not really essential to a theory of unemployment. Similarly, Mongiovi argues that the claim of a zero substitution elasticity is not correct, since 'a large number of highly liquid assets ... are capable of (partially) displacing money in the portfolio of agents. ... Chapter 17 ... obscures the fundamental issue, *which concerns not money but the theory of distribution*' (Mongiovi 1996: 113–14; emphasis added).

Mongiovi therefore infers that 'if money is what accounts for unemployment, it follows that in a non-monetary economy the postulates of marginalist theory hold and such an economy would tend to full employment'. This conclusion, however, is a *non sequitur*, as Mongiovi would have realized had he remembered his own argument that the non-monetary classical theory 'lacks a [determinate] theory of employment'. Hence, it does *not* follow that in a non-monetary economy, there is a tendency to full employment. Nothing can be said about a determinate full employment equilibrium in a non-monetary economy. There are, as Keynes (1936: 26) noted, an 'infinite range' of employment outcomes, and in a non-monetary classical economy 'Say's Law ... is equivalent to the proposition that there is no obstacle to full employment'. The absence of an obstacle to full employment in a Say's Law world with an infinite range of neutral equilibrium positions does not justify Mongiovi's claim that a non-monetary economy would automatically tend towards a full employment equilibrium.

This suggests that there may be something wrong with Mongiovi's attack on what Keynes deemed the two 'essential' zero elasticity properties associated with interest and money. Keynes (1936: 241) insisted that 'The attribute of "liquidity" is by no means independent of the presence of these two characteristics'. Before revealing the flaws in Mongiovi's argument regarding the two essential zero elasticity properties that Keynes attributes to *all* liquid assets, the reader should remember that Sraffian theory of value and distribution is merely a variant of classical theory. Consequently, it suffers the same deficiencies as classical theory – it cannot provide either a theory of money or a determinate theory of employment. Even when Mongiovi introduces something that he labels money into his Sraffian analysis, this Mongiovi money would be indistinguishable from any other producible commodities; it would simple be a *numéraire*.

Unfortunately, Mongiovi's common sense keeps getting in the way of his Sraffian logic. His native good judgement makes him recognize the need to provide an explanation for non-neutral money in a classical system where only relative prices matter and where money should therefore be neutral. For this he relies on a model developed by Pivetti (1985) that, in turn, is based on a remark (rather than a logical deduction) by Sraffa.

The reason for non-neutral money

Sraffa commented that 'the rate of interest fixed by the monetary authority regulates the rate of return on industrial capital'. In a Sraffian *competitive* economy where all commodities are produced by means of commodities, however, it would seem illogical to speak of a single monetary authority that somehow produces a money commodity that is not like any other commodity produced by industry.[3] If money is a producible commodity (i.e. if its elasticity of production is not zero as Mongiovi claims), then for the money producer to 'regulate' the rate of return on money, the producer would require monopoly power over this money commodity. The resulting economic system must encompass a monetary authority able to set a return on what it produces above what could be obtained by producing goods in a perfectly competitive economy. Accordingly, the claimed equality of rates of return on capital in all lines of endeavour – the fundamental conclusion of the neo-Ricardian theory of distribution – is undermined. If all other industries achieved the same rate of return as on money (as Pivetti's argument requires) then the equal rate of return in each industry would include a monopoly return equal to the mark-up set by the monetary authority on its own product.

This monopoly mark-up return Mongiovi (1996: 114) labels 'the long-term money rate of interest', which he claims is simply added to 'a historically rigid normal [competitive] net rate of return'. Following Pivetti, he argues that if there is an 'increase of *i by the monetary authorities*, [then this] *will entail an increase in money prices, and with a given money wage a decline in the real wage* [without any change in the real productivity of capital or labour] *and hence an increase in the gross profit rate*'.[4]

In my view it is not useful to talk about nominal money prices (presumably on all producible commodities) rising relative to money wages in a purely competitive economy where money is simply a *numéraire*. Instead, one can only point out that this Pivetti–Mongiovi argument implies that a monopolist monetary authority can affect the distribution of real income through some unspecified mechanism, and that this will have 'consequences for the composition, level and growth rate of output, and for employment' (Mongiovi 1996: 114). All the Pivetti model shows is that if some *ad hoc* monopoly entrepreneur produces the money commodity, then the resulting monopoly rents accruing to the monetary authority get passed through to the return of all capitalists. Only workers pay for these monopoly rents! A model that relies on an *ad hoc* monopoly to generate the assumed 'competitive' equalized real rate of return in each industry only muddies the waters when one is trying to explain not only the real determinants of distribution and values but also trying to provide a determinate theory of employment.

One might ask why Mongiovi prefers Pivetti's muddled analysis to Keynes's crystal-clear explanation of money prices, distribution and employment. Mongiovi (1996: 115) calls the liquidity preference explanation of unemployment 'murky' regarding value and distribution because it requires 'arguments about the pervasiveness of uncertainty in money economies . . . [even though] these arguments are not in themselves wrong . . . [and are] stating the obvious'. He favours the Pivetti model even though he admits that it can not capture the complex forces of a market economy. Why this model is superior to one that is based on the admittedly obvious pervasiveness of uncertainty that underlies Keynes's theory of the 'essential properties' of a non-neutral money is never made clear.

The two essential elasticity properties

In using the example of endogenous credit money to attack Keynes's invoking a zero elasticity of production as an essential property, Mongiovi has confused the elasticity of the quantity of money supplied function with the elasticity of production of money as a producible commodity. The elasticity of production involves a production function and is defined by Keynes (1936: 230) as the ratio of the percentage change in labour input for any given percentage change in the quantity of money produced. The elasticity of the money supply function, on the other hand, involves the ratio of the percentage change in the quantity of money supplied for any given percentage change in the price of money (the interest rate).

A zero elasticity of production means that there is no change in the number of workers in the money producing industry required to provide any given percentage change in the quantity of money supplied. An endogenous (credit) money supply system, on the other hand, usually implies an infinitely elastic quantity of money supply curve – the horizontalist argument of Moore (1988) – even though the credit money's elasticity of production is approximately zero. In essence, there will be little or no change in employment in the banking (credit supplying) industry to produce any change in the quantity of credit money supplied.

Mongiovi incorrectly takes the zero production elasticity argument to assume a given exogenous quantity of money – the verticalist argument of Moore (1988). In *The General Theory*, however, Keynes (1936: 232) warned that it 'would be inaccurate' to interpret this zero production elasticity as meaning that the money supply 'is rigidly fixed'. Moreover, in his finance motive analysis, Keynes (1937) expanded his monetary theory to include an endogenous overdraft system without retracting his essential zero elasticities analysis. Finally, Hahn (1977: 39) reinforced the zero production elasticity argument by demonstrating that 'any non-reproducible asset allows for a choice between employment-inducing and non-employment inducing demand'. In other words, Hahn demonstrated that the existence of an asset whose elasticity of production is zero provides a logical explanation of why unemployment equilibrium can exist.

Similarly, Mongiovi incorrectly accuses Keynes of being in error regarding the essential property of a zero elasticity of substitution. Mongiovi (1996: 113) argues that Keynes overlooked 'a large number of highly liquid assets that are capable of (partially) displacing money in portfolios'; i.e. there is a high elasticity of substitution among all liquid assets including money. What Mongiovi has failed to recognize is that this zero substitution elasticity property is between *all* liquid assets (including money) as a group *vis-à-vis* all commodities that are produced by means of commodities (Keynes 1936: 241; Davidson 1972: 195–7). Although all liquid assets have a zero production elasticity, there is a high elasticity of substitution between the different things that make up the group of liquid assets (including money) as a group. In fact, Keynes's speculative motive depends on significant substitution elasticities between each possible pair of liquid assets and provides the justification that permits Keynes to indicate that the speculative motive for holding money will have a rectangular hyperbola shape (1936: 201–2).

Many times in the past I have (Davidson 1972: 195–7; Davidson 1994: 95) made this point regarding the high elasticity of substitution among assets within the liquid asset grouping and the zero elasticity between liquid assets as a group and producible commodities. While citing my writings in other contexts, Mongiovi ignores my explicit analysis regarding this 'essential' substitution property in his determination to explain why the Post Keynesian macroeconomics of Davidson, Minsky, Chick and others that emphasize these elasticity properties, is wrong.

Non-ergodicity

Why does Mongiovi go so far out of his way to introduce the Pivetti model to denigrate Keynes's liquidity preference–uncertainty analysis? I believe the answer is obvious. Keynes's emphasis on uncertainty requires a non-ergodic system (see Davidson 1994). Sraffian analysis, on the other hand, requires the existence and persistence of 'long run centers of gravity' towards which the economy has a tendency to converge. This is similar to Newton's nineteenth-century celestial mechanics with an immutable gravitational constant. For the nineteenth-century Newtonian celestial mechanics system to hold, it was necessary to impose the ergodic hypothesis (see Samuelson 1969).

If Mongiovi were to admit that uncertainty is an important building-block for a determinate theory of employment, value and distribution, he would have to admit that the economic system is non-ergodic and that *persistent centres of gravity cannot exist*. In other words, the claim that centres of gravity determine long-run value and distribution is logically inconsistent with the acceptance of a non-ergodic system. Yet Mongiovi concedes that pervasive uncertainty exists in the real world. Such an admission means that Keynes was correct in not paying attention to the ergodic classical theory of value and distribution that Mongiovi advocates.

Because persistent centres of gravity cannot be assumed to exist in a non-ergodic world, unemployment can be an equilibrium phenomenon (as Keynes claimed), and not just a temporary disequilibrium phenomenon. By insisting on the existence of long-run centres of gravity (without proof) Mongiovi shares the same faith in the classical axiom of ergodicity – held with the same religious tenacity – as the rational expectations theorists (e.g. Lucas and Sargent 1981). Thus Mongiovi's criticism of Post Keynesian economics and his defence of the neo-Ricardian theory of value and distribution must be recognized for what it is – namely a variant of what correctly should be called New Classical economics.

Until Mongiovi clears his mind of the contrary centre of gravity notion, and rethinks the problem of money and the theory of employment from the beginning, he will be unable to comprehend the conceptual clues that Keynes and the Post Keynesians have been throwing at him. Instead, Mongiovi and other neo-Ricardians will continue to engage in a sterile debate about the importance of their classical (non-monetary) value and distribution theory for explaining the problem of unemployment in a money-using, market-oriented economic system. Such a controversy between the neo-Ricardian and Post Keynesian schools will only waste precious resources and energies, while encouraging the majority of our mainstream professional colleagues to take this squabbling as evidence that it is a waste of time to read this heterodox literature. Both the economics profession and the global economy that we live in will be much poorer for that.

CONCLUSION

This defence of Keynes and Post Keynesian theory has shown that Mongiovi (1996: 115) is wrong when he claims that 'most of the Post Keynesian literature ... is murky or ungrounded as regards value and distribution'. The writings of Keynes and the Post Keynesian are based on a well-articulated theory of prices and distribution applicable to a market-oriented, money-using production economy. Keynes and the Post Keynesians deliberately avoid becoming enmeshed in any variant of the classical theory of value and distribution because it has characteristics that 'happen not to be those of the economic society in which we actually live' (Keynes 1936: 3). As a result, it is not only useless for policy purposes but may have devastating consequences if put into practice.

NOTES

1 Weintraub was proud of a letter he received from Robertson, which stated that Weintraub's 1957 *Economic Journal* article correctly described the microfoundations of what Keynes meant by aggregate supply, or at least what Keynes should have meant. Thus one of Keynes's sharpest classical critics accepted the value and distribution theory used by Keynes and the Post Keynesians.

2 Only after the Second World War did economists attempt to find the sufficient conditions for a unique full employment equilibrium (see Arrow and Hahn 1971). As Clower (1965) noted, Walras's Law had to be added to Say's Law for marginalist theory to claim that endogenous market forces assured a unique full employment equilibrium.

3 After all, the title of Sraffa's book is *The Production of Commodities by Means of Commodities*. It does not explain how money is produced by a monetary authority unless the money is a producible commodity.

4 Note that Pivetti's high interest rate policy leads to high profit rates, whereas in the real world high nominal interest rates typically reduce market demand, lower profit expectations and cause entrepreneurs to reduce labour hiring.

REFERENCES

Arrow, K. and Hahn, F. H. (1971) *General Competitive Equilibrium*, San Francisco: Holden-Day.

Clower, R. W. (1965) 'The Keynesian Counter-Revolution: An Appraisal', in F. H. Hahn and F. Brechling (eds) *The Theory of Interest Rates*, London: Macmillan.

Davidson, P. (1972) *Money and the Real World*, London: Macmillan.

——(1994) *Post Keynesian Macroeconomic Theory*, Aldershot: Edward Elgar.

Davidson, P. and Smolensky, E. (1964) *Aggregate Supply and Demand Analysis*, New York: Harper & Row.

Hahn, F. H. (1977) 'Keynesian Economics and General Equilibrium Theory: Reflections on Some Current Debates', in G. H. Harcourt (ed.) *The Microfoundations of Macroeconomics*, London: Macmillan.

Keynes, J. M. (1936) *The General Theory of Employment Interest and Money*, New York: Harcourt, Brace & World.

——(1937) 'Alternative Theories of the Rate of Interest', *Economic Journal* 47:241–52.

——(1973) *The Collected Writings of John Maynard Keynes*, Vol. XIII, London: Macmillan.

——(1979) *The Collected Writings of John Maynard Keynes*, Vol. XXIX, London: Macmillan.

Lucas, R. E. and Sargent, T. (1981) *Rational Expectations and Econometric Practices*, Minneapolis: University of Minnesota Press.

Minsky, H. (1975) *John Maynard Keynes*, New York: Columbia University Press.

Mongiovi, G. (1996) 'Some Critical Observations on Post Keynesian Macroeconomics', in S. Pressman (ed.) *Interactions in Political Economy: Malvern After Ten Years*, London: Routledge.

Moore, B. J. (1988) *Horizontalists and Verticalists: The Macroeconomics of Credit Money*, New York: Cambridge University Press.

Pivetti, M. (1985) 'On The Monetary Explanation of Distribution', *Political Economy: Studies in the Surplus Approach* 1: 73–103.

Samuelson, P. A. (1969) 'Classical and Neoclassical Theory', in R. W. Clower (ed.) *Monetary Theory*, London: Penguin.

Sraffa, P. (1960) *The Production of Commodities by Means of Commodities*, Cambridge: Cambridge University Press.

Weintraub, S. (1957) 'The Micro-Foundations of Aggregate Demand and Supply', *Economic Journal* 67: 455–71.

—— (1958) *An Approach to the Theory of Income Distribution*, Philadelphia: Chilton.

9

HYSTERESIS AND UNCERTAINTY

Complementary or competing visions of evolving economic systems?

Mark Setterfield

Economists have been concerned with uncertainty and its effects on economic behaviour and outcomes for some time. But only recently has the term 'hysteresis' become popular in economic theory. Although interest in the influence of history in economic models and the idea of path dependence are not new (Currie and Steedman 1990; Setterfield 1995), the literature on hysteresis is more recent, having grown and developed since the mid-1980s.

Both uncertainty and hysteresis purport to deal with the dynamics of historical systems – i.e. systems whose dated outcomes unfold sequentially, and which at any point in time have a past and a future. A fitting contrast is the Arrow–Debreu–MacKenzie model of general equilibrium, which simultaneously determines all future outcomes in some initial period. Nevertheless, there is some consternation as to the extent to which the concepts of uncertainty and hysteresis are really compatible. Davidson (1993) is unambiguous in his conclusion that the resemblance between hysteresis and uncertainty is unproven,[1] a conclusion based upon his identification of a number of shortcomings in the concept of hysteresis. These include: a degree of determinacy not found in discussions of uncertainty; questions about whether hysteretic systems are 'truly historical'; a failure to specify the meaning of the 'long run' in calendar time; and a reliance on exogenous shocks to generate economic change. The point of this chapter is to suggest that while these criticisms are not entirely without merit, they apply to a particular (special case) characterization of hysteresis, and that even the claim that this special case represents an uncertain world may not be completely indefensible. Hysteresis is conceptually more general than this single characterization and is, in general, compatible with the notion of uncertainty.

The next two sections define the notions of 'uncertainty' and 'hysteresis'. We then consider the degree of complementarity between these concepts.

THE CONCEPT OF UNCERTAINTY

The term 'uncertainty' is used in economics in a variety of different ways and, as such, can take on a variety of different meanings (Lawson 1988). It is important, therefore, to begin by clarifying the term in its present use. By uncertainty, we mean fundamental uncertainty of the Knight/Keynes variety, as opposed to some form of probabilistic risk. In an environment of risk, agents need appeal only to probability theory in order to evaluate the future (i.e. form expectations). The presupposition is that for any stochastic process, the set of all future possibilities and their associated probabilities can be conceptualized (either objectively or subjectively) in the present. In an environment of uncertainty, however, probability theory is inadequate as a basis for evaluating the future. Hence Keynes argues that by using the term uncertainty, he does

> not mean merely to distinguish what is known for certain from what is only probable. The game of roulette is not subject, in this sense, to uncertainty .... The sense in which I am using the term is that in which the prospect of a European war is uncertain, or the price of copper and the rate of interest twenty years hence, or the obsolescence of a new invention, or the position of private wealth owners in the social system in 1970. *About these matters there is no scientific basis on which to form any calculable probability whatever. We simply do not know.*
>
> (Keynes 1973: 113; emphasis added)

In an environment of uncertainty it is *not* the case that all future possibilities and/or their associated (absolute or relative)[2] probabilities can be conceptualized in the present; at least some relevant features of the future are unknown to agents in the present. Agents know that they do not know about these relevant features, and must therefore form their expectations in an acknowledged state of partial ignorance. As a result, agents must rely in part on 'gut feelings' or 'animal spirits' to guide their current behaviours, which are oriented towards future outcomes.[3]

How is it that agents find themselves acting in an environment of uncertainty? In order to answer this question, we need to model environments of both risk and uncertainty. Modeling either risk or uncertainty necessarily involves a variety of hypotheses. In particular, we can distinguish between hypotheses concerning the nature of the economic environment, and hypotheses concerning agent perceptions of this environment. In what follows, we will characterize the former in terms of the evolution through time of a macroeconomic data generating process *(DGP)*, and the latter in terms of the relationship between agents' information sets and the future form of this macroeconomic *DGP*. This framework allows us to develop a typology of expectations formed under environments of risk and uncertainty, depending on how we characterize the macroeconomic *DGP*, agent information sets, and the relationship between the two.[4]

Suppose that we have two time periods, t = 1,2. Define $E(\mu_{t+1}|\Omega_t)$ as the expected value of μ_{t+1} in period t given current information Ω_t, where $\mu_t^T = (x_{1t}, \ldots, x_{nt})$, t = 1,2 is a vector of n macroeconomic variables that agents wish to forecast.[5] Define DGP_t, t = 1,2 as the macroeconomic data generating process in period t. DGP_t should be conceived as the precise configuration of the macroeconomic system (comprising all relevant structural equations, variables, constants and probability distributions) that is responsible for generating actually observed outcomes in period t. The issues we wish to examine are the nature of the relationship between DGP_t and DGP_{t+1} on one hand, and that between Ω_t and DGP_{t+1} on the other. The first relates to the evolution of the economic environment through time, the second to agents' current perception of their future environment.[6]

Suppose that $DGP_t = DGP_{t+1} = DGP^*$ and that $\Omega_t = DGP^*$. This captures the notion that there are stable (i.e. timeless) laws and probability distributions (denoted as DGP^*) governing economic outcomes in any period, and that agents know them ($\Omega_t = DGP^*$). This environment – which involves the formation of strong form rational expectations of μ_t on the basis of objective probability distributions – is an environment of risk.[7] Suppose, instead, that $DGP_t = DGP_{t+1} = DGP^*$ and $\Omega_t \neq DGP^*$, where Ω_t is, nevertheless, of the same dimensions as DGP^*. This latter statement is intended to denote that there is the same *amount* of information in Ω_t as in DGP^*, even though the information is quantitatively *different*. Agents are therefore aware of the size of the set of future possibilities from which future realized outcomes will be drawn, but they cannot (as yet) determine the objective value of each future possibility and/or its associated probability. Suppose further that if we were to consider subsequent periods $t = 3, \ldots, \infty$, we would find that

$$\lim_{t \to \infty} \Omega_t = DGP^*.$$

The idea here is that agents form a subjective impression of the future, but one that will eventually converge towards the 'true model' of the economy as they learn from past experience. This is again an environment of risk, based initially on subjective probability distributions, but which ultimately converges over time to an objective probability environment where, once again, strong form rational expectations are formed on the basis of the 'true model' of the economy.[8]

In contrast to the environment of risk described above is the environment of uncertainty, where agents do not know some information about the future DGP of the economy. They are thus unable to rely entirely on probability theory when forming their expectations.[9] Suppose, for example, that $DGP_t = DGP_{t+1} = DGP^*$, but $\Omega_t \neq DGP^*$, $t = 1,2$, and the dimensions of Ω_t are now strictly *smaller* than those of DGP^*. Now there is less information in Ω_t than in DGP^* – i.e. agents are not able to conceive the size of the set of future possible outcomes and their associated probabilities, much less the objective values of these possible outcomes and probabilities. Despite the existence of a stationary external reality (or 'true model') DGP*, agents here exist in a state of partial ignorance about the future due to bounded rationality. Without being aware (not even subjectively) of all future possibilities and their associated probabilities, agents find themselves in an environment of fundamental uncertainty.

In the bounded rationality environment described above, agents fail to know about the future because of some constraint or limitation on their individual faculties of computation. This is true despite the fact that there exists an external reality which is, in principle (individual computational limitations notwithstanding), knowable by a sufficiently large intelligence. Uncertainty is therefore characterized as a feature of agents' perceptions of their environment, not as a feature of the environment itself. However, this is clearly *not* how many post-Keynesians conceptualize the phenomenon of uncertainty (see Hoogduin 1987: 59f.; Davidson 1988, 1991; Lavoie 1992: 42–5). Suppose, then, that $DGP_t \neq DGP_{t+1}$ and $\Omega_t \neq DGP_{t+1}$, where the dimensions of Ω_t are once again strictly smaller than those of DGP_{t+1}. Note first that no DGP^* is postulated. This captures the notion that the laws and probability distributions governing economic outcomes are cultural and historical constructs which evolve over time – no immutable 'true' macroeconomic *DGP* exists. Furthermore, post-Keynesians conceive this evolution as occurring in a discontinuous and non-deterministic fashion, so there is no timeless law or 'meta *DGP*' which describes, mechanically, the transformation of the economy between periods *t* and *t*+1. Instead, evolution occurs as a result of historically specific 'originative actions' or innovations in products and production processes (Lavoie 1992: 44) and in behavioural responses, the latter a result of social interaction among agents (McKenna and Zannoni 1993; Hamouda and Smithin 1988). On this conception of the economic process there is no single, determinate true model governing economic outcomes that is independent of the economy's actors. Instead, agents are simultaneously creatures of their environment (i.e. they are engaged in learning based on past experience) and authors of their environment (i.e. they are capable of actions that do not unfold according to given laws of nature, but which mould reality of the present/future).[10] Because of all this, $\Omega_t \neq DGP_{t+1}$; indeed, we cannot have $\Omega_t = DGP_{t+1}$ because at least some of the information contained in DGP_{t+1} – that stemming from originative actions or innovations in period *t*+1 – is historically specific to this period and is not available to agents in period *t*. Once again, agents 'don't know what is going to happen and know that they do not know just what is going to happen' (Hicks 1977: vii), and so they exist in a state of uncertainty. Here, uncertainty is a product of the nature of the economic *environment*, rather than the nature of economic *agents* (as in the case of bounded rationality). The sense in which agents do not know the future is a sense in which the future is *unknowable in principle*, and has nothing whatsoever to do with any computational limitations suffered by economic agents themselves.

In sum, fundamental uncertainty exists when some aspects of the future (some possible outcomes and/or their associated probabilities) are not known to agents in the present. This ignorance is brought about either by bounded rationality, or by the evolutionary nature of the economic environment coupled with the historical specificity of information, so that the future is unknowable in principle. It is the latter view that accords most closely with the post-Keynesian conception of uncertainty and which will inform our subsequent comparison of hysteresis and uncertainty.

THE CONCEPT OF HYSTERESIS[11]

A great deal of attention has focused on the possibility of hysteresis in natural rate models of unemployment (Blanchard and Summers 1986; Jenkinson 1987; Layard, Nickell and Jackman 1991).[12] Indeed, it seems at times that the very term 'hysteresis' is held to be synonymous with changes in the natural rate of unemployment in response to prior deviations in the actual level of unemployment from the natural rate.[13] Apart from presupposing the existence of a natural rate, there is one main problem with this view. Simply put, the notion of hysteresis is far broader in meaning and application than its treatment within the natural rate framework suggests. Hysteresis is a potential property of *any* dynamic system, not just of the dynamics of disequilibrium adjustment in the natural rate hypothesis. It is, therefore, at this level of generality (i.e. in terms of the properties of any dynamic system) that we should seek to define and discuss the concept of hysteresis.

The term 'hysteresis' was first introduced in physics, where it was used to describe the propensity of ferric metals to retain magnetic properties brought about by the prior application of magnetizing forces, even after these magnetizing forces had been removed.[14] In general, if a dynamic system is hysteretic, earlier states of the system influence its later states. More specifically, hysteresis can be said to exist when the long run or final value of a variable depends on the value of the variable in the past, by virtue of the influence of this past value on the alleged exogenous variables, coefficients and structural equations which characterize the system that determines the variable.

To help better understand the concept of hysteresis, it is instructive to focus on two important features of the preceding definition. First, a central characteristic of hysteresis is that the long run or final value of a variable depends on past values of this variable. This distinguishes hysteretic systems from other dynamic systems whose short-run outcomes are path specific, but which ultimately converge to configurations defined and reached without reference to the path taken towards them.[15] There need be no constraint on the precise form that a hysteretic long-run outcome takes. In some systems, the long-run or final outcome is an equilibrium which exhibits no subsequent (endogenous) tendency to change over time. In other systems, the long-run or final outcome may be described by some regular periodic motion or limit cycle. In still others, there may be no final outcome as such, and the long-run value of the variable of interest may only be described as a long-run value because of its temporal distance from the present, measured in calendar time. Any of these different types of long-run or final outcomes may, in principle, be hysteretic, as long as they are path dependent in the manner previously defined.

Second, the definition of hysteresis given above lends itself to the ontological point made by Elster (1976) that the past has no being in the present. What, then, can it mean to regard the past as a determinant of current (and future) outcomes? Elster suggests that 'traces of the past' must be left in the present. For example, stocks of goods (such as fixed capital) or experience accumulated in the past may carry over into the present. In the preceding definition, these traces are explicitly recognized in the sensitivity of the current structural model to past values of the variable of interest. This leads to an obvious point of contrast between hysteretic systems and orthodox (deterministic) economic models. In the former, unlike the latter, the structure of a system is not regarded as a set of timeless data. Rather, it is treated as historically specific, so that any theoretical model of the system at a particular point in time is conditional on the current structure of the system (including tastes and preferences, technology and institutions), and must respect the propensity of this structure to change over time in response to the unfolding history of the system's outcomes.

In sum, hysteresis describes how long-run outcomes in a system may be influenced by past outcomes of the system. In orthodox equilibrium models of the economy, long-run (equilibrium) outcomes act as centres of gravity towards which any sequence of short-run (disequilibrium) outcomes is inexorably drawn. Hysteretic systems, however, possess the contrasting property that any long-run or final outcome to which they give rise is a product of the precise sequence of short-run outcomes (the prior adjustment path) that lead up to it. Orthodox equilibrium models, then, suggest that 'the future determines the past,' whereas with hysteresis 'the past determines the future'.

ARE HYSTERESIS AND UNCERTAINTY COMPATIBLE?

We are now in a position to evaluate the compatibility of uncertainty and hysteresis. As noted earlier, Davidson (1993) has expressed scepticism that hysteresis corresponds to a situation of fundamental uncertainty. The argument advanced here is that post-Keynesians should generally regard hysteresis and uncertainty as complementary.

We saw above that, at least in post-Keynesian economics, uncertainty is conventionally conceived as arising from features of an evolving economic environment, rather than from features of the individual agents who populate this environment. This is important, because were it not true, and were claims regarding the existence of uncertainty sustained mainly on the basis of hypotheses about agents' perceptions of their environment, there would exist a basic tension between the concepts of hysteresis and uncertainty. The former is unambiguously concerned with the properties of an evolving economic environment and not with the nature of the agents who inhabit it. The latter, however, would be concerned with the nature of agents rather than the properties of their environment. But because this characterization is inaccurate – because, in fact, uncertainty is conventionally regarded in post-Keynesian economics as arising from the nature of the economic environment and the historical specificity of information therein – no such tension exists. Instead, there is a compatibility between hysteresis and uncertainty in so far as both concepts are chiefly concerned with the properties of an evolving economic environment.

Upon closer inspection, this compatibility reveals a more profound complementarity. The environment that both concepts are ultimately seeking to characterize is one of historical time. Historical time comprises a unidirectional sequence of events; any present event exists in the context of a given and immutable series of prior events. This draws our attention to the possibility that the past matters in the sense that it may affect current and future (including long-run or final) outcomes. It is exactly this possibility that is captured by the definition of hysteresis given above. Indeed, the principle of hysteresis and the concept of historical time are compatible (Setterfield 1995). However, the notion of historical time also implies something about the *future*. If history does matter, the future cannot be predestined, since whatever happened in the past cannot, by definition, impact upon a predestined future outcome. Serious consideration of historical time therefore precludes the possibility that the future will unfold according to timeless and immutable 'laws of history' and probability distributions which, by definition, would indicate that history does *not* matter. Historical time therefore creates an environment of uncertainty, because it denies the possibility of there being a time-invariant 'true model' – either static or dynamic – which is knowable in principle. But if the concept of hysteresis is compatible with historical time and if historical time, in turn, creates uncertainty, then there is clearly some degree of complementarity between hysteresis and uncertainty. In this view, hysteresis describes precisely the sort of evolutionary process thought to characterize the economic environment in a state of uncertainty. It is not surprising, in light of all this, to find that some models of hysteresis appeal explicitly to uncertainty as part of the hysteretic process (Katzner 1993: 339–44),[16] while others address the conditions under which their dynamics are consistent with the existence of uncertainty (Setterfield 1994b).[17] Indeed, Katzner (1993: 343) has gone so far as to claim that '[t]he simpler, and more natural, way to conceive of hysteresis in economics ... is in the context of historical time and ignorance'.

Having established this, however, it is important to recognize that post-Keynesian scepticism surrounding the compatibility of hysteresis and uncertainty has not been entirely misplaced. What is demonstrated above is that the *general* concepts of hysteresis and uncertainty are complementary. However, it is well known that certain *specific* formal characterizations of hysteresis (in particular, the so-called 'unit root' characterization) severely impair the conceptual breadth and meaning of this process (Setterfield 1992, 1993, 1995; Katzner 1993; Cross 1993a). Post-Keynesian concerns regarding the compatibility of hysteresis and uncertainty make more sense if they are interpreted as concerns over the compatibility of unit root characterizations of hysteresis and uncertainty.[18] What is interesting, however, is that even in the case of the unit root characterization, the gulf between hysteresis and uncertainty may not be as wide as it initially appears. At the very least, the nature of unit root processes raises some important questions for post-Keynesians regarding the nature of uncertainty and how it should (or should not) be conceived.

Unit root processes and uncertainty

The unit root characterization of hysteresis is based on the following system of equations:

$$X_t = \alpha W_t \quad [1]$$
$$W_t = \beta X_{t-1} + \gamma Z_t \quad [2]$$

Upon substitution, we arrive at:

$$X_t = \eta X_{t-1} + \phi Z_t \quad [3]$$

where $\eta = \alpha\beta$ and $\phi = \alpha\gamma$. Conventionally, the long-run value of X can be determined by solving equation [3] for the steady state:

$$X^* = \frac{\phi Z^*}{1 - \eta} \quad [4]$$

However, if $\eta = 1$ – i.e. if the difference equation [3] has a unit root – then the steady state in [4] cannot be defined. Instead, in order to determine the value of X in any period t, we must appeal to equation [3] and its previous $t - 1$ iterations. The value of X in any period can now be summarized as:

$$X_t = X_0 + \phi \sum_{i=1}^{t} Z_i \quad [5]$$

The value of X in any period now depends on its own past values, as summarized by initial conditions X_0 and the history of all subsequent values of the variable Z. Note that the long-run value of X will also take the form described in equation [5], the 'long-run outcome' being defined here solely in terms of its temporal distance, measured in calendar time, from the initial period 0. With $\eta = 1$, X displays hysteresis.

Davidson (1993) levels three main criticisms at this characterization of hysteresis, each of which calls into question its correspondence with the post-Keynesian treatment of uncertainty. First, he criticizes the distinction made between 'full' hysteresis and 'persistence'. The latter occurs when $\eta \neq 1$, so that 'short-run' values of X display path dependence (as in equation [3]), but the 'long-run' value of X nevertheless converges to the predetermined steady state in equation [4]. Davidson (1993: 315f.) quite legitimately questions how long is the long run, and what is the relevance of the distinction between full hysteresis and persistence if we are effectively always in the short run and 'dead' in the long run? (Also see Setterfield 1992: ch. 2; Katzner 1993.) Failure to define the short run and long run in calendar time is a common feature of long-run equilibrium models. It is also a shortcoming of the unit root characterization in its attempt to distinguish between the permanent and temporary path dependence of full hysteresis and persistence respectively. However, note that when $\eta = 1$, long-run outcomes in unit root systems can only be defined as such in terms of calendar time. No long-run outcome independent of history exists to define the value of X, in marked contrast to the state of affairs when $\eta \neq 1$ and the steady state in [4], defined in terms of ahistorical data, is assumed to constitute the 'long-run' outcome of the system. This is surely affined with the post-Keynesian notion of uncertainty, in which the long run has no meaning independent of calendar time, since it is no more than a historically specific sequence of short runs.

Davidson (1993: 312ff.) also criticizes the unit root model of hysteresis because it possesses a degree of 'concealed determinism' which makes it incompatible with an environment of uncertainty. The concern here is that unit root models describe a process in which the *level* of some variable is path dependent, but in which rates of change accord, at some level of differencing, to a deterministic 'law of change' which is independent of history and which can be (at least in principle) known by economic agents. Hence ahistorical determinism re-enters the picture, albeit at a higher level of reasoning. To see this, note that equation [5] yields the result:[19]

$$X_t - X_{t-1} \equiv \Delta X_t = \phi Z_t \qquad [6]$$

If we suppose that $Z_t \sim (0, \sigma_Z^2)$ is an independently and identically distributed random error term for all values of t, then equation [6] provides agents with a law of change suitable for the formation of rational expectations. Given the preceding assumptions, rational expectations of ΔX_t formed by using equation [6], given by $E(\Delta X_t) = 0$, will differ from actual outcomes only by some constant multiple, ϕ, of any contemporaneous error Z_t. Clearly, the notion of uncertainty is reduced here to its meaning within the rational expectations hypothesis – that of errors, with strictly temporary effects on the economy,[20] which prevent agents from having perfect foresight. There is no role for animal spirits; agents can forecast on the basis of the true model, and knowing that this is the case, they will re-use the same forecasting model time and again despite any errors (and hence disappointed expectations) that they encounter over time. This is quite unlike behaviour under uncertainty, where agents do not know the future and know that they do not know the future, so that any disappointment of expectations may lead agents to re-evaluate all facets of their future-oriented behaviour, including the worth of any forecasting model that they are using. It seems, then, that unit root characterizations of hysteresis admit the possibility of a degree of determinism in economic evolution that is antithetical to the post-Keynesian notion of uncertainty.

The preceding argument certainly poses a problem for anyone who would argue that the unit root version of hysteresis is compatible with the post-Keynesian conception of uncertainty. However, there may be a caveat in this argument. While errors do not matter in equation [6] in the sense that they have no lasting effect on the value of ΔX_t, they *do* matter in equation [5], where the effect of random errors on the value of X persists indefinitely. Since random errors cannot, by their nature, be foreseen, we may have something approaching a state of fundamental uncertainty here, because agents cannot predict Z_t, but they know that we may have $Z_t \neq 0$ and that this matters because it affects long-run outcomes.[21] Will agents bet their shirts by entering long-run commitments governed by a process such as [5], the existence of equation [6] notwithstanding? Does not the answer to this question depend on their animal spirits – their psychological optimism or pessimism concerning the value of Z_t over the chosen planning horizon? Perhaps the more fundamental issue that underlies these questions is whether equations such as [6] are really important if it is the outcomes in [5] that matter to agents and that influence their behaviour.

Davidson's final criticism concerns the appeal in unit root systems to exogenous perturbations to explain any non-deterministic evolution of the economy. This exogenous shock rhetoric contrasts with the post-Keynesian conception of an endogenously evolving monetary production economy which underlies the existence of uncertainty. The notion of originative action or innovation is rooted in a philosophical belief in the possibility of spontaneous change from within the economy on the part of economic agents, even in the absence of exogenous shocks (see McKenna and Zannoni 1993). The idea here is that the economy evolves according to endogenous forces, but in a non-deterministic fashion, thus undergoing endogenously generated transformations that are not routinely predictable. The economy therefore creates its own future and, as a result, its own uncertainty, rather than having either of these imposed upon it from 'without' (whatever, precisely, this means).

However, we might question whether this amounts to anything more than a purely rhetorical difference between unit root characterizations of hysteresis and uncertainty. Is there any substantive difference between the notion of exogenous shocks and appeals to originative/innovative behaviour which cannot be predicted a priori? Is the latter simply a long-hand way of appealing to exogenous shocks, as when, for example, post-Keynesian economists describe agents as experiencing a sudden revision in their animal spirits?[22] Ultimately, if we accept that uncertainty exists in an environment where errors matter, is not the difference we are contemplating more apparent than real? Alternatively, of course, it might be objected that rhetoric *does* matter – that the language of 'exogenous shocks' brings with it the tacit assumption that the economy is essentially (i.e. but for shocks) a stable, self-regulating environment. Meanwhile, the language of endogenous (but non-deterministic) transformation is suggestive of stability only in Keynes's sense of there being apparent limits to the fluctuations caused by change-inducing features inherent in the economy (Brown 1981: 120). Might the overtones of language contribute significantly more to the content of a model than many economic theorists are wont to admit?

It is important to note that none of the preceding arguments are intended to defend the unit root characterization of hysteresis. The flaws of this characterization are well known, especially to the present author (Setterfield 1992, 1993, 1994b, 1995). The unit root approach attempts to reduce hysteresis to a special case,[23] when, in fact, it is itself a special case of this process. But even this limited characterization of hysteresis may not be entirely inconsistent with the concept of fundamental uncertainty. Moreover, as argued above, the general concepts of hysteresis and uncertainty are complementary.

Should we seek complete consistency?

One final question remains to be addressed, and this is essentially a question of the pros and cons of 'philosophical purism' versus those of 'modelling pragmaticism'. In short, *should* we judge models of hysteresis by the criterion of complete consistency with fundamental uncertainty? Are we foregoing something crucial if we do not, or is this an unnecessarily high-mannered approach to adopt?

Any model of hysteresis that generates uncertainty, and which is therefore consistent with the maxim that there are no laws of history, will be of considerable philosophical appeal to post-Keynesians. But should post-Keynesians be sufficiently flexible to consider *two levels* of historical time – a lower level which is admitted for purposes of model building and a more radical high level which defines the philosophical high ground?[24] As Setterfield (1995) argues, there exist a number of useful organizing concepts (such as hysteresis, cumulative causation and lock-in) which may not all be entirely faithful to the notion of (high-level) historical time, but do at least 'promise to take us beyond the extreme stasis of orthodox equilibrium theory'.

An example may help to illustrate what is at stake here. Cross (1993b: 306ff.) uses a Ewing loop to illustrate hysteresis. His diagram is reproduced, in a slightly amended form, as Figure 9.1.

In the Ewing loop, a system subject to an exogenous shock moves, in response to this shock, from its initial configuration *A* to a new configuration *B*. However, when the shock is removed, the system adjusts to a new configuration *C* – it does not return to its original position *A*. Hence the system is hysteretic – its long-run outcomes depend on its own past history. The configuration *A* can, however, be restored by the application of some appropriate counter-shock, which would move the system along the trajectory *CDA*.

This latter feature is criticized by Davidson (1993: 318) for being incon-

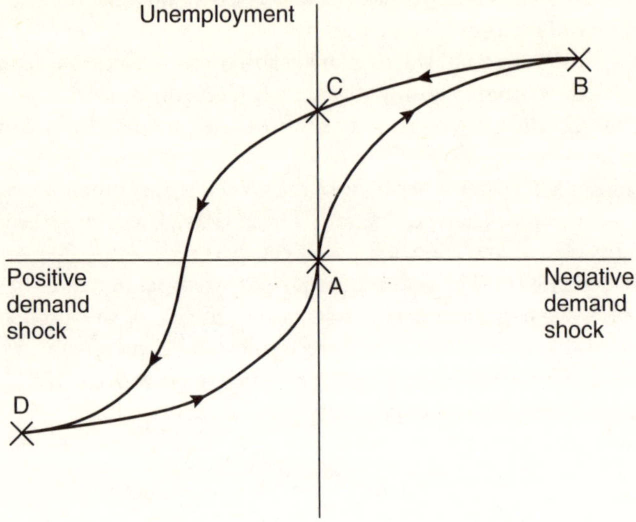

Figure 9.1 Hysteresis and the Ewing loop

sistent with historical time. In the Ewing loop, shocks are *irreversible* in the sense that their removal will not lead to the restoration of initial conditions. However, they are *revocable* (see Georgescu-Roegen 1971: 197), since some subsequent process (or shock) *can* be relied upon to restore initial conditions. Worse still, in the Ewing loop revocability can be brought about in a deterministic fashion. But any form of revocability (much less deterministic revocability) can be thought of as being antithetical to the notion of historical time (Setterfield 1995), since movement through time changes the stocks of experience that agents possess. These stocks of experience, accumulated since the initial conditions of a system existed, cannot easily be eradicated if, indeed, they can be eradicated at all (Hodgson 1992: 758). Yet this is precisely what the restoration of initial conditions would require. There is, therefore, a fundamental incompatibility between the Ewing loop and high-level historical time, where post-Keynesians typically ground the concept of uncertainty.[25]

However, there are useful lessons to be learned from the Ewing loop, even if it is compatible only with a low-level conceptualization of historical time. If the exogenous shock in the Ewing loop is a policy decision regarding aggregate demand, and if the configurations *A*, *B* and *C* correspond to unemployment outcomes, the Ewing loop suggests, contra the orthodox wisdom of the natural rate hypothesis, that changes in aggregate demand can have permanent effects on unemployment because long-run unemployment outcomes are not determined independently of the past history of realized unemployment outcomes and hence macroeconomic policy. Can post-Keynesians afford to maintain the philosophical high ground if it means rejecting models that are at least partially consistent with post-Keynesian concerns regarding the influence of historical time, and which make salient policy points? Is not discussing the philosophical high ground associated with historical time, but subsequently looking for ways to 'lock up' (without ignoring) its effects in order to engage in practical modelling exercises the hallmark of the research methodology practised by Keynes and the post-Keynesians (see Kregel 1976)?

CONCLUSIONS

It is perhaps useful to end by again quoting Katzner's (1993: 343) suggestion that '[t]he simpler, and more natural, way to conceive of hysteresis in economics . . . is in the context of historical time and ignorance'. In principle, it seems, there is no necessary contradiction between the concepts of hysteresis and uncertainty. Certain specific models of hysteresis may fall short of the philosophical mark set by many post-Keynesians in their treatment of uncertainty, but even here the differences between hysteresis and uncertainty are, to some extent, minor. Furthermore, in a modelling context, deviations from 'high-level' historical time may even be desirable and/or necessary. This conclusion seems consistent with the modelling strategy of Keynes and the post-Keynesians. In short, it appears that post-Keynesians should treat hysteresis and uncertainty as essentially complementary concepts.[26]

NOTES

1 Davidson (1993: 311) does suggest that confluence may yet be demonstrated, which partly motivates the present paper.

2 The notion of relative probability refers here to the evaluation of some event being more or less likely to occur than some other event with which it can be compared.

3 Note that uncertainty is not completely demobilizing; agents can and do continue to form expectations and pursue future-oriented activities in environments of uncertainty. Moreover, partial ignorance of the future does not mean that behaviour is irrational. As will become clear in what follows, partial ignorance is not a feature of agent choices (for example, a perverse intent to overlook certain information), but arises because of constraints on individual decision-making with respect to the future that cannot be alleviated. For further discussion of behaviour under uncertainty, see Davidson (1988) and Lavoie (1992).

4 This typology differs schematically, but not in principle, from Davidson (1988: 330), which also attempts to define 'uncertainty' in ways that can be understood by the mainstream.

5 We shall not pursue the issue as to how the composition of the vector μ_t is chosen. Note, however, that we make no supposition that agents know all relevant macroeconomic variables that need to be forecast in period *t*, or that they *can* know this in period *t*. In characterizing μ_t, we suppose only that $n \neq 0$ – i.e. that in the present period agents are interested in forecasting the future values of *some* set of macroeconomic variables.

6 By associating the form of the information set Ω_t with agents' perceptions of their future environment we are implicitly assuming that agents' perceptions are

objective, in that they vary only with the available information, Ω_t. This assumption involves no loss of generality in the current context, and does not rule out the possibility that agents' behaviour may ultimately reflect subjective influences – especially if it is realized that perceptions of the future are subject to partial ignorance.

7 We could write $DGP_t \neq DGP_{t+1}$, but in this case the rational expectations hypothesis would likely suggest that $\Omega_t = DGP_{t+1}$ on the basis of agents' knowledge of some intertemporally stable, deterministic 'meta DGP' governing the evolution of DGP_t over time. Hence the presentation above suffers no real loss of generality by writing $DGP_t = DGP_{t+1} = DGP^*$ and therefore conceiving DGP_t as stationary.

8 Note that if $\Omega_t \neq DGP^*$ and $\lim_{t\to\infty} \Omega_t \neq DGP^*$, and the dimensions of Ω_t and DGP^* are identical, then we have a situation akin to the subjectivist environment of risk associated with Friedman and Savage. See Lawson (1988) for further discussion.

9 Agents may use the *rhetoric* of expected value maximization associated with environments of probabilistic risk even if, in principle, probability theory does not provide a complete basis for decision-making with regard to future outcomes (Palley 1993: 17).

10 This is Davidson's (1988: 331f.) non-ergodic environment, whereas the previous scenarios correspond to his ergodic environment.

11 This section draws heavily on Setterfield (1995).

12 The notion of a non-accelerating inflation rate of unemployment (NAIRU) is sometimes preferred to that of a natural rate in these models. See Setterfield (1994a) for further discussion.

13 For example, Rutherford (1992) defines hysteresis as '(t)he hypothesis, applied to the study of unemployment, which states that a level of unemployment does not have a tendency to return to an equilibrium rate and certainly not the natural rate of unemployment'.

14 See Cross and Allen (1988) for further discussion.

15 The case of damped cycles in the multiplier accelerator model of the trade cycle provides an example of such a system. See Setterfield (1992: ch.2) for further discussion.

16 For Katzner, agents in an environment of uncertainty are learning by doing as history unfolds period by period. As a result, 'the steady alterations in the epistemic statuses and decision opportunities of individuals as they learn of and experience new things ... do not permit a return to an earlier state' (Katzner 1993: 343). In other words, a form of hysteresis exists; any long-run or final outcome that attains is the product of the precise path taken towards it, due to the influence of this adjustment path on individuals' choice sets and stocks of experience.

17 For Setterfield, hysteresis is caused by asymmetries in the adjustment of what are defined as 'deeply endogenous' variables along disequilibrium time paths. If the nature and likelihood of these adjustment asymmetries are time dependent and historically specific, and cannot, therefore, be known a priori, agents populating the hysteretic environment will exist in a state of uncertainty.

18 Davidson's (1993) criticisms of hysteresis are very much directed at the unit root characterization of this process.

19 Equation [5] implies that:

$$X_t = X_0 + \phi \sum_{i=1}^{t} Z_i$$

and:

$$X_{t-1} = X_0 + \phi \sum_{i=1}^{t-1} Z_i$$

It therefore follows that:.

$$X_t - X_{t-1} = \phi Z_t$$

See also Katzner (1993: 325f.).

20 Note that the permanent effect of errors – and hence the influence of history – present in equation [5] gets expunged from equation [6], which is written solely in terms of the current value of Z_t.

21 Note that questions regarding the suitability of treating uncertainty as an environment where 'errors matter' – something with which not all post-Keynesians may feel comfortable – are left begging here. However, this issue is addressed in detail below.

22 These issues beg the very question of what we mean by 'endogenous' and 'exogenous' forces in economics.

23 That it is not altogether successful in this attempt is evident from Setterfield (1992: ch. 2, 1993) and Katzner (1993).

24 The distinction between levels of historical time is due to Marc Lavoie and was communicated to me in a personal correspondence dated 13 July 1994.

25 Notice that the same criticism could also be made of the unit root model discussed earlier. Hence in equation [5], whilst any shock $Z_i \neq 0$ will have a permanent effect on X_t, it can be offset in any subsequent period, in a manner that restores initial conditions, by the appropriate counter-shock $Z_j = -Z_i$, $i \neq j$.

26 I would like to thank Steve Pressman for comments on an earlier version of this chapter. Any remaining errors are, however, my own.

REFERENCES

Blanchard, O.J. and Summers, L.H. (1986) 'Hysteresis and the European Unemployment Problem', in S. Fischer (ed.) *NBER Macroeconomic Annual*, Cambridge, Mass.: MIT Press.

Brown, E.K. (1981) 'The Neoclassical and Post-Keynesian Research Programs: The Methodological Issues', *Review of Social Economy* 39: 111–32.

Cross, R. (1993a) 'On the Foundations of Hysteresis in Economic Systems', *Economics and Philosophy* 9: 53–74.

——(1993b) 'Hysteresis and Post Keynesian Economics', *Journal of Post Keynesian Economics* 15: 305–8.

Cross, R. and Allen, A. (1988) 'On the History of Hysteresis', in R. Cross (ed.) *Unemployment, Hysteresis and the Natural Rate Hypothesis*, Oxford: Basil Blackwell.

Currie, M. and Steedman, I. (1990) *Wrestling with Time*, Ann Arbor: University of Michigan Press.

Davidson, P. (1988) 'A Technical Definition of Uncertainty and the Long-Run Non-Neutrality of Money', *Cambridge Journal of Economics* 12: 329–37.

——(1991) 'Is Probability Theory Relevant for Uncertainty?', *Journal of Economic Perspectives* 5: 129–43.

——(1993) 'The Elephant and the Butterfly; Or Hysteresis and Post Keynesian Economics', *Journal of Post Keynesian Economics* 15: 309–22.

Elster, J. (1976) 'A Note on Hysteresis in the Social Sciences', *Synthese* 33: 371–91.

Georgescu-Roegen, N. (1971) *The Entropy Law and the Economic Process*, Cambridge, Mass.: Harvard University Press.

Hamouda, O.F. and Smithin, J.N. (1988) 'Some Remarks on "Uncertainty and Economic Analysis" ', *Economic Journal* 98: 159–64.

Hicks, J.R. (1977) *Economic Perspectives*, Oxford: Oxford University Press.

Hodgson, G.M. (1992) 'The Reconstruction of Economics: Is There Still a Place for Neoclassical Theory?', *Journal of Economic Issues* 26: 749–67.

Hoogduin, L. (1987) 'On the Difference between the Keynesian, Knightian and the "Classical" Analysis of Uncertainty and the Development of a More General Monetary Theory', *De Economist* 1: 52–65.

Jenkinson, T. (1987) 'The Natural Rate of Unemployment: Does It Exist?', *Oxford Review of Economic Policy* 3: 20–6.

Katzner, D.W. (1993) 'Some Notes on the Role of History and the Definition of Hysteresis and Related Concepts in Economic Analysis', *Journal of Post Keynesian Economics* 15: 323–45.

Keynes, J.M. (1973) *The Collected Writings of John Maynard Keynes*, Vol. 14, *The General Theory and After*, London: Macmillan.

Kregel, J. (1976) 'Economic Methodology in the Face of Uncertainty: The Modelling Methods of Keynes and the Post Keynesians', *Economic Journal* 86: 209–25.

Lavoie, M. (1992) *Foundations of Post-Keynesian Economic Analysis*, Aldershot: Edward Elgar.

Lawson, T. (1988) 'Probability and Uncertainty in Economics', *Journal of Post Keynesian Economics* 11: 38–65.

Layard, R., Nickell, S.J. and Jackman, R. (1991) *Unemployment: Macroeconomic Performance and the Labour Market*, Oxford: Oxford University Press.

McKenna, E.J. and Zannoni, D.C. (1993) 'Philosophical Foundations of Post Keynesian Economics', *Journal of Post Keynesian Economics* 15: 395–407.

Palley, T.I. (1993) 'Uncertainty, Expectations and the Future: If We Don't Know the Answers, What are the Questions?', *Journal of Post Keynesian Economics* 16: 3–18.

Rutherford, D. (1992) *Dictionary of Economics*, London: Routledge.

Setterfield, M.A. (1992) 'A Long Run Theory of Effective Demand: Modelling Macroeconomic Systems with Hysteresis', unpublished PhD thesis, Dalhousie University, Canada.

——(1993) 'Towards a Long Run Theory of Effective Demand: Modelling Macroeconomic Systems with Hysteresis', *Journal of Post Keynesian Economics* 15: 347–64.

——(1994a) 'Using the NAIRU as a Basis for Macroeconomic Policy: An Evaluation', in B.K. MacLean and L. Osberg (eds) *The Unemployment Crisis: All For Nought?*, Cheektowaga, NY: McGill-Queens University Press.

——(1994b) 'Adjustment Asymmetries and Hysteresis in Simple Dynamic Models', Trinity College mimeo.

——(1995) 'Historical Time and Economic Theory', *Review of Political Economy* 7: 1–27.

Part IV

POLICY ISSUES

10

DEFICITS IN OUR UNDERSTANDING

Transformational growth and the role of government

Edward J. Nell

Applied economics is inherently historical in nature. The structure and functioning of markets and other economic institutions must be studied in the historical period where they are located. If markets and institutions change, guiding principles and policies that work well in one period may be completely inappropriate or ineffective in another. Using a model from one era to analyse the market behaviour of another is thus liable to result in confusion.

We can see historical differences in the working of markets in the post-war USA. Policies that were effective in the earlier part of the period have not worked well lately. Inflation has proved difficult to control. Unemployment has risen and productivity growth has fallen. Unemployment and inflation have also both increased at times. The balance of payments has deteriorated and the USA has become a net debtor nation. But there was a time when economic policies did work.

The Golden Age lasted from the end of the war to the beginning of the 1970s; a second age, of baser metal, runs from that point to the present. In the first period growth was strong, inflation and unemployment were low, and policy measures seemed to help the economy. In the second, growth was weak, inflation and unemployment were high, and policies often failed. Table 10.1 presents this contrast.

In the second period unemployment averaged nearly 50 per cent more than in the first period. Moreover, both discouraged workers and underemployment errors (part-time work counted improperly as full-time) were especially

Table 10.1 The golden age versus recent economic performance

	1948–69	*1970–94*
Unemployment	4.7%	6.7%
Capacity utilization	84%	81%
GNP growth	3.8%	2.4%
Productivity growth	3.1%	1.3%
Inflation	2.6%	5.5%

Source: Citibank, CITIBASE 1994

prominent during the latter period. Estimates of capacity utilization confirm that there were more idle resources in the second period. Far from pressing on resources, as advocates of crowding out would have it, demand in the second period has been insufficient to employ all the labour and capital available. As might be expected, with a substantial pool of idle resources the average rate of GNP growth was lower in the second period (about two-thirds of its former level). Productivity growth performance was even worse; it fell in the second period to less than half the rate of the first period.

Despite the absence of demand pressure, inflation surged. Measured as the annual percentage change in the GNP price deflator, the inflation rate in the second period was more than twice that of the first period. In general, the picture is one of sluggish markets and greater inflation beginning in the 1970s.

TRANSFORMATIONAL GROWTH

These changes suggest a major structural shift in the economy. Most conventional accounts, however, attribute our problems either to random shocks – like OPEC's price hikes – or to the ill effects of intervention itself. The theory of transformational growth seeks to explain changes in market behaviour by examining the interplay between markets and technology. It holds that what markets do is drive innovation.

A new technological order is now emerging to displace the system of mass production. Faster communications, computerized control over production, electronic funds transfers, robots and automation have all changed the economic world. One consequence of this new technology is that the economy does not operate in the same way. Inflation is more easily triggered; firms are more skittish about capital spending; expansion draws in imports faster. Likewise, policies will not have the same effects as before.

Most interpretations of weak economic performance during the last two decades have been based on a set of economic principles that arose in the era prior to mass production. Conventional microeconomics, as far as it actually applies to anything at all, describes an economy of flexible prices and supply-and-demand adjustments – the Victorian world of Alfred Marshall. In that world, employment and output tended to remain comparatively fixed in the short run, and prices carried the burden of adjustment. That era, of course, gave birth to neoclassical theory, the same theory that lives on in today's textbooks and policy debates, although the contemporary version is far more sophisticated.[1]

Not surprisingly, this theory implies that governments should behave like Victorian governments – following the ideal of the night-watchman state rather than the interventionist, welfare state. In the world of Victorian economics, a rise in deficit spending might well drive up interest rates, and crowd out private investment.

However, the world of today is strikingly different from the Victorian world. In a mass production economy output and employment are flexible, but prices tend to be fixed, varying with productivity but not with sales. Both money prices and money wages tend to drift upward; but output and employment tend to be unstable. Adjustment in a mass production economy works through the multiplier–accelerator mechanism, and this is decidedly not stabilizing.

The past two decades mark the displacement of mass production in favour of a new technological order, one whose outlines are only just emerging. We can expect that this economy will adjust differently, just as the mass production system worked differently than the craft-based economy that preceded it. So the Keynesian policies suited to mass production may no longer be effective; a new approach may be needed. But it does no good to try to analyse this change with a theory based on economic principles that describe the markets of a bygone age.

The theory of transformational growth takes the view that the working of markets reflects the character of the technology; therefore the working of markets changes over time. Contrary to conventional theory, competitive markets do not allocate scarce resources optimally; they do not help to resolve social problems by reaching Pareto optimal positions. Markets, in fact, do not or need not reach equilibrium. Of course, they may do any or all of these things sometimes; but their chief function and chief importance is that they stimulate innovations and, through competition, spread them throughout the economy. Markets are the midwives of new technology.

New technologies, in turn, change the way that markets work. Technology determines costs; when technology changes, costs change. It is not just that technology reduces cost; rather, it is the character of the costs that matters (for example, which costs are fixed, which are variable, and to what degree). When costs change, and especially when their character changes, the strategies of firms must change. If cost changes are large enough or important enough, the way that the market adjusts may change.

An interactive pattern emerges. The process of market adjustment creates problems for firms. Some features of the process can be particularly troublesome. Some costs will be unpredictable or liable to vary suddenly and excessively, or will be large and fixed regardless of the market. Solving these problems gives rise to new technologies. Competition spreads them, and the new cost structure permits firms to develop different strategies in the market, giving rise to a new set of adjustment problems, which in turn can be expected to stimulate a new set of innovations (Nell, forthcoming).

Prior to 1914 (when the foundations of modern economics were developed) the price mechanism operated in ways that tended to stabilize the economy – for small shocks, at any rate. Given craft-based technologies, output and employment could not be readily adapted to fluctuations in sales; hence prices were flexible, more flexible than money wages. The result was a system of adjustment that behaved more or less as described by Marshall, with falling demand curves and rising supply curves, the latter based on marginal costs. Even today residual elements of this mechanism can be found in some sectors. But the production system's rigidity and its dependence on craft methods (and therefore on skilled craftspeople) led to the development of the technology of mass production, which fundamentally changed the core of the system. With mass production, large multi-divisional corporations replaced small family-run craft firms. Operating with greater flexibility, firms could adjust output and employment to sales.

But the effect of adjusting employment and output to variations in demand, when generalized throughout the economy, was to ensure that any given change in sales would be magnified. The post-war economy, based on mass production and the modern corporation, contains an inherently unstable market mechanism. Small fluctuations in output and employment are transformed into large ones by some variant of the multiplier–accelerator process. Prices, for the most part, are flexible only upwards, and the pressures causing inflation are in general not stabilizing. The traditional price mechanism, where supply and demand adapt to one another in a stable process, is not to be found.

In the absence of a stabilizing price mechanism, the economy is prevented from swinging out of control chiefly by a large government sector, whose expenditures move in a counter-cyclical fashion – the so-called 'automatic stabilizers' instituted after the Second World War. (These, however, may not be sufficient, and may need to be supplemented by active policy.) Prior to the First World War, government spending in the advanced economies tended to lie below 10 per cent of GNP; after the Second World War it rose to over 20 per cent. Counting transfer payments the increase was even greater.[2] And government spending continued to rise throughout the post-war period, reaching 36 per cent in the USA, 44 per cent in the UK and even higher elsewhere. Larger governments provided infrastructure, regulation, and through the welfare state, support for mass consumption. Together with counter-cyclical measures, this provided for an era of strong and stable prosperity.

Mass production, however, posed problems. Very briefly, low costs required long production runs, which meant that a given product design had to serve everyone. Customizing was expensive. Effective production was heavily dependent on union cooperation; quality control was difficult and time-consuming. Business lacked detailed control over processes. Given the distribution of income, markets tended to become saturated; while they still might grow, they grew more slowly. At a certain point, everyone who could afford one (and many who could not) had a car and a television.

A new technology – flexible mass production or computerized automation – has arisen to solve these problems, and this has begun to undermine the post-war system. With the new technology, some say, there has emerged a 'new competition', and a new leaner, more flexible, corporation (Best 1992). The new system is still an embryo; it is hard to know exactly how it will look or how it will work. What is clear is that it will be different. Production processes have become intermediated. Components are 'sourced' from the cheapest worldwide producers, and assembly plants are located near cheap labour. One effect has been to weaken the labour movement and hold down wages. New forms of communication, faster transport and computer control have created an international system, but the new technologies are still in their infancy. That is enough to create uncertainty among investors, particularly when consumer markets are growing more slowly and showing greater volatility.

The counsel of despair: policy will not work

Transformational growth suggests that the troubles that began in the early 1970s have deep roots, and require government to rethink its approach to the economy. Policies that worked for a quarter century will have to be revised, but the government will have to remain as a stabilizer.

The old theory of price adjustment implies that governments are powerless, except possibly to make things worse. It is a view held strongly by many professional economists. This approach explains the failure of demand management in the 1970s and 1980s by suggesting that markets learned to anticipate and offset the effects of government policies. Expanding the money supply might temporarily lower real wages and increase employment; but once money wages catch up to prices, unemployment would again rise to its natural level. The only permanent effect of policy intervention is thus higher prices.

Others have argued somewhat differently. For example, Peterson (1994) claims that deficit spending drives up interest rates, reduces investment, strengthens the dollar and cuts exports. In yet another version, it is held that government deficits soak up savings, leaving only the residue for private investment. Or government expansion might lead to inflation, reducing real wages and consumption, which then reduces private investment. In each case expansionary policies become self-defeating.

These arguments are based on economic principles that were developed in the era prior to the First World War, an era when prices were decidedly flexible in both directions. There was a price mechanism then, and it tended to stabilize the economy.[3] Under such conditions expansionary policy would be counteracted, while contractions would be automatically reversed. But this model is simply irrelevant for understanding the world of the last forty years; there is no such price mechanism. Deficits bear no systematic relation to interest rates, real or nominal. Relative prices vary with productivity; money prices only rise. Real wages vary pro-cyclically. Corporate savings exceed household saving, and companies grow by investing retained earnings. The Victorian economy of the family firm has been supplanted by the world of large transnational corporations (Nell 1988; Nell and Phillips 1995; Nell, forthcoming).

Despite these fundamental structural changes, the older theory has recently regained popularity. The weak performance of the economy has discredited interventionism, which is blamed for not controlling inflation. One consequence of the resurgence of the night-watchman theory is that governments have become less activist. This is unfortunate, for the evidence suggests that expansionary policies work, although they will have to be modified to suit the new conditions. Yet this argument cannot get off the ground until we overcome the Victorian view that government activity should be minimal, lest it lead to disaster.

The effectiveness of expansionary policies

Let us compare policy that tilts towards expansion with policy favouring austerity. In general, Democratic administrations have favoured expansionary policies while Republican administrations have favoured policies leaning towards austerity and control of inflation. There have been exceptions, of course. The Carter administration, especially in the last two years, retreated from expansion, Nixon adopted Keynesian expansionist measures before the election of 1972, and Reagan expanded military spending while permitting large deficits. However, both Nixon and Reagan supported deregulation, cut government social spending and supported high interest rates and tight money. With few and minor qualifications, Democrats do lean towards expansion while Republicans lean towards austerity.

Table 10.2 looks at the economic performance of three Democratic administrations (Truman, Kennedy–Johnson and Carter) plus the first year of the Clinton administration, as well as three Republican administrations (Eisenhower, Nixon–Ford and Reagan–Bush).

This comparison is quite striking in several respects. First, the Democrats outperform the Republicans in all four categories! The contrast is most marked in productivity growth and GNP growth. Average productivity growth during the Democratic years was 3 per cent; average Republican productivity growth comes out at 1.7 per cent. Even with the dismal record of the Carter years, Democratic performance is nearly twice as good as the Republican record. The GNP growth picture is almost as extreme – Democrats average 4.7 per cent, Republicans 2.3 per cent. Unemployment averages 5.5 per cent for the Democrats and 6.1 per cent for the Republicans, closer than we might have expected. Somewhat surprisingly, even the Republican record on inflation is worse than the Democrats.

Second, the weakest Democratic performance comes during the Carter years. Unemployment during the Carter years is close to the Nixon–Ford record and lower than Reagan–Bush. GNP growth under Carter is better than either of these Republican administrations. The disasters are in productivity growth and inflation.

Third, the strong performance of the golden age is largely concentrated in the Truman and Kennedy–Johnson years. The Eisenhower record, while the best of the Republicans, still has a lower GNP growth rate than Carter (the weakest of the Democrats). In general, it seems that the more expansionary

Table 10.2 Economic performance in Democratic and Republican administrations

	Democrats		*Republicans*	
Unemployment	1948–52	4.3%	1953–60	4.9%
	1961–8	4.8%	1969–76	5.8%
	1977–80	6.5%	1981–92	7.1%
	1993	6.8%		
	Mean = 5.5%		Mean = 6.1%	
Inflation	1948–52	2.9%	1953–60	2.4%
	1961–8	2.5%	1969–76	6.4%
	1977–80	8.2%	1981–92	4.2%
	1993	2.2%		
	Mean = 4.1%		Mean = 4.3%	
Productivity growth	1948–52	4.3%	1953–60	2.5%
	1961–8	3.3%	1969–76	1.4%
	1977–80	0.3%	1981–92	1.4%
	1993	1.4%		
	Mean = 3.0%		Mean = 1.7%	
Real GNP growth	1948–52	5.6%	1953–60	2.2%
	1961–8	4.7%	1969–76	2.5%
	1977–80	2.8%	1981–92	2.4%
	1993	2.8%		
	Mean = 4.7%		Mean = 2.3%	

Source: Citibank, CITIBASE 1994

party has had the better economic record. Contrary to the conventional wisdom, administrations can do something about the economy.[4] Policy matters! Other things also matter, of course, but the unfashionable claim here is that an expansionary policy tends to lead to higher growth, lower unemployment and better economic performance. But such a policy today has to be based on understanding how the economy has changed. We turn now to an examination of what has happened.

THE ELEMENTS OF AGGREGATE DEMAND

Macroeconomics textbooks explain that aggregate demand consists of total consumption, plus investment, plus net exports, topped off with government spending. We now consider these elements of aggregate demand in turn. We will show that each component grew more slowly, became more volatile and shifted in composition away from manufacturing towards commercial or service activities.

Consumption

During the post-war era household consumption grew at about the same pace as GNP. However, the components of household consumption did not all behave in the same way. Figure 10.1 expresses the major components of consumption as a percentage of US GDP. (Some remarks that follow are based on statistical analysis and a more detailed disaggregation of the figures.)

Consumption of services has come to comprise an increasing percentage of GDP, and exhibits the highest growth rate. Durables show little growth, maintaining a relatively constant share of GDP. Non-durables show a decline in both growth and as a percentage of GDP. Durables fluctuate the most, except during the 1960s, when they grew strongly and more rapidly than GDP. They stagnate again during the 1980s, then grow rapidly in the mid-1980s before flattening out again.

At the beginning of the post-war period non-durables made up nearly half of all personal consumption spending, and more than the services category. By 1960 services exceeded non-durables as a share of consumption. Some of this may be attributable to the rise of fast-food services, replacing home consumption. But much of the decline stems from the fact that non-durables have a low income elasticity, meaning that the market is easily saturated. Once a home is heated adequately, households will not spend more on heating when its income rises. If markets are to continue to expand, something must rise to compensate for such slower than average growth. That has been services (and to a slight extent, durables). But the growth of services has been slower since 1974, and virtually flat, though volatile, since 1980.[5]

Overall, the growth of consumption has slowed since the early 1970s. Consumption spending has been more volatile, and has shifted markedly away from goods and towards services.

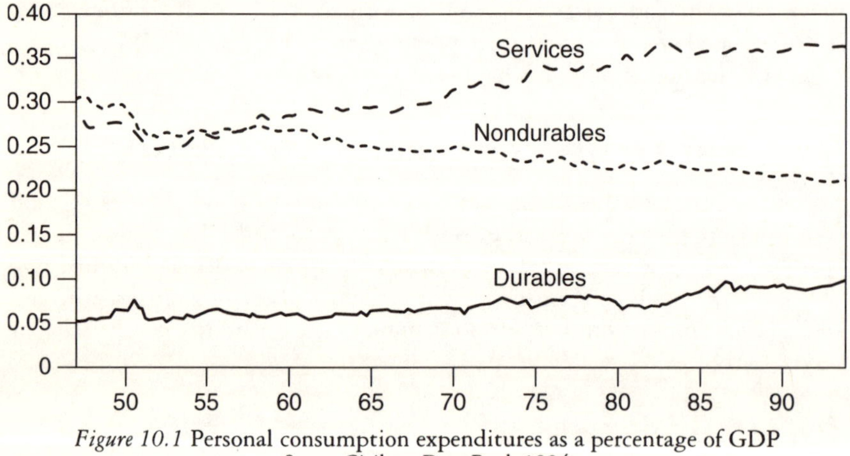

Figure 10.1 Personal consumption expenditures as a percentage of GDP
Source: Citibase Data Bank 1994

Business investment

Investment behaviour repeats this pattern, which should be no surprise since investment depends, to a large extent, on consumption. The slower or more irregularly consumption grows, the lower the level of investment tends to be, other things being equal (which, of course, they seldom are). We can see this from Table 10.3, which examines business investment relative to GDP. In general, investment grew faster than the economy during the 1960s, but slower than the economy thereafter. In addition, after the 1960s, larger fluctuations in investment are evident.

Table 10.3 Business investment relative to GDP

Years	*1947–69*	*1970–93*
Investment in producers' durable equipment/GDP		
Mean	11.53	8.69
Standard deviation	1.12	2.29
Nonresidential investment/GDP		
Mean	7.27	5.99
Standard deviation	1.02	1.27

Source: Citibank, CITIBASE 1994

A look at annual growth rates confirms this. Until 1970, the annual growth rates are relatively small and are either positive or very slightly negative (aside from the Eisenhower slump and the great boom of the mid-1960s). After 1970, however, we see greater volatility and a weaker overall performance.

Other measures confirm both of these developments. For example, taking statistics from the *IMF Financial Statistics Yearbook*, the ratio of investment to GNP, defined as gross fixed capital formation plus change in stocks, can be seen to fluctuate more widely after 1970, and to have trended downward on average. The same trend appears even more sharply in net private domestic nonresidential fixed investment in relation to GNP.

Also, just as in consumption, we see evidence that investment has shifted away from manufacturing to offices and commercial activities. Table 10.4 illustrates this point. We see three different categories of investment expenditure relative to gross fixed business investment. The pattern of business investment has clearly shifted toward service-related equipment (computing machinery and commercial equipment) and commercial structures. What has declined is the fraction of business investment devoted to manufacturing plants and equipment. This shift has surely contributed to the slow-down in productivity growth.

Table 10.4 Categories of business investment (as a percentage of gross fixed business investment)

	1958	*1986*
Computing and accounting machinery	1.3%	16.2%
Electrical and communications equipment	2.8%	9.3%
Commercial structures	9.3%	11.1%

Source: IMF *Staff Papers*, March 1989

Construction

Although private construction is included in private investment, and public construction under government expenditure, the trends in both public and private construction are so striking that they deserve special mention. Net private domestic residential fixed investment (relative to GDP) declined strongly over the entire post-war period, but the fluctuations become wider after 1970. New housing starts show a somewhat similar picture, although the downward trend is not so noticeable. However, the increase in volatility is clear.

Finally the annual growth rates of public construction show a clear downward drift, and increased volatility compared to the 1960s.[6] Public infrastructure has not kept pace with the growth of GDP either. OECD (1993: 75) figures show a decline in the public capital stock relative to GDP from a peak of 52 per cent in the late 1960s to 42–3 per cent in 1990. Gross public investment has similarly turned down. Since public investment in infrastructure contributes to private productivity growth, this slow-down in public construction and public investment has played a role in the productivity growth slow-down.

Net exports

In principle, foreign trade should be stabilizing. Ideally, at full employment exports and imports should balance. When aggregate output rises above the full employment level, the trade balance turns negative, reducing demand pressure; and when output falls below full employment, a positive trade balance provides an economic stimulus.

In the golden age this almost seemed to be the case. During the first half of the post-war era, net exports provided a small but positive stimulus to the US economy. Beginning in the early 1970s this stimulus vanished, reappeared briefly, and then disappeared for good in the mid-1970s. From then on, net exports have been negative although they fluctuated a great deal (see Figure 10.2).

Looking at a decomposition of net exports, it is evident that consumer durables and non-durables followed very similar patterns. Their balances were generally positive, but declining slightly, during the golden age; then they became more volatile, slumping sharply in the 1980s. The balance on services

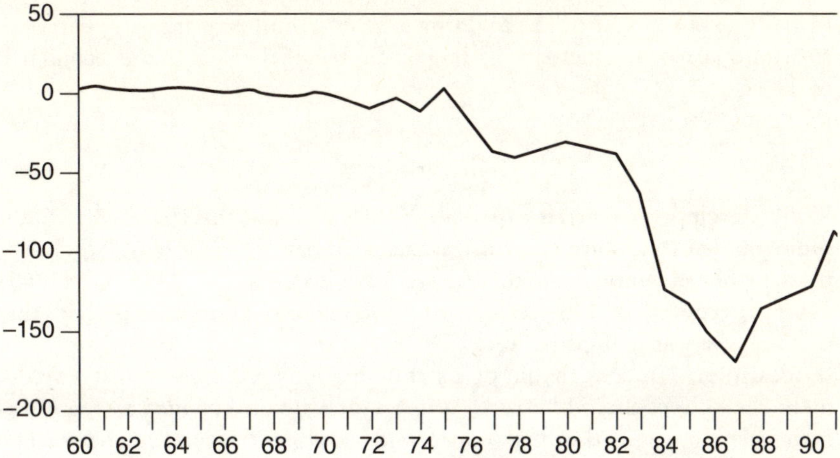

Figure 10.2 US net exports (in billions of 1987$)
Source: Citibase Data Bank 1994

developed in a completely different manner. It was slightly negative in the 1960s, turned strongly positive in the 1980s, fell back to zero, and then gained strongly in the late 1980s (see Figure 10.3).

A detailed examination of specific goods shows that the loss of export markets was wide-ranging, although computers remained strong until the end of the 1980s. Automobiles turned negative about 1968 and sank steadily thereafter, until turning up somewhat at the end of the 1980s. Industrial supplies went negative briefly in the mid-1970s, but (although fluctuating) remained positive thereafter.

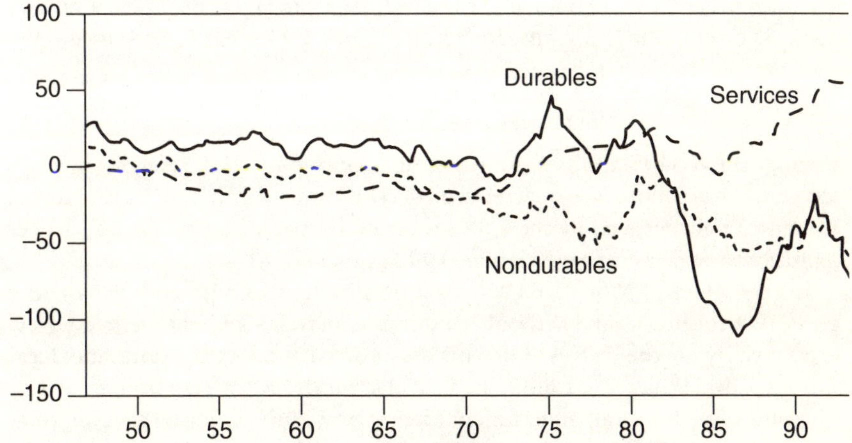

Figure 10.3 US net exports, disaggregated (in billions of 1987$)
Source: Citibase Data Bank 1994

In short, exports went from providing a small stimulus in the early period to creating a large, but fluctuating, drag on aggregate demand in the second half of the era.

Government

While developed countries experienced difficulties in the 1970s and 1980s, some countries and some administrations fared better than others, largely due to the policies implemented.[7] As we have seen, in the USA Democrats generally compiled a better record of economic performance, but that performance was still rather weak.

Ideally, government should be a stabilizing force. At close to full employment the budget should balance. When aggregate output increases, government spending will diminish, since unemployment insurance and welfare spending will fall, but with higher incomes, tax receipts will rise. Things are just the reverse when output falls – government spending rises and tax collections fall. Therefore, a rise in output will reduce demand stimulus and a fall will increase it. This requires that the full employment budget be balanced, and that automatic stabilizers be in place. In fact, this has not been the case.

According to demand management theory, under these circumstances, discretionary policy must be applied. It is the job of fiscal policy to pick up the slack when there is a long-term slow-down, leaving monetary policy to deal with short-run fluctuations. If long-term developments undermine the ability of effective demand to grow and maintain the desired level of employment, taxation and government spending should be adjusted to provide the required stimulus. This is usually thought of as deficit spending; but a stimulus is provided even when the budget is balanced, if part or all of the taxation falls on business or household savings. In fact, this issue is of great significance.

Taxation

During the 1940s and 1950s taxes on corporate and household savings accounted for almost one-quarter of Federal revenue. In the 1960s this fell to around 15 per cent, and by the 1980s this fell to between 5 per cent and 10 per cent (*Economic Report of the President*, 1992, Table B-78).

In the 1940s, 1950s and 1960s the government budget thus provided a greater stimulus, even without running a deficit. Federal deficits grew substantially in the 1980s, but this was partially offset by state and local surpluses. In 1989, for example, the Federal deficit was 15.5 per cent of Federal revenue, but the total government deficit was only 6.7 per cent of total government revenue. Of this 7.9 per cent was raised by taxes on savings. Thus a balanced budget in the late 1960s, when 15–16 per cent of revenue came from corporate taxes (with state and local surpluses almost the same), would have provided as much stimulus. Changes in taxation have progressively reduced the impact of deficit spending because of the smaller proportion of revenue raised by taxation falling on savings and other withdrawals.

Government expenditure

We have seen that all the other major components of aggregate demand grew more slowly, and fluctuated more sharply, in the second half of the post-war era. We now ask whether the government spending tried to counteract these developments.

Figure 10.4 shows that governments did nothing of the sort. Federal spending has not contributed at all to growth and, indeed, has acted as a drag on growth. State and local government expenditures grew more steadily than Federal government expenditures. But even state and local spending slowed down from 1970 to about 1983. Apart from the Korean War and the 1960–8 period, total government spending has grown more slowly than output.

Breaking down Federal spending, Figure 10.5 shows that the flat level in real terms is made up of more or less offsetting growth patterns for the whole economy.

Far from providing an offset to the decline in the growth of private markets, government spending has been shrinking as a percentage of GDP, while staying relatively flat in real terms. Yet for years there has been an outcry against excessive government spending, and a widespread belief that we do not have the money to increase government spending. Much of the outcry over government spending has been generated by the rapid growth of transfer

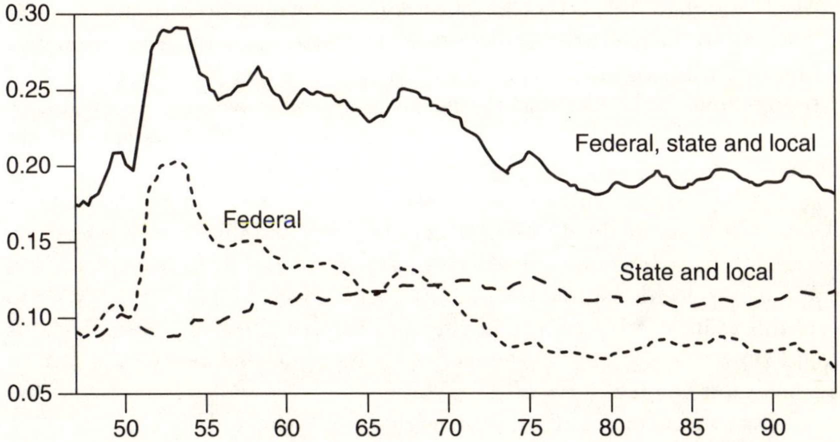

Figure 10.4 Government spending: Federal, state and local (as a percentage of GDP)
Source: Citibase Data Bank 1994

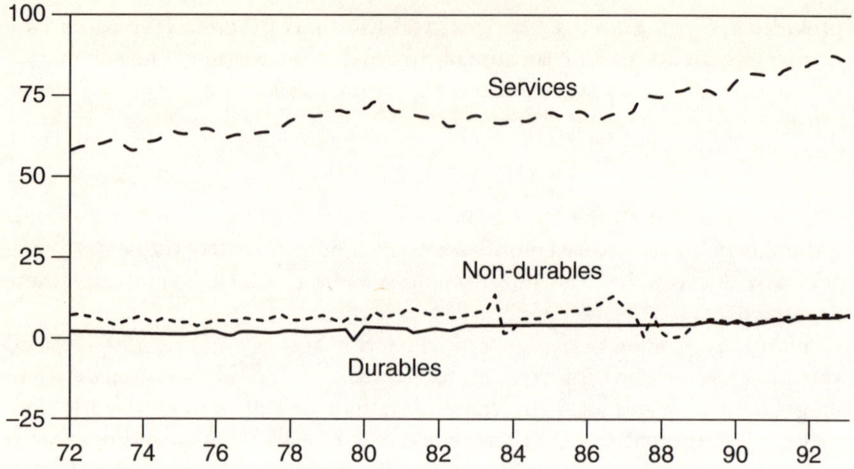

Figure 10.5 Federal government non-defence purchase (in billions of 1987$)
Source: Citibase Data Bank 1994

payments and the rising cost of the Federal debt. Both of these have risen at an exceptional rate, and concern over both is understandable. But overall government demand for goods and services has failed to grow in real terms and has actually declined in relation to GDP. This has created a very significant drag on the economy, rather than the stimulus that was needed.

NEW RELATIONSHIPS IN THE MARKET

Several important insights can be taken from this analysis of spending patterns. Most obviously, resources are available for faster growth. Poor economic performance during the second half of the post-war era is due not to lack of resources, but to the fact that the labour and productive capacity already in place have not been put to use, largely as a result of inappropriate government policy.

Second, poor performance has become cumulative or self-reinforcing. As demand grows more slowly, becomes more volatile and shifts towards services, investment also slows down, becomes more volatile and shifts from plants and equipment towards commercial activities and offices. It is not implausible to read this as interacting cause and effect. Multiplier theory suggests that this could slow down aggregate demand even more. Therefore, the interaction would exacerbate the initial effect.

The same kind of cumulative interaction might come about in other ways. Consider the impact of a slower growth in demand on productivity. With weaker demand, and a shift in the composition of investment, productivity growth can be expected to slow down. But this means that real wages will now grow more slowly, and wage disparities are likely to widen. This will create consumer uncertainty, and lead to slower growth in household spending; that is, it will exacerbate the trends in consumption. But this will react back on investment, through adjustments in the capital stock, reducing the growth of capacity, and further reducing productivity growth in a deepening spiral. In short, an unstable cumulative interaction could develop between demand and productivity growth.

This may help to explain changes in the unemployment–inflation tradeoff. During the golden age unemployment and inflation moved inversely; now they appear to move together. If changes in the pattern of demand growth brought a slow-down in productivity growth, the effect could well have been to raise unit labour costs. This could happen if productivity growth became more uneven, while wage settlements were obliged to maintain traditional relativities. Sectors in which productivity was rising would make settlements based on the productivity gains, but other sectors would insist on maintaining their customary relationship. This would lead to pressure for price increases, and undermine US competitiveness, leading to rising imports and a weaker exchange rate. Thus a slow-down in growth, accompanied by a rise in volatility and a shift away from manufacturing, could have led to inflationary pressures through its effects on productivity and unit labour costs.

Other factors also led inflation and unemployment to move together. Inflation has many causes. The oil shock increased a basic price, one that entered directly or indirectly into the cost of almost everything. This set off a cost-inflation spiral. At the same time the oil shock caused a deterioration of the balance of trade, which reduced aggregate demand and therefore tended to raise unemployment. Attempts to control inflation through tight monetary policy will raise interest rates and make them more volatile. When the restrictions are severe enough unemployment increases; but the additional uncertainty over credit and the higher charges for interest add to the costs of business. These costs tend to get passed on to consumers in higher prices, at least in those sectors where businesses have a degree of control over prices. Thus monetarist policies can lead to price increases and rising unemployment.

The slow-down in the growth of markets, especially in the second half of the era, was quite widespread. It shows up in all components of aggregate demand, as does the increase in volatility and the shift away from manufactured products towards services. It is not likely that this is the only consequence of policy; rather it is part of the pattern of development and capital accumulation. The emergence of new technologies increases uncertainty among firms over whether and when to invest in a new process or product, and whether and when to abandon old ones. New forms of communication have permitted long-distance control over production processes, making it possible to locate plants in distant and low-wage regions, while at the same time making it easier to shift capital funds about. One result has been the emergence of worldwide competition together with worldwide sourcing. This has led, in turn, to growth in world trade.

However, a rise in world trade can have perverse effects. Nations are not equally competitive. A rise in trade benefits nations unequally, leading to balance of payments deficits for some and surpluses for others. Deficit nations tend to contract while surplus nations tend to expand, and this is supposed to lead to adjustment. But surplus countries cannot expand above full employment. Nor will they be willing to permit their exchange rate to rise without limit. Deficit nations, likewise, will not be willing to permit a free fall in their currency. Moreover, if imports are inelastic, devaluation triggers inflation. Hence contraction in the deficit countries has become the chief means of adjustment. Far from providing a stimulus, more trade can mean more stagnation.

Rather than offsetting these changes, policy measures employed in the 1970s and 1980s made things worse. Instead of enlarging government purchases (especially of goods), supporting investment at home to diminish its volatility, spending on infrastructure to promote productivity growth and taking action to improve the balance of payments, the reverse was done. Successive administrations cut back on government, deregulated, encouraged capital flight and opened markets, thereby allowing the US foreign balance to deteriorate. This is not to deny that a case could be made for these policies, or some of them at least, on long-term grounds. But such gains, if any, must be balanced against the costs of the stagnation that they bring.

POLICY IMPLICATIONS

The preceding analysis suggests that policy should be devoted to offsetting the pattern of growth slow-down and volatility increase. The problem is not that government is growing too fast, as is commonly believed, but that it has been growing too slowly. Government spending underwent the same changes that we found in private spending – it stagnated, became more volatile and shifted from manufacturing toward services. In particular, too little spending has been devoted to public investment in infrastructure, education, health, transportation, research and development, and protection of the environment. These are areas where government spending would not only help to increase demand, but also help to promote productivity growth.

Why did government policy fail? This is a complex matter. One reason is that the Democratic Party came to favour austerity more. Fears of inflation and the need to defend the dollar overcame the commitment to high employment. All advanced countries have faced similar difficulties in the second period. But a few did succeed with expansionist governments. Austria, Japan, Norway and Sweden managed to maintain high employment and low inflation, as did Germany until the austerity-minded Kohl government came to power.

In the USA, however, a political consensus formed in support of austerity. An important factor has been the weakening labour movement. There are many factors underlying this, but the impact of new technology in reducing the importance of blue-collar labour seems critical. As their base in a working class has deteriorated, progressive political forces have retreated. Yet without a strong political push, an expansionist programme cannot overcome business resistance to government intervention.

The new relationships also make it clear that old-fashioned expansion through fiscal and monetary policies will not do the job. Even a wisely managed programme of increasing demand and promoting productivity could get into trouble. Any policy sufficient to offset poor US economic performance would have to provide a strong and persistent stimulus to demand, one that grows faster than GDP. But this could lead to a substantial rise in imports and perhaps set off a run on the dollar. Even with no run, a lower exchange rate, accompanied by a sharp rise in demand, would increase the prices of primary products, triggering inflation. In the present political climate this is not acceptable. Moreover, if price inflation outruns wage increases, real wages will fall, reducing consumption; this may have a negative effect on investment. Expansion is no longer a simple matter.

However, if a US expansion were accompanied by expansionary policies by our major trading partners, US exports would rise. Imports might rise still faster, but the pressure against the dollar would be much less, and there would be less chance of inflation. This would have to be a systematic and coordinated expansion, jointly managed by all major advanced countries, with arrangements for financing any trade deficits caused by the expansion. Such an approach requires a degree of international cooperation that is not imaginable at present. Only limited institutional arrangements for international cooperation currently exist, while the political climate favours austerity.

Helpful though it would be, coordinated international expansion is not enough. Also needed is long-term management of the transition to a new technological framework. Keynesian policies were essentially short term. Long-term development requires managers trained in policy issues and equipped with the necessary powers. They must be able to impose price controls if inflation threatens to get out of hand, or to halt trading if speculation threatens a run on the dollar. But even such short-term measures will be of little use unless they are exercised in support of a long-term programme. In the long run, preventing inflation will require a domestic incomes policy – either a TIP (tax-based incomes policy) or a 'social contract'. Income supports will have to be provided to those not employable in competitive labour markets. To maintain a strong dollar, there must be a reasonable balance on foreign accounts, which requires investment and technology policies to encourage a strong competitive position. This means that investment will have to be encouraged and subsidized. There will also have to be investment policies to encourage the right amount and type of capital expansion, and to control its volatility. Labour policies will need to be developed to spur productivity growth, while central banks cooperate to prevent speculative runs on any currency.

Policy failures over the last twenty-plus years teach us that long-term policy must encourage productivity growth and the development of competitive positions in new technologies. The theory of transformational growth tells us that no intervention is not a correct policy response. The free market, working through flexible prices, flourished in the last century and gradually gave way to the multiplier–accelerator system of mass production. This system may now be yielding to new patterns of adjustment. Traces of flex-price markets can still be found in the advanced countries, and are widespread in the craft-based sectors of the developing world. Otherwise, free markets, where deficits crowd out productive investment and savings govern growth, exist only in the imagination of conservative economists. To fall back on non-intervention is to accept long-term stagnation. It is also to endanger our competitive position. The new technologies are so expensive and so risky, that without government participation, licensing and regulation, companies will not be able to undertake such investment.[8]

NOTES

1 Modern neoclassical theory is presented as an abstract theory of rational choice under constraints rather than a practical theory of market adjustments.

2 The interwar years provide a mixed picture of governments seeking, with varying degrees of success, a new role in relation to the economy.

3 The price mechanism worked so long as fluctuations were small. But the financial system was unstable, resulting in periodic crises with widespread bankruptcies. *Overall*, the system showed considerable volatility but within this the markets for goods tended to act as a stabilizer (see Nell and Phillips 1995; Nell forthcoming).

4 The Korean and Vietnam wars may, in part, account for these differences. Yet it is not so obvious that wars could explain the contrast. Vietnam contributed little during the booming years of 1960–65 and lasted through most of Nixon's period. Also, Reagan boosted defence spending, and Bush had the Gulf War. Furthermore, the Kennedy–Johnson period had the lowest inflation rate of the Democrats and the second lowest overall, not something the war could help.

5 The growth of services does less than might appear to offset the increasing sluggishness in non-durables and the growing volatility of durables. The largest component in the category of consumer services is the imputed value of services from owner-occupied housing. These imputed services are not on the market, so the rise of this category does not represent increased spending. When this item is removed the growth of consumer demand after 1970 becomes even weaker (Nell 1988).

6 Recent studies (Aschauer 1989, 1990; Munnell 1990) claim that public infrastructural spending will promote private productivity growth, and conversely, that the decline in public investment in infrastructure helps to account for the sluggish growth of productivity beginning in the 1970s. Other studies have come to similar conclusions. A comprehensive survey is presented by Uimonen (1993), with additional analysis and tests for cointegration and structural stability.

7 Austria, Norway, Sweden and Switzerland managed to maintain low unemployment and low inflation throughout the entire second period, while still managing respectable growth rates.

8 An earlier version of this chapter was presented at the New School for Social Research, in honor of the author's appointment to the Malcom B. Smith Chair of Economics. The author thanks Stephanie Clark for an exceptional job of data preparation and also for assistance in editing.

REFERENCES

Aschauer, D. (1989) 'Is Public Expenditure Productive?', *Journal of Monetary Economics* 23: 177–200.

—— (1990) *Public Investment and Private Sector Growth*, Washington, D.C.: Economic Policy Institute.

Best, M. (1992) *The New Competition*, Cambridge, Mass.: Harvard University Press.

Munnell, A. (1990) 'Why Has Productivity Growth Declined? Productivity and Public Investment', *New England Economic Review* January/February: 3–22.

Nell, E. J. (1988) *Prosperity and Public Spending*, London and Boston: Unwin Hyman.

—— (forthcoming) *Keynes After Sraffa: The General Theory of Transformational Growth*.

Nell, E. J. and Phillips, T. F. (1995) 'Transformational Growth and the Business Cycle', *Eastern Economic Journal* 21: 125–46.

OECD (1993) *Economic Survey: United States*, Paris: OECD.

Peterson, P. (1994) *Facing Up: How To Rescue the Economy From Crushing Debt and Restore the American Dream*, New York: Simon & Schuster.

Uimonen, P. (1993) 'Public Debt, Public Investment, and Productivity Growth', unpublished PhD dissertation, New School for Social Research.

11

A KEYNESIAN FRAMEWORK FOR STUDYING INSTITUTIONAL CHANGE AND EVOLUTIONARY PROCESSES

John Cornwall and Wendy Cornwall

This chapter deals with institutional and evolutionary change at the macroeconomic level. As the title suggests, our analysis focuses on institutional change that is related to economic causes rather than to unexplained exogenous factors. In addition, the chapter deals with the impact of such institutional changes on macroeconomic performance. This joint interaction of economic performance and institutions provides a framework for studying the evolutionary processes that transform economies.

As in traditional Keynesian analysis, the level and growth rate of aggregate demand are singled out as the driving forces behind movements of aggregate economic activity; but equally important, these forces influence the shape, speed and direction of institutional change and evolutionary processes. While Keynesian forces also affect tastes and technologies, here we confine our enquiry to their effects on institutions.

Institutions – i.e. norms, rules, laws and customs – bring orderliness to social and economic life by governing behaviour. They thus act simultaneously as cognitive devices, providing information about expected behaviour, and as constraints on that behaviour. Our interest lies in the relationship between economic performance and institutional change. It is undoubtedly true that exogenous events, for example military conquest, may bring about institutional change (see Olson 1982). However, the focus of this chapter is endogenously generated institutional change, specifically change brought about as part of the normal functioning of the capitalist economy.

The next section offers a brief description and criticism of the mainstream neoclassical framework for modelling macroeconomic dynamic processes. It also gives some details about our method of modelling economic development, and discusses the differences and similarities between our approach and those adopted by others for dealing with similar issues.

Subsequent sections take up the main task, which is to illustrate the explanatory power of our approach. To this end, the paper explains macroeconomic developments in eighteen developed capitalist economies – roughly the OECD economies – from the 1930s until the present.[1] Although there were variations in the economic performances of the OECD economies – some experienced higher unemployment than others – their development paths were similar in many respects. These include trends in inflation and unemployment rates, unionization, the distribution of economic and political power and sectoral patterns of output and employment. This is the result of such influences as similar macroeconomic policies, increasing economic interdependence through trade and capital market integration, and similar tastes and technologies. These common features allow us to compare the economic records of these economies and 'test' the generality of our explanation of evolutionary developments.

APPROACHES TO MACROECONOMICS

The mainstream neoclassical paradigm models dynamic macroeconomic processes within an equilibrium framework. In neoclassical growth theory, the long-run equilibrium path of the economy is determined entirely by a few exogenous variables (tastes, technologies and endowments) which act as structural constraints on the interaction of the endogenous variables. In 'well-behaved' models, temporary disturbances cause only temporary deviations from the equilibrium path; the system always returns to its original equilibrium path in the absence of permanent change in the exogenous variables. Clearly, the long-run growth path of the economy is independent of the history of its performance – the system is ahysteretic, or path or history independent. Of particular significance, aggregate demand plays no role in determining this equilibrium; it merely adjusts passively to aggregate supply forces.

Evolutionary economics

The evolutionary approach that we use contrasts sharply with the mainstream approach. Evolutionary economics regards neoclassical equilibrium analysis as inappropriate for studying dynamic processes. The neoclassical model, with its assumptions of full employment and balanced growth, cannot explain economic change over time. We also reject the view that the behaviour of an economy is usefully modelled as being independent of prevailing institutions and their transformation over time. Finally, the assumption that the long-run performance of the economy is unaffected by influences on the demand side, and therefore by its history, is unacceptable.

Evolutionary economists point out that to model dynamic processes, neoclassical economists must arbitrarily break up the 'historical flow of events'. Only then can they distinguish between the short-run impact of endogenous forces when the system is out of equilibrium and the determination of long-run movements of the system that depend only upon exogenous forces. In contrast, the key idea underlying the evolutionary approach is that macroeconomic development must be modelled as the transformation of a system over time, resulting from endogenously generated change (Witt 1991).

From our evolutionary perspective the long-run economic performance of an economy often induces significant changes, not only in the alleged exogenous variables of neoclassical analysis, but also in institutions, the chief concern of this chapter. Furthermore, because current performance affects the institutional framework, it also affects future performance. In other words, this framework interprets movements of macroeconomic variables over the long run as responses to endogenous changes in the past, not exclusively as responses to exogenous forces. As a result, the long-run position of the system depends upon the historical path that it has actually experienced; the system is hysteretic. Moreover, within an evolutionary framework, shocks do not simply generate temporary deviations from some exogenously determined equilibrium path; they may divert the system to a radically different path of development.

The political economy tradition

Clearly history matters, but it is not only historians who have stressed the central place of change in the development of capitalism. Such a concern has a long pedigree within our own discipline. For many early economists, change was capitalism's overwhelming characteristic, making capitalist development incomprehensible except in its historical context. As Heilbroner (1985: 143) notes, all the great political economists describe 'dramas of social as well as material evolution' brought about by capitalism. A common theme in these works is that periods of economic malfunction are inherent in capitalist development. This is fundamentally different from neoclassical analysis, which attributes malfunction to imperfections or to exogenous shocks. Arguably the most influential among these early writers was Marx, who envisaged a process driven by the central need of capitalism to amass capital. Marx recognized within capitalism the inseparability of economic from institutional change, influenced by endogenously generated periods of serious malfunction.

These insights have inspired other theories of long-run economic development stressing recurrent malfunction. Most envisage an evolving capitalist system dominated and transformed by radical changes in technologies over the long run. We distinguish two strands here – theories that rely exclusively upon economic mechanisms, and those that include institutional change as an integral part of the process.

The long cycle school

The first group includes various versions of long cycle theory. While the very existence of long cycles is controversial, the methodology used by its proponents is of interest. Their objective is to explain regular long-run swings in economic activity. The driving force of these swings is the pattern of investment initiated by technological change, which is treated as an exogenous variable. This work stems from the ideas of Kondratiev (1935), who originally proposed cycles of some fifty or sixty years, generated by investment in long-lived capital, primarily infrastructure. Van Gelderen (1913) also proposed cycles of similar periodicity, driven by new technologies such as the introduction of electricity or by the opening up of new territories. Schumpeter (1939) developed these ideas, and attributed long fluctuations to the clustering of innovations based on the introduction of one or more new technologies.

In these theories, the eventual overexpansion of capacity and market saturation reduced profitability, causing the downturn. There is no convincing explanation of, and no agreement about, how the upturn originates. Demand is assigned at most a passive role, and institutions none at all.[2] This 'supply-side' character, and implied inevitability, of cycles denies any role to aggregate demand.

The regulation school

These omissions are to some extent remedied in the proposals of the regulation school (Aglietta 1982; Boyer 1987; Lipietz 1986). Regulationists combine Marxian with Kaleckian (or Keynesian) macroeconomics to form the basis for an institutionalist analysis of capitalist transformation in this century. As a result, demand is important, particularly as it affects the balance between consumption and investment spending. A central theme, reminiscent of Veblen (1899, 1919) and American institutionalists (Commons 1961; Ayres 1962), is that the 'wrong' political and social institutions impede economic progress and that periods of severe malfunction are caused by a mismatch between institutions and the economy. Like the long cycle theorists (including Schumpeter), regulationists emphasize technological change; but true to their Marxian roots, their main concern is with how it alters the way that production and investment are carried out. They view capitalism as a series of episodes, each with a different technological base, which determines the internal organization of firms, including work itself. To realize the potential of this technical base, there must be a compatible institutional superstructure. If the technology changes, a new institutional superstructure is needed. Whenever there is a mismatch between the technology and the institutional superstructure economic crisis follows, and persists until appropriate institutions are established. For example, assembly-line mass production needs institutions that enable mass consumption. These were not developed in the early part of this century, thus leading to the Great Depression. By the end of the Second World War they were established, allowing for rapid growth and increased prosperity.

While the regulationists stress the importance of institutions, and trace out an endogenous process of decay within each episode, they do not explain how the new institutional superstructure arises; hence there is no clear link between different episodes, and no endogenous theory of institutional change.

A Keynesian evolutionary process

Unlike neoclassical growth theory, the theories just discussed envisage the dynamics of capitalism as something other than merely economic growth; they are concerned with radical structural change or economic development. These structural changes are primarily unexplained changes in technology. Even for the regulation school, developments in technology are the initiating and dominant forces leading to institutional change and altered economic performance. This contrasts with the evolutionary approach, where the economic performance of an economy is itself a factor inducing institutional change. And because institutions affect economic performance, the way is open to formulate an evolutionary (i.e. endogenous) explanation of economic development.[3]

Thus in the short run, a given institutional framework will constrain economic performance, but over a longer period performance will lead to changes in institutions which, because of their very nature as constraints, will act to alter future economic performance. This causal chain can in principle repeat itself, generating an endogenous theory of change in which institutional change plays a central role. The remainder of the chapter uses this institutional–evolutionary framework to explain macroeconomic developments in the post-Second World War period.[4]

Fluctuations in aggregate demand, aggregate output and unemployment are singled out as direct sources of institutional change. Also emphasized are their indirect effects on institutions via their impact on per capita incomes and productivity. For example, expected and actual profits, and the strength and type of business investment outlays, will vary with the general level of economic activity. This will affect the rate of growth of productivity and per capita incomes and significantly influence the institutional framework.

THE IMPACT OF THE 1930S AND THE SECOND WORLD WAR ON INSTITUTIONS

Following the Great Depression, preparations for war rapidly reduced unemployment everywhere to historically low levels. One important result of this was a loss of the belief that high unemployment was simply an act of God. Increasingly the view developed that appropriately used aggregate demand policies could reduce unemployment. Moreover, the personal hardships experienced during the 1930s and the war years generated a widespread belief that the benefits of capitalism should be more equally shared. Prominent among these benefits was a guaranteed job for any who wanted one. Once the reconversion from war was complete, the commitment to full employment reinforced the growing power of organized labour. It also spurred the development of political parties that included full employment policies as an essential part of their political programme. In short, the prolonged high unemployment of the 1930s and its reduction during the conduct of a war helped to initiate institutional changes that were self-reinforcing and persisted for almost a quarter of a century. These centred on new attitudes, laws and policies, accepted both by the public and their political and economic leaders, for dealing with problems of unemployment, deprivation and inequality.

ECONOMIC PERFORMANCE IN THE GOLDEN AGE

These changes marked a turning point in economic policy. Most OECD governments made quite clear their intention to implement aggregate demand policies should private sector demand fail to provide full employment. This guarantee of economic stability encouraged private sector investment, reducing or even eliminating the need to actually use the policies. In addition, governments promoted export growth, further increasing aggregate demand.[5] The resulting strong and persistent booms in investment and exports, with occasional use of aggregate demand management, reduced unemployment rates throughout the OECD to unprecedented low peacetime levels. They remained there for over two decades. For the entire 1960–73 period, the average rate of unemployment in the eighteen OECD economies was 2.3 per cent. If the high unemployment economies (Canada, Ireland, Italy, the United Kingdom and the USA) are excluded from the sample, the remaining thirteen economies experienced an average unemployment rate of 1.5 per cent (Cornwall 1994: table II.1).

During this period of high and growing levels of aggregate demand, rates of growth of labour productivity and per capita incomes achieved historical highs everywhere except in the USA. Rapid growth of incomes accelerated the transformation of all these economies. Agriculture declined in importance, as both the industrial and service sectors grew. Eventually the service sector rose to dominance in terms of employment, if not output. Associated with these movements were shifts in the organization of production and in the institutions of the industrial relations systems. The prolonged period of rising incomes also provided a growing financial base for the extension of the welfare state, further reinforcing the rising economic and political power of labour brought by full employment, affluence and greater unionization.

The inflation record of the period requires special consideration since it is reasonable to assume that authorities would have restricted aggregate demand if tight labour markets had generated politically unacceptable rates of inflation. During the golden age, inflation rates remained at acceptable levels everywhere, and did not depend on whether countries experienced high or low unemployment. To understand this, it is first necessary to note that during the period there was no positive correlation between rates of inflation, on the one hand, and union strength and political party control on the other. This, in turn, requires a distinction between the power that events conferred on labour during the full employment conditions of the period and labour's use of this power to achieve its goals. Powerful unions and pro-labour governments do provide labour with the muscle needed to obtain large money wage increases and the political strength to gain government support for full employment policies. Serious inflation problems can result if labour exerts this increased economic and political strength to the full. In most OECD economies, the adoption of social bargains averted this danger during the golden age.

Among the OECD economies two types of labour market strategies were adopted to protect and increase real wages. They will be referred to as a social bargain strategy and a market power strategy. The latter was adopted in the five high unemployment economies. Here, labour attempted to achieve a fair real wage by maximizing the rate of money wage increase possible under prevailing labour market conditions. Since their market power increased when unemployment fell, this labour strategy produced the familiar negative relationship between rates of unemployment and inflation, the Phillips curve. Moreover, even at unemployment rates that included large numbers of involuntarily unemployed workers, inflation rose to politically unacceptable rates. Such economies faced what will be referred to as an inflationary bias. Policy-induced high unemployment was the only means available for containing inflation and, as a result, employment goals were relaxed in these economies even before 1974.

Most of the OECD economies, however, adopted a social bargain strategy. In cooperation with capital and government, labour accepted the need for and desirability of money wage restraint in the interest of achieving national goals such as wage and price stability and international competitiveness. In return labour was promised full employment and, depending upon the country, other rewards such as generous welfare benefits, rising real wages, improved industrial relations, and a role in developing, implementing and monitoring the bargain. For those countries that concluded a social bargain, it proved to be a successful instrument for restraining inflation even at full employment. As a result, high unemployment was not necessary for restraining inflation in most of the OECD economies, allowing them to attain both low unemployment and low inflation. All things considered, during this period most economies were free to pursue a relatively independent aggregate demand policy because they were relieved of unacceptable inflation problems at full employment.[6]

The determinants of labour market strategy

The strategy that a particular country adopted (and whether it experienced acceptable rates of inflation at low rates of unemployment) depended largely on the historical development of its economic and political institutions. Consider some of the institutional features of those countries that implemented a successful social bargain. First, in all these economies the notion that somehow 'market forces' or 'invisible hands' on their own would generate a favourable macroeconomic performance was never a widely accepted doctrine. Rather, the general belief was that a well-functioning economy, one that could simultaneously achieve low inflation and unemployment, required a deliberate, cooperative effort at moulding institutions to provide these results.

Second, by the post-war period these social bargain economies had evolved cooperative industrial relations systems. The essential feature of such an industrial relations framework is the conscious effort by both labour and management to find cooperative solutions to potentially harmful industrial relations problems. Unresolved, these could result in serious adverse macroeconomic outcomes, especially high inflation. Third, in these economies there existed a tradition of government leadership to reconcile potentially conflicting interests that might lead to inflation rates in excess of government targets. Fourth, early in the post-war period the low unemployment economies altered their tax structures in order to remove large inequalities in the post-tax, post-transfer distribution of income.

In contrast, a belief in invisible hands, the presence of an adversarial industrial relations system, a denial that government had a conciliatory role to play in industrial relations, and a relatively unequal distribution of incomes were ingrained institutional elements in those economies where labour adopted a market power strategy.[7]

First summary

The causal chain connecting the historical events considered so far can be summarized as follows. Macroeconomic developments from the 1930s until the end of the golden age can be characterized largely as an evolutionary process with negative feedback. Put simply, the early period of poor economic performance contributed to superior performance later. The low unemployment (and high growth) of the golden age was a phase in an endogenous evolutionary development dating back to the economic breakdown of the 1930s. Linking the 1930s and the Second World War with the golden age period were the institutional changes induced by the poor economic conditions in the earlier part of the period. These changes paved the way for post-war prosperity by altering the institutional constraints that in the past had prevented the acceptance of full employment conditions. Mass unemployment was now seen as avoidable, employment for all was considered an economic right and political parties were both willing and able to implement the necessary programmes.

THE END OF THE GOLDEN AGE

In retrospect, by the late 1960s the accelerating inflation in many countries signalled the end of the golden age. By the early 1970s inflation rates reached unacceptable levels, inducing governments to respond with restrictive aggregate demand and high unemployment policies. Numerous causes of the Great Inflation of the late 1960s and early 1970s have been cited and their alleged relative importance is still a matter of great controversy. Without too much simplification it is useful to divide opinion into two general camps, which will be referred to as the human error explanation and the institutional change explanation. Underlying these different explanations of the Great Inflation lies an even more fundamental difference in beliefs about the ability of capitalism to regulate itself.

The human error explanation starts from the premise that in the absence of shocks, the private sector is inherently stable with strong full employment tendencies. Based on the quantity theory of money, this view asserts that, provided the monetary authority follows a money supply growth rule, the economy will experience full employment growth, with a constant rate of inflation. Deviations from this growth path will be due to shocks, especially those resulting from intervention by the monetary and fiscal authorities. Based on these premises, it follows that any acceleration or deceleration of inflation rates will be due to acceleration or deceleration in the rate of growth of the money supply as inflation is always and everywhere a monetary phenomenon.

One of the most influential examples of this theme is the OECD-sponsored McCracken Report. While recognizing that several factors were involved in the acceleration of inflation during the late 1960s and early 1970s, the report concludes that 'the most important feature was an unusual bunching of unfortunate events unlikely to be repeated on the same scale, the impact of which was compounded by some avoidable errors in economic policy' (OECD 1977: 103). While institutional changes in the form of rising aspirations and expectations by the public, especially by labour, played a role in the acceleration of inflation rates, the report treats these changes as reversible. To return to a state of low rates of inflation *and* unemployment, they advise a policy of slow recovery in demand. This is to give time enough for inflationary aspirations and expectations to be permanently reversed.

In contrast, the institutional change explanation of inflation starts from the basic premise that the private sector of a capitalist system is inherently unstable, subject to periodic episodes of poor macroeconomic performance, one of which is a high rate of inflation. The expression that inflation is a monetary symptom of distributive conflict helps to convey the essence of this school's explanation of inflation. And while perhaps agreeing with the human error school (and the monetarists) that inflation is always and everywhere a monetary phenomenon, the institutional change school finds such a remark little more than a cliché.

Thus they might agree that restrictive monetary polices can halt inflation, but only at great unemployment cost. After all, there is a limit to the velocity of circulation of money. But to determine the underlying causes of inflation and its cure, it is necessary to proceed differently. The first step is to ascertain the nature and amount of unemployment at the level of aggregate demand consistent with a reasonably stable rate of inflation.[8] If this level of aggregate demand eliminates most of what would be considered involuntary unemployment, we can infer that periods of accelerating inflation (in the absence of shocks) are monetary phenomena, i.e. too rapid increases in the rate of growth of the money supply and aggregate demand. Here the policy implications for reducing inflation are straightforward.

On the other hand, if the level of aggregate demand consistent with non-accelerating inflation is associated with a high unemployment rate that includes a large proportion of involuntary unemployment, the institutional change view would conclude that it is misleading to call inflation a monetary phenomenon. Rather it is rooted in conflict over the distribution of income and its cure requires a resolution of this conflict through policy-induced institutional change. To use the earlier terminology, in this case the economy is subject to an inflationary bias.

The institutional change explanation of the Great Inflation centres on adverse changes in the institutions surrounding the labour market that intensified the conflict and thereby increased the inflationary bias. Under these circumstances, inflation rates were higher at every rate of unemployment, including the full employment rate. Any rate of inflation could now be contained only at a higher rate of involuntary unemployment.

OPEC and other shocks: a digression

Our explanation of the Great Inflation as the outcome of an endogenous process of interaction between economic performance and institutional change stands in sharp contrast to the reliance on exogenous shocks found throughout the literature dealing with the end of the golden age. Referred to in the McCracken Report (OECD 1977) as an 'unusual bunching of unfortunate events', these shocks include the OPEC price hikes, as well as the rapid run-up of other commodity prices in the early 1970s. One can argue that this bunching was not really unusual, but the straightforward result of rapid demand growth. As long as the OECD accounts for the lion's share of world output, and experiences a prolonged growth boom, there will be demand pressure causing upward movement in raw materials prices. In short, such price movements could have been predicted, given some supply information. And because of the size of the OECD, they might well be regarded as endogenous.

What of the OPEC price rise in 1973–4? For the entire 1960s and the early 1970s the American oil companies controlled the price of oil, keeping it at $2.50 per barrel. Thus, the price of oil declined relative to other raw materials throughout this period. It was declining in real terms as well throughout the period, and more rapidly as inflation accelerated in the late 1960s.[9] It was the golden age boom, with its strong demand for oil, that eventually gave OPEC the power to impose the price hikes.

The *cause* of the price shocks is at root the same prolonged growth boom that caused the institutional changes leading to the end of the golden age. There can be very little question that these shocks had an effect. The question is, did they simply expose the developing weakness of the institutional framework, amplifying and accelerating a process already under way? Or did they cause the process, with only the superficial institutional effects implied in the McCracken Report? We argue for the former. The shocks during the period temporarily amplified the rise in inflation rates and kept high rates of inflation in the system longer; but even in their absence inflation had become a more serious and long-run problem. The shocks thus reinforced an established endogenous process.

The increasing inflationary bias

The position adopted here is that institutional change was the key factor in the Great Inflation. It had lasting effects on these economies, increasing the inflationary bias and transforming potential inflationary forces into actual ones. While admitting that this is highly speculative, although no more so than competing hypotheses, we maintain that both empirical and theoretical considerations support our view.

The empirical support is based on the unemployment and inflation records of the OECD economies over the post-Second World War period. Beginning in 1979–80, highly restrictive aggregate demand policies were applied throughout the OECD to combat the accelerating inflation. Concentrating on the seven largest OECD economies, restrictive aggregate demand policies successfully reduced inflation by the mid-1980s to rates experienced in the 1950s, but at a great cost in unemployment. Over the 1980–6 period, unemployment rates averaged 7.3 per cent in the G7 countries. More significantly, only in 1987 did unemployment fall noticeably below this average (to 6.7 per cent); although this was high by post-war standards, inflation rates accelerated. Furthermore, inflation rates continued to rise (until the recession beginning in 1990) although unemployment fell by a little over 1 percentage point.

The worsening inflation problem can be rephrased in terms of the worsening inflationary bias. Inflation rates in the G7 averaged 2.9 per cent in the 1960–8 period, the same as the 1987 rate. However, the average unemployment rate in the earlier period was only 2.8 per cent compared to 6.7 per cent in 1987. A similar worsening of the inflationary bias occurred in most of the other OECD economies during this period (Cornwall 1994: table 9.1)

This suggests that the OECD economies have developed an increased inflationary bias, despite efforts from the mid-1970s to rid capitalism permanently of the inflation problem.[10] Rates of inflation that in the early post-war period were associated with relatively low rates of involuntary unemployment are now associated with much higher involuntary unemployment rates. A corollary of this worsening inflation–unemployment tradeoff is that full employment now leads to higher, and to politically less acceptable, rates of inflation.

Theoretical support for the institutional change explanation of the Great Inflation comes in both right-wing and left-wing versions. Both versions reflect the view that the prolonged period of full employment following the Second World War undermined the golden age (Brittan 1975; Flanagan, Soskice and Ulman 1983; Phelps Brown 1968; Goldthorpe 1978; Korpi 1991; Perry 1975; Soskice 1978). Each considers inflation to be symptomatic of a conflict between capital and labour over the distribution of national income. A necessary condition for this conflict is a relatively equal distribution of power in industrial relations. No such equality existed in the pre-First World War period. One result of this was that wage settlements were largely the outcome of take-it-or-leave-it offers to labour by a powerful business class. From the end of the Second World War until the mid-1970s, there was a dramatic shift in the distribution of power toward labour for three reasons: full employment, an expanded welfare state and expanded unionization. Prolonged periods of full employment, and the additional safety nets provided by an enlarged welfare state increased the ability of workers to withhold labour by quitting and eventually taking up other jobs. Increased unionization further increased labour's ability to exert its market power by disrupting production through strikes.

During the golden age the power of labour was at a historical high in developed capitalist economies. As explained earlier, this power coexisted with money wage restraint at the time as labour adopted a social bargain strategy in most economies. This strategy implied labour's general acceptance of the fairness of distributional outcomes. Consequently, this reduced attempts to alter the distribution of incomes by means of accelerated money wage demands and increased strike activity. The centre of distributional conflict shifted from the market to the government.

To a large extent the rising inflationary bias in the late 1960s and the 1970s can be traced to the end of social bargains beginning in the second half of the 1960s in the European economies, thus leading to a rapid acceleration in the rate of wage inflation (Soskice 1978; Perry 1975; Flanagan *et al.* 1983). The main factor behind the shift to market power strategies was a perceived unfairness in market-determined distributional outcomes. In explaining this institutional change in the labour market, and indeed the increase in the inflationary bias in economies such as the USA and Canada, it is essential to consider the forces undermining the once widely held belief in the fairness of the system.

The spread of unfairness perceptions

To explain the sources of the wage explosion in the second half of the 1960s, economists usually cite a sequence of temporary disturbances. However, social scientists outside economics saw these events as symptomatic of a developing trend in public attitudes, especially on the part of labour. This involved greater questioning of the fairness of market-determined distributional outcomes.

The argument can be put best in terms used more commonly by sociologists (Goldthorpe 1978). In a modern market economy the distribution of national income requires ethical, as well as political and legal, legitimacy if distributional conflict is to be minimized. This is particularly true when after-tax and after-transfer incomes are distributed unequally. To put it otherwise, economic advantages conferred by the market require status or 'prestige entitlements' if they are to be generally acceptable and devoid of divisive implications. In the early stages of capitalist development, religion, geographical stability, differences in education and inherited privilege provided this legitimation. However, as capitalism developed, rising geographic mobility, the decline of organized religion, the spread of education and the suffrage and the increasing commercialization of life in general undermined this legitimation of economic inequalities, calling into question the fairness of market capitalism.

To some extent the growth of the welfare system temporarily blunted this unease, but the trend was one of freeing the less economically advantaged from the constraints imposed by their own sense of inferiority. Feelings of deference and loyalty in society, in industrial relations and at the factory declined. Two important and related effects were the Great Inflation of the late 1960s and early 1970s, and a more serious inflationary bias facing most OECD economies ever since.

CONCLUSION

Just as the 1930s were important in initiating institutional changes that favourably affected macroeconomic performance in the golden age, successful performance in the latter period eventually induced institutional changes that would also have a negative feedback on performance. Unfortunately in this case the effect was to bring the golden age to an end. Since then the unemployment records of the OECD economies have remained noticeably inferior to those of the golden age. It is true that inflation is of little consequence today, but that is to be expected, given the prolonged period of severely depressed conditions leading up to the present. Almost all developed capitalist economies are now trapped in a condition of mass unemployment with rates of growth of productivity and per capita incomes that are only a fraction of their golden age values.

Restrictive aggregate demand policies to curb the Great Inflation were initiated throughout the OECD in 1973 or 1974. A period of prolonged stagnation following the imposition of the restrictive policies was not anticipated by most government leaders and economists. The McCracken Report was published after the restrictive aggregate demand policies had been in effect long enough to reduce inflation rates below their 1973–4 peaks.

Indeed they had fallen enough to allow the authors of the report to conclude optimistically that the economies would soon be restored to health. As stated in their policy recommendations:

> In the short-run the aim should be to follow a recovery track explicitly to let the memory of unfavourable initial conditions erode and expectations improve. The longer-run framework, however should provide a constant reminder to government, business and labour that high rates of inflation lead inevitably in time to loss of sales and loss of jobs.
>
> (OECD 1977: 181)

Events have not justified the optimism of this statement. After two decades of stagnation, monetary authorities still find it necessary to remind governments, business and labour that restrictive aggregate demand policies will remain in force until they behave themselves. The basic problem, still not well understood, is that the difficulties leading to the Great Inflation were more profound than those recognized by the report's authors or by the economics profession at large. Realization of the full employment goal before the early 1970s was a major factor altering the institutions of the labour market in the OECD economies. The shift to a market power strategy in so many economies signalled the end of social bargains as a policy instrument to contain inflation. The failure to develop instruments that would restrain inflation in a way that would permit a return to full employment has been the main cause of two decades of mass unemployment.

Accordingly, a necessary condition for a return to full employment first involves developing a good institutional–policy fit, in this case developing policies that will induce institutional change. Of central importance, recovery requires policies that lead labour to return to social bargain strategies in their wage bargaining or, as in the case of the two North American economies, to implement such a strategy. Without this, stimulative aggregate demand policies to reduce unemployment cannot be used; they would lead to politically unacceptable rates of inflation. The inability to induce the required institutional changes through policy is sufficient to prevent a return to anything like the golden age of the 1950s and 1960s.

To find solutions to the current economic problems, we must first understand how they arose. This cannot be done within the mainstream equilibrium framework. Malfunction is not a self-reversing interlude caused by exogenous shocks. It is inherent in capitalism, part of the process of capitalist development. Modelling capitalism as an evolutionary process, in which economic performance and institutions interact, provides the means to understand and explain both good and poor performance. In our analysis, superior macroeconomic performance is dependent upon successful policy intervention. The historical episode of malfunction discussed is an example of the inability to develop the policy instruments needed for success. Only by focusing on the evolution of the institutional framework can this need for new instruments be seen, as changing institutions can and do cause a poor institutional–policy fit.[11]

NOTES

1 The small and less developed OECD economies (Greece, Iceland, Luxembourg, Mexico, Portugal, Spain and Turkey) are not considered here.
2 While this is true of Schumpeter's business cycle theory, he (Schumpeter 1942) recognized the importance of institutions elsewhere.
3 Economic performance can also induce changes in technology and tastes, which then affect economic performance. However, as already indicated, the focus of this paper is institutional change.
4 An earlier study by Cornwall (1994: xxi) used the term 'institutional–analytical' to describe this approach; however, 'institutional–evolutionary' better conveys the endogenous causes of change emphasized in this chapter.
5 The Bretton Woods Agreement provided exchange rate stability and tariff reductions stimulated exports. Export demand interacted with investment to maintain high growth rates of aggregate demand and output.
6 For reasons not covered in this chapter, these economies were also relieved of serious balance of payments constraints on their aggregate demand policies.
7 For a fuller treatment see Cornwall (1994: ch.5).
8 The text statement is not meant to convey support for the concepts of the NAIRU or natural rate of unemployment.
9 From the period 1960–8 to 1968–73 inflation tripled in the European OECD countries, from 1.6 per cent to 4.8 per cent. This was a severe problem for the oil-producing states, for not only was the price of oil set in US dollars, but they held large balances of so-called petrodollars.
10 This average increase in the inflationary bias was reflected in movements in unemployment and inflation rates in every OECD economy studied, although the size of the increase varied from country to country.
11 Financial support for this research by the Social Sciences and Humanities Research Council of Canada is gratefully acknowledged.

REFERENCES

Aglietta, M. (1982) *Regulation and Crisis of Capitalism*, New York: Monthly Review Press.

Ayres, C. (1962) *The Theory of Economic Progress*, New York: Schocken Books.

Boyer, R. (1987) 'Regulation', in J. Eatwell, M. Milgate and P. Newman (eds), *The New Palgrave: A Dictionary of Economics*, London: Macmillan.

Brittan, S. (1975) 'The Economic Contradictions of Democracy', *British Journal of Political Science* 5: 130–59.

Commons, J. R. (1961) *Institutional Economics*, Madison: University of Wisconsin Press.

Cornwall, J. (1994) *Economic Breakdown and Recovery*, Armonk, N.Y.: M.E. Sharpe.

Flanagan, R., Soskice, D. and Ulman, L. (1983) *Unionism, Economic Stabilization and Incomes Policies: European Experience*, Washington: Brookings Institution.

Gelderen, J. van (1913) 'Springvloed: Beschouwingen over Industrieele Ontwickeling in Prijsbeweging', *De Niewe Tijd* 18: 253–77, 369–84, 445–64.

Goldthorpe, J. (1978) 'The Current Inflation: Towards a Sociological Account', in F.

Hirsch and J. Goldthorpe (eds), *The Political Economy of Inflation*, Cambridge, Mass.: Harvard University Press.

Heilbroner, R. L. (1985) *The Nature and Logic of Capitalism*, New York: Norton.

Kondratiev, N. D. (1935) 'The Long Waves in Economic Life', *Review of Economic Statistics* 17: 105–15.

Korpi, W. (1991) 'Political and Economic Explanations for Unemployment: A Cross-national and Long-term Analysis', *British Journal of Political Science* 21: 315–48.

Lipietz, A. (1986) 'Behind the Crisis: The Exhaustion of a Regime of Accumulation: A "Regulation School" Perspective on Some French Empirical Works', *Review of Political Economics* 18: 12–32.

OECD (1977) *Towards Full Employment and Price Stability*, Paris: OECD.

Olson, M. (1982) *The Rise and Decline of Nations*, New Haven: Yale University Press.

Perry, G. (1975) 'Determinants of Wage Inflation around the World', *Brookings Papers on Economic Activity* 2: 403–35.

Phelps Brown, E. (1968) *A Century of Pay*, London: Macmillan.

Schumpeter, J. A. (1939) *Business Cycles*, 2 vols, New York: McGraw-Hill.

—— (1942) *Capitalism, Socialism and Democracy*, New York: Harper & Brothers.

Soskice, D. (1978) 'Strike Waves and Wage Explosions, 1968–1970: An Economic Interpretation', in C. Crouch and A. Pizzarno (eds), *The Resurgence of Class Conflict in Western Europe since 1969*, vol. 2, New York: Holmes & Meier.

Veblen, T. (1899) *The Theory of the Leisure Class: An Economic Study of Institutions*, New York: Macmillan.

—— (1919) *The Place of Science in Modern Civilisation and Other Essays*, New York: Huebsch.

Witt, U. (1991) 'Reflections on the Present State of Evolutionary Economic Theory', in G.M. Hodgson and E. Screpanti (eds), *Rethinking Economics: Markets, Technology, and Economic Evolution*, Aldershot: Edward Elgar.

Part V

NEW DIRECTIONS IN POLITICAL ECONOMY

12

BEYOND POLITICAL ECONOMY

Ingrid H. Rima

The term 'political economy' has become outmoded and has largely been dropped from the lexicon of mainstream economists. Its decline dates, in large part, to Alfred Marshall's choice of the title *Principles of Economics* for his 1890 treatise. For Marshall, this choice was intended to ensure the scientific status of the 'engine of analysis', which he created to focus on the problems of value, price and income distribution. His choice also reflected the view, principally associated with John Neville Keynes's *Scope and Method of Political Economy* (1891), that the hard scientific core of economic theory should be insulated from particular ideologies and moral principles. This would make the discipline 'value free'; however, one further consequence was that economics became separate from practical advice on matters of policy.

The works of Marshall and J. N. Keynes also paved the way for the subsequent conceptualization of economics as the science of allocating scarce resources among competing uses (Robbins 1932). The vision of Robbins, in turn, laid the groundwork for the static models of maximization and equilibration employed by contemporary economic positivists who, in their purest articulations, insist that the market-clearing mechanism renders economic policy unnecessary and, perhaps, even pernicious.

The contrary view – that policy formulation is among the chief tasks of the economist, and that the principal role of economic theory is to provide its proper foundation – is a substantive departure from views now held by the mainstream. Although John Maynard Keynes was schooled in the Cambridge tradition, he aligned himself with this contrary view in a pair of lectures given in 1924 and 1926 that were subsequently published as 'The End of *Laissez-Faire*' (Keynes 1971–89:IX). His disassociation from the so-called 'Treasury view' of the efficacy of the gold standard called into question the viability and suitability of nineteenth-century *laissez-faire*, which Keynes (1971–89:IX, 286) viewed as chiefly expressing 'the needs and wishes of the business world of the day'. Keynes's (1936) subsequent articulation of a theory of aggregate effective demand then laid the theoretical foundation for what is now termed the 'Keynesian revolution'. It provided a substantially new model for the functioning of the macroeconomy, and a theoretical foundation for establishing appropriate mechanisms within government to move the economy in the direction of achieving national policy goals.

A parallel intellectual revolution, which was similarly a response to the economic (and political) tumult of the inter-war period, was taking place in Germany during the 1920s and 1930s. While Keynes was railing against the Treasury's commitment to balanced budget, and its support of free trade and the gold standard, Adolph Lowe (1893–1995) was laying the intellectual foundation for what he termed 'political economics'.[1] Lowe held a politically sensitive post in the Weimar republic. His position involved the practical planning and management of the currency reforms that brought the great hyperinflation under control. In 1921 he became Director of Research at the Institute of World Economics at the University of Kiel, where he established a research centre for the study and control of business cycles through regulation and planning. His work on cycles, and the prospect for their control via planning, provided the basis for his development of 'instrumental analysis' as a technique for directing a politically free economy along the path of economic growth.

The ideas of Lowe remain known only to relatively few, despite his long and active professional life at the New School in New York City. Lowe emigrated to New York from England in 1941 after being fired by Hitler from his prestigious academic post at the University of Frankfurt. Yet, like Keynes, his work as a political economist challenges the conventional wisdom that economic outcomes can safely be left to the operation of the market mechanism. 'Political economics', as Lowe explained in *On Economic Knowledge* (1965), undertakes to relate the processes of the economic core to the sociopolitical environment. Its conceptual roots can be traced to Adam Smith's system of equilibrium growth and to Keynes's principle of aggregate demand. From these models of analysis Lowe derives a logic of causality that centres on the macroeconomic goals towards which the system is to be directed.

The object of instrumental analysis, as Lowe (1965:11–12) envisioned it, is to 'search for the economic means suitable for the attainment of any stipulated end'. The technique of instrumentalism takes the macroeconomic outcomes, which the majority of a country's citizens have identified as a desirable starting point, and then seeks to develop a strategy for achieving these desired outcomes.

Despite its commitment to personal freedom, this instrumentalism is certain to require a level and degree of public management that is likely to make it politically unacceptable to an electorate like the USA or Britain, except under emergency economic conditions that are as devastating as the German hyperinflation of the inter-war years or the US depression of the 1930s.

The situation may, however, be different for those economies in eastern and central Europe that are making the transition toward private property and a market system. These countries, and the economists engaged in studying economies undergoing transition, are more likely to view their problems as a unique opportunity for rethinking economics, and for reshaping the method of arriving at economic knowledge and formulating economic policy. The transition to capitalism from socialism is a transformation for which there is no historical precedent, and for which classical political economy may offer more informed guidance than that offered by traditional mainstream economics. If Lowe's instrumental political economics is to find practical application in this century, or in the early decades of the twenty-first century, it is most likely to occur in relation to the problems of these newly developing capitalist economies.

The present chapter seeks to examine this broad terrain. The first section makes the historical case for instrumentalism that was articulated by Smith in his argument for the provision of public goods, and then carried forward by Thomas Malthus, David Ricardo, and James and John Stuart Mill. The enthusiastic participation of these thinkers in the policy debates of the nineteenth century is in marked contrast with the reluctance that Alfred Marshall felt, in the century that followed, to contribute directly to public policy in the interest of social betterment.

The second section of this paper focuses on *The General Theory* and the New Deal, drawing on some recently articulated interpretations about the professionalization of economics in America and Britain. It attempts to interpret these events as a bridge to the development of an instrumentalist approach in economics.

The third section focuses on the challenge presented by events in eastern and central Europe, where countries previously aligned with the former Soviet Union are making the transition to capitalism. The needs of these countries, and their unwillingness to give up entirely the social services on which their populations have come to rely, offer a unique opportunity for rethinking, and so reshaping, the task of economic science and the method for arriving at economic knowledge and policy.

The fourth section of the chapter offers some comments regarding the possibilities for instrumentalism in developed economies undergoing global restructuring. The last section offers some reflections on the future possibilities for an instrumentalist approach taking hold in economics.

PRECURSORS OF INSTRUMENTALISM

The conventional wisdom has it that the *laissez-faire* tradition in economics began with the publication of the *Wealth of Nations* by Adam Smith (1776). According to this view the role of government should be limited to defence against external and internal enemies. Yet this interpretation is a gross oversimplification. Smith identified the goals of political economy as 'first to provide a plentiful revenue or subsistence for the people', and second 'to supply the state or commonwealth with a revenue sufficient for public services' (1776:397). Smith was concerned to develop a bill of particulars to guide the allocation of some inputs and outputs from the private to the public sector in order to correct the failings of mercantilism and the agricultural system, both of which he regarded as 'subversive of the great purpose which [they] mean to promote' (1776:650–1).

Although Smith's system is predicated on the vision of a self-regulating economy in which policy intervention is either unnecessary or harmful, he also believed that the ideal of self-regulation via market processes becomes realizable only subsequent to institutional changes that eliminate mercantilist controls from the system. It is thus clear that, notwithstanding the determinism of the invisible hand, there is an implicit instrumental premise in Smith's system of natural liberty. Smith envisioned a science that would enable the statesman or legislator to propel the society towards a plentiful sustenance for its inhabitants, and also to 'supply the commonwealth with a revenue sufficient for the (requisite) public services' (1776:398).

Smith conceived of an economic order that was in the process of 'becoming', as mercantilist restrictions were driven out or fell into disuse. His focus was on policy measures that would contribute toward realizing 'the natural order' in which the invisible hand would function to move the system towards the macroeconomic objective of 'opulence'. This conception of political economy is thus fully compatible with the development of a science that studies politically related questions such as the distribution of income, and examines instruments of social control that encourage behaviours compatible with socially desirable actions.

In nineteenth-century England there was no national objective that had higher priority than the pursuit of economic growth. Growth is closely associated with the question of the way in which capitalist production generates a social surplus, and the effect that the division of the surplus between capital accumulation and consumption has on the capacity of the economy to reproduce and continue to grow. Two critical points emerge from this early phase of capitalist development. First, accumulation of capital becomes the driving force both for nations and for the capitalist class. Second, capitalism has a *political* aspect; for the state is both a defender and a promoter of business interests. The state operates, in effect, as a *visible* hand. The reform of the Poor Laws and the Corn Laws, which were so central to the writings of Malthus and Ricardo, focused on removing latent mercantilist restrictions in order to improve labour mobility while at the same time providing a cheaper food supply for the growing population of England. The focus of Malthus, Ricardo and other classical political economists on the cost of the food supply reflects their concern with the problem of the sharing of the nation's product among the three great social classes in the form of wages, profit and rent; that is, with the issue of income distribution.

Smith was the first English thinker (he was anticipated by Turgot's (1767) *Reflections on the Formation and Distribution of Wealth*) to integrate the problem of income sharing into his analysis. But it was the later classical economists, specifically Ricardo and John Stuart Mill, who gave special focus to the questions of income shares and policy. Ricardo, who served in Parliament, and his contemporaries, Thomas Malthus, James Mill and John Stuart Mill, all addressed these practical problems in their economic writings. They were *political economists*, rather than pure theorists; their policy perspective is apparent in the extent of their concern with such questions as the Corn Laws and Poor Laws, and the relationship between these policy matters and income distribution.

BRIDGES TO INSTRUMENTALISM

Despite prominence of Smith and other classical political economists in Britain, the scientific study of political economy was held in relatively low repute in Britain. This is especially noteworthy when contrasted with the German university system, and its French and American counterparts. Political economy was not even part of the qualifying examinations that civil servants were required to pass (Winch 1990:50–2). From the 1890s onwards, the British university system was more committed to serving the interests of the business community than it was to training future civil servants. This perception of the proper role of the university in teaching economics as a discipline is very much in evidence in the preface to Marshall's *Industry and Trade* (1919), as well as in his earlier paper 'The Social Possibilities of Economic Chivalry' (Marshall 1907). Political economy was incorporated into the programme of study for prospective civil servants, principally for service in India. Yet the men who held chairs of Political Economy at Cambridge, London's University College and Oxford had no prescribed duties for engaging in scholarly research relating to the interests of the state.

The evolution of political economy as the science of using economic knowledge to shape social outcomes found a considerably more congenial environment in the USA than it did in England. The American belief was that universities, in addition to emphasizing intellectual values, had a responsibility to directly serve the needs of society. Accordingly, political economy was more widely incorporated into American universities. It was more likely to be added to the final year's course in moral philosophy (as part of the liberal arts curriculum) in American universities and colleges than in Britain, the country where political economy originated (Coats 1985:349). In England, on the other hand, emergence of a broader conception of the state as having a purposive role in guiding economic life was considerably delayed, despite early beginnings there of political economy.

When founding the London School of Economics, Sidney and Beatrice Webb envisioned expanded research roles for governmental departments, and also a separate official body devoted to economic intelligence. John Maynard Keynes went a bit further in envisioning a public service organized along the lines of the civil service to run the business side of government. His idea bore some fruit when the Labour government implemented the Economic Advisory Council, which provided Keynes with a platform to promote the role of the economist in government to provide 'deliberate and purposeful guidance'. He was optimistic that the employment of economists in government 'would provide guidance for the evolution of our economic life' (Howson and Winch 1977:21). More specifically, Keynes called for 'deliberate control' of currency and credit by a central institution, and for 'intelligent judgment' about savings and investment (Keynes 1971–89:VIII, 287). Far from trusting Marshall's enlightened and chivalrous business leader, Keynes looked to the possibilities of 'build[ing] up in this country a great public service running the business side of public concerns recruited from the whole population with the same ability and the same great traditions as our administrative civil service' (Keynes 1971–89:XIX, 646).

It is ironic that despite his high expectations about the future role of professional economists in shaping public policy, the views of Keynes were largely rebuffed by authorities at the Treasury and the Bank of England. Nor were they readily embraced in the USA. There was no reply from the oval office when Keynes wrote to President Roosevelt on 31 December 1932:

> You have made yourself the trustee for those in every country who seek to mend the evils of our condition by reasoned experiment within the framework of the existing social system ... if you succeed, new and bolder methods will be tried everywhere, and we may date the first chapter of a new economic era from your accession to office.
>
> (Keynes 1971–89:XXI, 289)

The relevance of Keynes's analysis to diagnosing the US Depression did not become apparent until the 1937 economic decline was linked to the accumulation of payroll taxes in the Social Security Trust Fund without any spending offset such as the veterans' bonus, whose final payment had been made in 1936. It was not until 1938 that President Roosevelt approved the proposal to support purchasing power by means of government spending. However, professional economists had little to do with this proposal or with the dissemination of Keynes's ideas in the USA.

It was not until Harvard Professor Alvin Hansen prepared a White Paper on employment policy for inclusion in the 1944 Democratic platform that the message of Keynes had an impact in the USA. Congress utilized this position paper as a basis for enacting the Employment Act of 1946, which mandated the goal of reducing unemployment to not more than 4 per cent. The 1946 Employment Act also established the Council of Economic Advisors as a body of professional economists to advise the President about economic matters. In effect, establishment of the Council of Economic Advisors indicates that a broader conception of the state's role in guiding economic life had emerged in the USA, and that professional economists were to become a critical resource for its success.

The policy role of government was reaffirmed again towards the end of the 1950s when the deteriorating condition of the US economy prompted demand management to promote full employment, real output growth and price stability by harnessing both fiscal and monetary tools. Analogous views were also gaining acceptance in the UK, where A.W. Phillips (subsequently of Phillips curve fame) used his background in engineering to conceptualize the economy as operating much like a hydraulic system. His model implied that fiscal and monetary measures can be used to maintain national income at an equilibrium level with low unemployment and high levels of output (Phillips 1950).

Jan Tinbergen's (1959:37–84) macroeconomic model of the Dutch economy, which grew out of his business cycles work at the League of Nations, his (1939) 48-equation model of the US economy and his (1951) macroeconomic model of the UK economy, also date from this era. Dutch policy made it the responsibility of government to develop policies that encapsulate a full range of social welfare objectives, including a fair distribution of income and wealth, full employment and economic growth. Tinbergen developed a social democracy policy model, which joined the free market with investment and planning. It had much in common with the kinds of proposals favoured by policy advocates in the USA and the UK, among them Alvin Hansen (1947, 1949), William Beveridge (1944) and Abba Lerner (1944).

Conceptually speaking, Lowe's instrumentalism is rooted in the same intellectual soil that sparked the great wave of interventionism growing out of widespread acceptance of full employment as a priority policy objective. This objective ultimately became encapsulated in the large macroeconometric models of the sort pioneered by Lawrence Klein (1947a, 1947b). Incomes policy (which was implicit in the *General Theory*) to contain inflation without sacrificing employment also came to the fore at this time (Weintraub 1940, 1946).

On a theoretical level, the less than full employment equilibrium model developed by Keynes (1936) became engulfed by the so-called 'neoclassical synthesis' soon after publication of Hicks's 'Mr. Keynes and the Classics' (1937). Later, mistrust of interventionism was given expression in monetarist and supply-side theory and policy. These became the prelude for the 'new classical' macroeconomics put forward by Lucas, Rapping, Sargent and Wallace. These North American academics presented a powerful and concerted front *against* policy intervention (Lucas 1980:200). These most recent developments in macroeconomics have taken place within an intellectual milieu that has become transformed by mathematical formalism and econometrics (Rima 1994). They have diverted attention, not only from social and political reality, but also from the more basic question of the relevance of political economy in the sense in which it was conceived by Robbins (1981). In its predilection for a *laissez-faire* policy perspective the profession thus appears to have come full circle since Marshall. For the time being at least, the majority of the American electorate shares the perspective of a very limited role for government.

Neither mainstream theory nor political conservatism, however, is likely to ameliorate the problems of the formerly collectivized economies previously aligned with the Soviet Union. The transition requirements of these economies raise the question of whether there is a theoretical prototype that can be drawn upon for guidance. The only case study that history offers of an emerging market economy (if, indeed, any exists) is the primary stage of capitalism that developed in England between the mid-eighteenth and mid-nineteenth centuries in tandem with the Industrial Revolution.[2] This period is, of course, also the era of classical economics that was ushered in by Adam Smith's *Wealth of Nations* (1776), whose chief concern was to explain the 'progress of opulence among the various nations'. The section that follows explores the similarities between emerging market economies in eastern and central Europe and early capitalism.

THE CHALLENGES OF EASTERN AND CENTRAL EUROPE

Classical political economy is best conceived as offering a model that represents linkages among the processes of production, income distribution, accumulation (investment) and growth in an economic system characterized by classes of persons whose claims to income derive either from their status as wage earners or earners of property income. When classical political economy is conceived in this way, it is seen to have relevance to economies that are in different stages of development. Thus one can envision, at one end of the spectrum, the newly emerging market economics, several of which are predominantly agrarian and most akin to England at the time that Adam Smith was writing. At the other end of the spectrum are the highly industrialized economies of western Europe and North America. In between are the governmentally subsidized capitalist economies of the Pacific region and the Third World economies of Asia, South America and Africa which still languish far behind. Each can be explained in terms of a suitably modified model. The common point of departure for all is their vision of a market economy as having the potential for moving them forward towards greater opulence. With the constraints of scarcity loosened by technical progress, the potential for growth in the newly privatized economies of central and eastern Europe is no less dramatic than that envisioned by Smith when mercantilist restrictions were driven out or fell into disuse. According to Smith, policy measures were a prerequisite for realizing 'the natural order' in which the invisible hand could function to move the system towards the macroeconomic objective of 'opulence'.

There is an important analogy between Adam Smith's argument that the natural order requires measures to bring about changes to make it compatible with the functioning of the 'invisible hand' and the requisites for successful take-off from a pre-industrial state that Adolph Lowe recognized. Lowe

(1965:309) noted that historical experience 'coincides with the main conclusion of theoretical analysis: as a rule, no pre-industrial region ... is capable of lifting itself by its own efforts out of its pseudo-equilibrium of stagnation'. This observation relates equally to newly privatized economies. Their challenge is to transform their formerly collectivist economies, which made so little progress towards growth that their lack of success called forth an overthrow of the system, even though they provided for basic consumption needs in the form of public goods (but at the expense of political freedom and economic efficiency).

It is relevant to note that the political restructuring initiated by the 1989 revolutions in eastern and central Europe is *not* ushering in *laissez-faire* systems of uncontrolled capitalism. The goal of these countries is to avoid the worst of the social dangers inherent in economic *laissez-faire*, while at the same time achieving a state of economic opulence. Each of the former Soviet bloc countries presents a unique problem, so that the challenge is to devise a package of 'road maps' by which one country at a time can effect a transition that is designed to address its own set of specific problems. In addressing this challenge, the modern state is not simply a consumer of useful knowledge about the functioning of the economy; it is also a producer of economic knowledge when it employs civil servants who are trained in economics, and when it seeks out the assistance of professional economists to 'determine organizational rules that are appropriate to the realization of a specific macro-goal' (Lowe 1965:252). This is the *instrumental* aspect of generating economic knowledge which is based on 'regressive inference from an end to the means, from a given effect to a suitable cause or causes' (Lowe 1965:252).

Lowe conceives of political economics as a theoretical science whose major task is to devise an analytical technique that will move the economy onto a desired growth path. This calls for the derivation of public controls that are suitable for transforming motivational and behavioural patterns into patterns that are goal-adequate. It is also clear that the reforms of the eastern and central European economies are likely to entail a level of supervision and guidance that may well rival the production planning system that preceded it. Establishing a market economy will require a comprehensive new infrastructure along with new laws; in particular, laws to govern the ownership of property and contractual relationships.

The definition of property rights is basic to privatization, and is pivotal to the way in which new market economies are likely to function. It is also necessary that there be a social consensus in favour of reform, along with the political authority to proceed, if reconstruction is to occur. Given these prerequisites, there are at least three tasks for economists to perform. The first is to identify what societal dangers are likely to accompany reprivatization and deregulation. The second is to enlighten the public about the alternative economic states that are feasible, given the available resource base and the level of technological knowledge. The third is to identify the set of alternative measures suitable for attaining a terminal state, which reflects society's desire for the efficiency aspects of a market system, without giving up social provision of what they consider essential goods and services.

Political economics thus has the potential for becoming an instrument for reshaping the outcome of uncontrolled market processes in the former command economies of central and eastern Europe. Conceivably, these formerly planned economies can achieve their microeconomic goals for more efficient resource use and also achieve higher growth rates with less uncertainty by availing themselves of a Lowe type of instrumentalism.

Lowe (1965:262) has described his methodology as being analogous to activity analysis and to linear programming, input–output analysis and operations research, which are its major branches. He also makes reference to economic projections, such as those developed by the National Planning Association in Washington, D.C. What these techniques have in common with instrumental analysis is their concern with identifying the means for achieving stipulated ends. In terms of welfare economics, this procedure would be expressed as identifying the 'optimum method for producing a given "commodity bundle"'. In the language of linear programming, the process would be described as the maximization or minimization of some 'objective function' subject to certain 'constraints'. Again, expressed in the language of Leontieff's output analysis, the procedure is concerned with determining the input–output levels for all industries contributing to the production of a particular set of goods.

The common thread in all these procedures is that when the technical requirements compatible with the production of specified outputs are known, the problem of identifying what is the appropriate behaviour of the underlying micro-units is implicitly solved. These techniques are consistent with what Lowe envisions instrumental analysis is capable of achieving, especially when combined with Jan Tinbergen's (1952) theory of economic policy, which has the further capability of evaluating the compatibility of goals and facilitating dynamic equilibrium.[3] The problem to be addressed by instrumental analysis is to identify what configuration of sectoral organization and resource distribution will assure steady economic growth over time. Thus the role of instrumental analysis is to design 'goal-adequate' public controls; i.e. controls that are consistent with democratically established macroeconomic goals. From a conceptual perspective, the problem of enabling an economy to proceed from a centrally planned economy to a market economy is appropriately viewed as identifying the traverse from one growth path to another.

SOME GLOBAL CHALLENGES FOR MATURE CAPITALIST ECONOMIES

The emergence of the European Economic Community and the North American Free Trade Association (and its likely Pacific rim counterpart), and the expressed willingness of the G-7 countries to provide financial support and assistance as the Community of Independent States (the former Soviet Union) moves towards a free market, may portend increased support for the production of what Kindleberger (1986) has termed 'international public goods'. If so, a fertile new area for research in political economy may emerge, one that has much to learn from classical political economy. When judged by modern standards, the scope for public sector activity was extremely circumscribed in Book V of *The Wealth of Nations* (Smith 1776); yet international economic support to provide public goods like the International Monetary Fund, a World Bank and the European Central Bank (if and when it becomes a reality) is a reasonable extension of Smith's vision of the scope of political economy.

The European Community has already taken steps to eliminate impediments to trade among its member states. The seemingly natural tendency that nations have towards mercantilistic restrictions on imports can be curbed only to the extent that nations work together towards their joint removal. A consensus also appears to have emerged among members of the European Community that a monetary and political union is an essential complement to their trading community. Twelve nations of the European Community signed the Maastricht Treaty in February 1992 which commits all members except Britain to introduce a common currency and establish a European central bank before 1999. This development would transfer monetary policy, which is traditionally a crucial tool of governmental economic control, to a transnational board. There thus appears to be agreement among nations that 'international linkage' problems require cooperative efforts to prevent crises like the 1929 crash.

Thorny problems nevertheless remain on the horizon. In particular, the French are fearful about surrendering authority over domestic monetary affairs to a European central bank, while the Germans are equally reluctant to give up the Deutschmark. The site of the new central bank, whether it is to be in London, Frankfurt, Barcelona, Amsterdam or elsewhere, is also a matter of contention. On the other hand, there appear to be greater prospects for international financial cooperation, because of the levels of opulence realized in Germany, Japan and the USA. The rich countries of the world increasingly appear to be willing to 'tax' themselves in order to support the internationalization of certain controls.

The world-view of the nineteenth century was predicated on a finite land supply and diminishing returns, whereas contemporary political economists are thinking in terms of models that analyse an economy while it expands in historical time. As technological progress frees humankind from the constraints of nature that dominated the dismal perspective of classical economics, the less relevant the Malthus–Ricardo vision of a zero-sum game becomes. As the twenty-first century approaches, the struggle by humankind will be seen less in terms of an intractable nature, and more in terms of an enlarged surplus and a greater prospect for accumulation and growth. Thus, the pessimistic prognosis of classical political economy may not be as near to hand as might have been thought when the stagnation theses of the 1930s gained serious attention. The economic reasons for 'beggar thy neighbour' policies may become less compelling so that nations may become more favourably disposed toward free trade and the provision of international public goods, especially if their increasing opulence improves the affordability of the 'price tag' (Kindleberger 1986). Nevertheless, the quest among nations to improve their relative positions, though it be at the expense of their neighbours, is a historical reality and remains a source of international conflict.

The happy prospect of easing resource constraints through science and technology will, of course, help. Yet these gains are likely to be offset by limits to growth that come from another direction – a massive population explosion. The finite capacity of spaceship earth (to use Kenneth Boulding's descriptive metaphor) to absorb additional waste, the gradual exhaustion of essential natural resources and the progressive deterioration of the environment pose problems whose complexities are almost beyond comprehension.

It is also all too clear that private enterprise economies are, in fact, *not* endowed with self-regulating mechanisms that can reliably be counted on to ameliorate negative outcomes. It is for this reason that *instrumental analysis* as a means for achieving society's economic goals has particular relevance in the context of the approaching twenty-first century. The critical need is not only for value judgements as argued for by Robbins (1981). Also necessary is an approach identifying the optimal adjustment path from among a set of possible paths in order to design public controls and institutions to encourage business, household and government behaviours at the national level that are consistent with desired global outcomes. Instrumentalism provides such an approach.

SOME CONCLUDING THOUGHTS

The complexities of instrumentalism at the global level clearly preclude specifics about institutional changes and policies. Nevertheless, there is a fundamental specific which is relevant to the current disinterest in political economy. Since Marshall, economists have chiefly been concerned with tendencies toward equilibrium. For a generation of economists trained in probability theory and econometric techniques, reliance on equilibrium modelling techniques has produced a mathematically explicit theory of general equilibrium in which households and firms are envisioned as jointly solving static maximizing problems. Statistical verification by means of the method of least squares and regression analysis has supported the perception of economics as a predictive science. When joined with the notion of 'rational expectations', the inference is that economic models are useless for policy formulation, because economic actors are envisioned as having the capability of correctly anticipating the likely effect of policy changes (Rima 1994). Much of the economics profession thus became indifferent to political economy as a discipline that envisions a positive role for the state in maintaining satisfactory levels of employment, and for encouraging economic growth.

Nevertheless, there is a segment of the profession that does have an interest in economic policy. They derive their building blocks from a wide range of intellectual sources, including the Cambridge traditions of Marshall, John Maynard Keynes and Piero Sraffa; American institutionalism; Fabian socialism; and even Marx and the 'New Left'. The concern of these modern political economists is with economics as both a moral science and a social science in the service of human betterment. They consider mainstream theory to be irrelevant precisely because of its conclusion that optimal outcomes will automatically come into existence if only artificial impediments to the operation of the price mechanism are either avoided or eliminated. Thus a rethinking of neoclassical theory would appear to be an essential first step in the rehabilitation of political economy.

The prevailing disinterest in political economy is closely linked to the underlying assumptions of mainstream theory; the most critical of these is the assumption that in the absence of impediments that derive from various restraints of trade, the price mechanism is capable of bringing about a result that is Pareto optimal. They thus have no basis for trying to further a tradition that is properly thought of as 'instrumentalist'. Indeed, a substantial number of economists believe that members of the profession should return to their traditional concern with pure theory (Arndt 1991). This view brings to mind Keynes's (1971–89:XXI, 496–7) disillusion about the 'rule of the Treasury School'. Keynes clearly confronted the source of resistance to his theoretical insights and their implications for public policy, when he concluded that 'it is my fellow economists, not the general public, I must convince' (Keynes 1971–89:VII, vi). Sixty years after Keynes's lament about his fellow economists, the profession remains indifferent, if not hostile, to political economy. The prospect for a substantial change in perspective among economists seems dim, unless they are driven to recognize the necessity for international coordination of the domestic policies among the world's leading economic powers.

NOTES

1 Lowe preferred the term 'political economics'. However, it is relevant to distinguish Lowe's political economics from the political economy of Lionel Robbins (1981), who draws the distinction between economic science as relating to the technical apparatus of the discipline, and political economy as covering that part of our sphere of interest which involves judgements of value. Political economy, thus conceived, is unashamedly concerned with the assumptions of policy and the results flowing from them.

2 The reform experiences of China and some Latin American economies also offer some insight into the transition from a predominantly agricultural economy to a

more industrialized economy. However, the analogies break down because these reforms did not involve an attempt to shift toward a market-directed economy.

3 Economists familiar with such modern techniques as activity analysis, input–output analysis and Tinbergen's 'theory of economic policy and operations research' are conversant with methodologies that are concerned with achieving multiple postulated goals and evaluating their compatibility. The focal point of these procedures is to identify how to achieve the desired ends in the least costly way.

REFERENCES

Arndt, W. H. (1991) 'The Purposes of Political Economy', *Methodus* 3,2:113–16.

Beveridge, W. (1944) *Full Employment in a Free Society*, London: Allen & Unwin.

Coats, A. W. (1985) 'The Educational Revolution and the Professionalization of American Economics', in W.J. Barber (ed.) *Breaking the Academic Mould: Economics and American Higher Learning in the 19th Century*, Middleton, Conn.: Wesleyan University Press.

Hansen, A. (1947) *Economic Policy and Full Employment*, New York: McGraw-Hill.

—— (1949) *Monetary Theory and Fiscal Policy*, New York: McGraw-Hill.

Hicks, J. (1937) 'Mr. Keynes and the Classics: A Suggested Interpretation', *Econometrica* 7:147–59.

Howson, S. and Winch, D. (1977) *The Economic Advisory Council 1930–1939: A Study of Economic Advice During Depression and Recovery*, Cambridge: Cambridge University Press.

Keynes, J. M. (1936) *The General Theory of Employment, Interest and Money*, New York: Harcourt Brace Jovanovich.

—— (1971–89) *The Collected Writings of John Maynard Keynes*, 30 vols, London: Macmillan. (Identified in the text by the volume number.)

Keynes, J. N. (1891) *Scope and Method of Political Economy*, London: Macmillan.

Kindleberger, C. (1986) 'International Public Goods without International Government', *American Economic Review* 76,1:1–13.

Klein, L. (1947a) 'The Use of Econometric Models as a Guide to Economic Policy', *Econometrica* 15:111–51.

—— (1947b) 'Theories of Effective Demand and Employment', *Journal of Political Economy* 55:108–31.

Lerner, A. (1944) *The Economics of Control: Principles of Welfare Economics*, London: Macmillan.

Lowe, A. (1965) *On Economic Knowledge: Toward a Science of Political Economics*, Armonk, N.Y.: M.E. Sharpe (2nd edn 1977).

Lucas, R. E., Jr. (1980) 'Rules, Discretion and the Role of the Economic Advisor', in S. Fischer (ed.) *Rational Expectations and Economic Policy*, Chicago: University of Chicago Press.

Marshall, A. (1890) *Principles of Economics*, London: Macmillan.

—— (1907) 'The Social Possibilities of Economic Chivalry', *Economic Journal* 17:7–29.

—— (1919) *Industry and Trade*, London: Macmillan.

Phillips, A. W. (1950) 'Mechanical Model in Economic Dynamics', *Economica* 17:283–305.

Rima, I. (1994) 'Numeracy and the Development of Economic Analysis', *Journal of the History of Economic Thought* 16:188–201.

Robbins, L. (1932) *An Essay on the Nature and Significance of Economic Science*, London: Macmillan.

—— (1981) 'Economics and Political Economy', *American Economic Review* 71,2:1–10.

Smith, A. (1776) *The Wealth of Nations*, New York: Modern Library Edition (1937).

Tinbergen, J. (1939) *Statistical Testing of Business Cycle Theories*, 2 vols, Geneva: League of Nations.

——(1951) *Business Cycles in the United Kingdom, 1870–1914*, Amsterdam: North-Holland.

——(1952) *On the Theory of Economic Policy*, Amsterdam: North-Holland.

——(1959) *Selected Papers*, Amsterdam: North-Holland.

Turgot, A. R. J. (1767) *Reflections on the Formation and Distribution of Wealth*, in R. L. Meek (ed.) *Turgot on Progress, Sociology and Economics*, Cambridge: Cambridge University Press.

Weintraub, S. (1940) 'Inflation and Price Control', *Harvard Business Review* 18:429–36.

——(1946) 'Monopoly Pricing and Unemployment', *Quarterly Journal of Economics* 61:108–24.

Winch, D. (1990) 'Economic Knowledge and Government in Britain: Some Historical and Comparative Reflections', in M.O. Furner and B. Supple (eds) *The State and Economic Knowledge*, Cambridge: Cambridge University Press.

13

SOME SUGGESTIONS FOR COMPLICATING THE THEORY OF MONEY

Kevin D. Hoover

> It is very funny about money. The thing that differentiates man from the animals is money. All animals have the same emotions and the same ways as men. Anybody who has lots of animals around knows that. But the thing no animal can do is count, and the thing no animal can know is money.
>
> Men can count, and they do, and that is what makes them have money.
>
> Gertrude Stein, 'All About Money'

HICKS'S PROGRAMME

The title of this chapter intentionally echoes the title of John Hicks's (1935) famous paper 'A Suggestion for Simplifying the Theory of Money'. Like that paper it is intended to be a prolegomenon to an as yet unwritten monetary theory. However, the monetary theory it foreshadows is to be constructed differently.

For centuries the central problems of monetary theory have been to articulate the relationship between money and prices and between money and real quantities. The oldest monetary theory, the quantity theory of money, starts from the well-established empirical generalization that (for some definitions of money at least) there is a rough proportionality between changes in the quantity of money and changes in the price level. The quantity theory attributes that correlation to the causal efficacy of money over prices. If changes in the stock of money cause proportional changes in all prices, then money is 'a veil' without real effects. One irony of the modern quantity theory is that its adherents usually believe that control of the money supply is essential, even though money is a veil. This is usually justified by distinguishing between long-run neutrality and short-run non-neutrality, but inevitably some hand-waving is involved.

Going back at least to Hume (1742a, 1742b), quantity theorists recognized that prices cannot adjust instantaneously to increases in the stock of money. To the degree that they do not, real quantities must be affected. But the argument that money affects prices and output is more elliptical than is usually appreciated. Indeed, in the hands of Milton Friedman, the most prominent modern advocate of the quantity theory, it presents a genuine puzzle. According to Friedman (1956), the essence of the quantity theory is the stability of the demand function for money. At first blush, this seems an odd formulation, because the demand function is usually written to indicate the amount of money that economic agents would choose to hold conditional on prices, interest rates and income. The implicit causal direction is thus from these various factors to money. Yet the quantity theory asserts just the opposite causality – money determines prices and income. Friedman presumes that the supply of money is exogenously determined and that agents consult their demand functions; if they find excess supply, they try to rebalance their portfolios by purchasing goods or financial or real assets, putting pressure on prices and rates of return.

This seems plausible, but is in fact puzzling. A 1 per cent increase in the stock of, say, M1 is a very tiny percentage increase in total social wealth. Friedman's (1957) own permanent-income hypothesis holds that only the yield from additions to wealth should go toward consumption, so the pressure on prices would appear to be infinitesimally small. Friedman (Friedman and Schwartz 1982: 29–31) would concede that the first-round effect is indeed small, but that the process continues as money flows from agent to agent, each trying to rebalance his portfolio. That the 1 per cent increase in M1 must ultimately increase prices by 1 per cent is then not a conclusion drawn from any detailed description of the mechanism through which prices rise. Instead, it comes from the assumption that changes in the stock of money do not increase real output in the long run, and that money supply must ultimately equal money demand. Not only does this appear to be question-begging, but it places an almost metaphysical faith in the tendency of an economy to converge to market-by-market static equilibrium.

This account of the transmission mechanism explains why the question of how to define money has loomed so large and proved so slippery. For Friedman's account to be plausible money must be the transactions medium, the asset that agents typically acquire as a byproduct of spending on real goods and services.[1] Historically, however, the assets that play this role keep changing – from coins, to banknotes, to cheques against bank accounts, to cheques against money-market mutual funds – so the quantity theory must be constantly reoriented to new primary causal agents. In Hume's day the claim was that changes in the amount of precious metals caused changes in prices and income. In Friedman's youth, changes in notes, coins and cheque deposits were claimed to be the causal agents. With every financial innovation there is a proposal to reorient the quantity theory. The definition of money also affects the very facts that the quantity theory is meant to explain: the proportionality of money and prices depends on the judicious definition of money. Indeed, Friedman (Friedman and Schwartz 1963: 649–50, *passim*; 1970) explicitly advocates defining money as the financial asset most closely correlated with nominal GNP. Once again, questions are begged.

Hicks wrote his essay on money twenty years before Friedman's restatement of the quantity theory. The main points of this essay are easily summarized.

First, Hicks castigates monetary theory for not analysing money using the same microeconomic tools (value theory) that economists use for other problems. Instead, quantity equations are tacked on to models of barter. But Hicks notes that since people choose to hold money, money must have marginal utility, and should be subject to the same theoretical analysis as the holding of real assets or the consumption of real goods.

Second, Hicks notes that the central puzzle of monetary theory is that people hold money despite the fact that other assets have higher rates of return. He writes (1935: 66):

> This, as I see it, is really the central issue in the theory of money. Either we have to give an explanation of the fact that people do hold money when rates of interest are positive, or we have to evade the difficulty somehow. It is the great traditional evasions, which have led to Velocities of Circulation, Natural Rates of Interest, *et id genus omne*.

Third, to explain the puzzle of rate-of-return dominance Hicks appeals to frictions that money helps to overcome, such as risk and transactions costs.

Hicks's programme for monetary theory follows immediately from his critical position. A successful monetary theory had to be based on the analysis of individual choice; in more recent language, he advocates establishing microfoundations for monetary theory. A successful monetary theory also needs to be a general equilibrium theory – one that accounts for why individuals hold money and how their choices help to determine prices and/or real allocations for the whole economy. Furthermore, a successful monetary theory will recognize that asset choice is about the future and therefore will take expectations seriously. Finally, a successful monetary theory must recognize that money is a stock, which both influences and is influenced by real flows; it will therefore treat the stock/flow distinction carefully. This programme for monetary theory is remarkably fresh. We recognize the central concerns of contemporary monetary theorists in the issues that he outlines.

GENERAL EQUILIBRIUM MICROFOUNDATIONS

Despite this freshness, I want to argue that the programme that Hicks advocated for monetary theory has been a failure – a heroic failure, but a failure none the less. To heterodox economists, declaring the general equilibrium programme for monetary theory a failure may seem uncontroversial; declaring the attempt heroic might appear to concede too much.

The general equilibrium approach requires some justification and defence. Mark Blaug (1990: 228) observes that general equilibrium theory changed from the 1930s, when models were viewed as potential analytical tools for empirical economies, to the 1980s, when they were regarded as ideal, non-empirical models used to demonstrate principles. Frank Hahn (1984: 45–6, 135–7) argues that general equilibrium models are useful not because they model Adam Smith's invisible hand, but because they show just how stringent the conditions are under which Smith's results can be proven; they thereby adumbrate the features of the actual economy that prevent it from operating like a general equilibrium model.

While Blaug is deeply suspicious of this argument, I think there is good reason to accept the general point with respect to monetary theory. Monetary theory would advance enormously if we could provide an idealized model of the behaviour of money in an economy-wide context. The failure of money to find a suitable place in general equilibrium models is a clear indication of the wide lacuna in our understanding of the operation of money. If we cannot capture its operation in an idealized context, what hope have we of capturing it in more realistic contexts?

The difficulty of embedding money in a general equilibrium model concerns how to connect holding money to the real choices of individual agents. Patinkin (1956) attempts to connect the monetary and the real by assuming that real money balances (M/p) give consumers utility because they provide services by permitting uncoordinated fluctuations in expenditure and receipt flows. Once money enters into consumer decision-making in this way, Patinkin argues, the ordinary mechanisms of the Walrasian model establish of the price of money ($1/p$) along with all other prices.

It turns out that Patinkin's model works only in highly restricted circumstances. If utility functions are restricted in such a way that there are no distribution effects, then relative prices are fixed by the conditions of barter equilibrium and any arbitrary price can stand in for the general price level p, since every price is a scalar multiple of every other. Hahn (1965) showed that, absent such restrictions, if there is an equilibrium in which money has a well-defined value, then there is necessarily another equilibrium in which its value is zero (i.e. there is a barter equilibrium), and also that a monetary equilibrium may not exist at all. That for every monetary equilibrium there is a barter equilibrium is a consequence of Patinkin's failure to assign any *essential* role to money: no economic possibilities are foreclosed in the absence of money. That monetary equilibrium may not exist at all is a consequence of the peculiar feature that the real value of money (i.e. its characteristic that is analogous to the *quantity* of any other good) depends on the prices of other goods. As prices are adjusted to find the market-clearing price vector, the quantity of money, unlike the quantities of any other goods, changes and may change in ways that drive the system further into disequilibrium.

In response to these difficulties Hahn (1973) argues that the mechanism of monetary exchange must be more fully specified so that it becomes evident how money expands the opportunity set of the economy. Hahn is surely right here, but there are other lessons to be learned from Patinkin. The Walrasian model solves two economic problems – it establishes relative prices, and it assures that the economic system is consistent and feasible at those prices. Expositions of the Walrasian model typically focus on the first problem. They sometimes even glory in demonstrating that a decentralized economy is feasible and that each agent need only consult prices (and not the actions of other agents) in order to give the 'correct' quantity response. This 'invisible hand' result is, however, parasitic on the highly centralized information processing of the Walrasian auctioneer (or the mathematical equivalent, the mapping rule of prices into prices to which a fixed-point theorem is applied to prove the existence of equilibrium). The Walrasian model works only because there is, implicitly at least, somebody in the model whose business it is to know everyone else's business.

Money is redundant in a true Walrasian economy. The most important function of money in reality is as a means of accounting for relative values and settling imbalances that arise in trading at those relative values. Such functions are unnecessary in a Walrasian world because the auctioneer knows enough to set relative prices in such a way that imbalances never arise. A programme to create a successful monetary theory is, therefore, unlikely to find the Walrasian model a happy starting point.

THE MAIN ALTERNATIVE MONETARY MECHANISMS

As a result, monetary theorists have, by and large, attempted to explain frictions and describe the mechanisms through which money overcomes them. But they have attempted to maintain the Walrasian framework, and this has created problems for these alternative approaches. Let us now look at four of the principal mechanisms in the current literature.

The overlapping-generations model

While most monetary theories concentrate on the role of money as a means of conducting transactions, the overlapping-generations model stresses the fact that money is a store of value, a means of moving wealth from one period to another.[2] The central idea of the overlapping-generations model is that individuals want to shift resources from earlier parts of their lives to later parts, but they cannot do so directly since resources do not store well (e.g. strawberries spoil). A solution is to trade for real resources in the future with people who want real resources today. Unfortunately, if the young want to give up resources in their youth and the old want to consume more than they have, such trades would be infeasible – for the old will die before the young can be repaid. Money overcomes this friction. The young sell to the old, carry the money into their own old age, and buy from a new generation of young people.

The overlapping-generations model, however, fails to solve the central problems of monetary modelling. Its principal difficulty is that it does not explain the fact, noted by Hicks, that money is held despite its low rate of return. Simple versions of the model rely on there being no means of shifting resources forward in time except money. If there were time-using productive processes (the analogy would be wheat growing rather than strawberries spoiling), they would provide a better means of shifting resources through time. Since money is held *only* for its ability to store value, no one would choose to hold money when better stores of value were available.

Many attempts have been made to explain rate-of-return dominance in an overlapping-generations framework. None has been successful. If real returns are stochastic, risk-averse agents will sometimes hold money as a way of reducing risk even though real returns on assets are positive on average (Wallace 1981). While this is true, the range of stochastic yields is far too narrow to explain commonly observed differences of five or ten percentage points between the yields of money and other assets. Intermediation costs could explain a premium (interest foregone) on money (Bryant and Wallace 1979). But actual intermediation costs in the real world (think of the service fees on money-market mutual funds) are simply too small to account for observed differential yields. If certain people (the relatively poor) cannot hold assets because of legal restrictions on intermediation (e.g. banks are forbidden to issue one-dollar bearer bonds at interest) then money might be dominated in rate of return but still held by the poor (Wallace 1983). Again, this is true in principle, but does violence to the facts. A wide range of interest-bearing assets can be purchased by the poor in small denominations. Furthermore, the rich as well as the poor hold money. The puzzle about why people hold money remains.

The cash-in-advance model

Cash-in-advance models focus on the role of money as a means of exchange.[3] As Clower (1967: 5) puts it: 'money buys goods, and goods buy money, but goods do not buy goods'. In the cash-in-advance model, people may have real resources, but they cannot barter them for other goods. Instead they must sell them for money. Only with money can people purchase goods.

Clearly, a comprehensive cash-in-advance requirement is too strict; some goods are in fact bartered directly. Lucas (1984) and others have investigated models in which there are both cash goods, which are subject to the constraint, and credit goods which are not.

But the principal difficulty with the cash-in-advance model is that it is not a good description of the economy. While it is true that one must have coins in hand to use vending machines, the largest transactions by value are made on credit, with settlement coming some time later. As credit-card use advances, this point becomes more obvious. What is less obvious is that the cash-in-advance constraint has never been pervasive. For hundreds of years many, and perhaps most, transactions have been carried out on credit – personal accounts with grocers or tailors, trade credit and wages paid in arrears. Money seems central to the economic system, yet it does not seem essential to possess money in advance of purchase.

Liquidity-cost models

Another way to model money is to assume that the possession of money reduces the real cost of obtaining consumption or production goods. Holding money is consumption foregone, but failing to hold money raises the costs of obtaining consumption goods. The demand for money is determined by balancing these opposing costs.

The principal objection to this approach is that it is question-begging. The nature and size of the liquidity costs, and the exact mechanism through which money is supposed to reduce them, are never clearly specified.

Liquidity-cost models have been used to justify the model of money in the utility function, in spite of Hahn's criticisms of Patinkin for using this technique. Feenstra (1986) demonstrates that for any particular specification of liquidity costs there is a model with money in the utility function that delivers the same equilibrium. Suppose that agents optimize a utility function $U(C_t, C_{t+1}, C_{t+2}, \ldots)$, where C is real consumption and the subscripts indicate current and future periods, subject to a budget constraint in which money enters as a liquidity cost measured in terms of reduced consumption. Feenstra demonstrates that the problem can be recast as one in which agents optimize a different utility function $U^*(M_t, X_t, X_{t+1}, X_{t+2} \ldots)$, where M is real money balances and X is consumption plus liquidity costs. The solution to each optimization problem generates exactly the same paths for consumption and money holdings. This result follows from the duality relationship between direct and indirect utility functions. It would appear, then, that if the liquidity-cost model could be justified, so could the money-in-the-utility-function model. Feenstra's result, however, is only valid, as he himself observes, for an economy with a single commodity. In such an economy there are no relative prices to induce the distribution effects that threaten the existence of equilibrium.

Beyond that, even in the restricted range of its validity, Feenstra's result says that for a particular utility function, U, and a particular specification of liquidity costs, there exists a particular isomorphic utility function, U^*. This function, U^*, however, is unlikely to belong to the class of utility functions commonly used in monetary models. Indeed, the form of U^* is dictated by the form of U and of the liquidity-cost function, and is likely in practice to be quite peculiar. Thus, Feenstra's result is highly limited: even if we were happy to model only a single-good economy, and even if we were happy with the specification of liquidity costs – assumptions unlikely to be fulfilled – there is no general support in Feenstra's analysis for choosing some particularly tractable utility function that includes money and using it as the basis for monetary analysis.

Search models

Search models are perhaps the most radical attempt to view money as a response to particular frictions.[4] Their central notion is that people have goods to trade and limited preferences over which goods to consume, so the process of finding suitable trading partners can be arduous. With direct barter, agents must find another agent who both has a good they want and who wants the good they have (Jevons's famed 'double coincidence of wants'). If agents believe that some undesired goods may be used to purchase desired goods, indirect barter is possible: I trade oranges for cigarettes, even though I do not smoke, because I believe that I can trade cigarettes for coffee at a later stage. If any commodity comes to be universally regarded as the preferred intermediary in trades, then that good is essentially money. Most work in search models has concentrated on detailing the conditions under which particular goods take on the role of money and on the efficiency improvements from monetization.

Search models may give some insights into how particular objects historically became money, but they do not help to understand a developed monetary system. The problem here stems from the fact that the friction that money overcomes is ignorance of where to find the goods that we wish to purchase. Money is valuable because the average time involved in locating preferred consumption goods is lower in a monetary economy than in a barter economy. But is this really a problem? I do not need to search randomly for groceries; I go to the same grocer each week. If I want a bolt I go to the hardware store; if I want aspirin I go to the pharmacy. Even when I do not know immediately where to find a good, my search is directed through informational resources such as the *Yellow Pages* or the advice of my neighbour. Holding intermediate goods is not a relevant part of finding my preferred consumption good, although there is undoubtedly a monetary aspect to the transactions involved in securing it.

In search models people can trade only when they find someone to trade with. Money improves consumption possibilities because it increases the probability of finding a willing trader. The average time to find two trades (what I have got for money and money for what I want) is lower (and therefore the consumption loss is lower) than the time to find one trade without money. The search metaphor is one of undirected trade and random mixing. The point about knowing where to find the grocer is that in any developed economy trade is directed, not random, and the fundamental friction is not search (finding the appropriate trade), but the difficulty of arranging the trade in a suitable way: valuing it appropriately (one function of a unit of account), and keeping it fair and honest. The issue is not just that I know where the grocer is, but that I know where the university (my employer) is, and that the grocer knows where the university (that his child attends) is. Search is not the issue; coordination is.

A NEW PROGRAMME FOR MONETARY THEORY

Search models are on the right track in that they reject the Walrasian model as a basis for monetary theory. They go wrong because they are mesmerized by the task of isolating why some particular good (gold, silver, fiat paper) becomes the preferred intermediary in transactions, and because they wrongly characterize the informational constraint that we face. Like some attempts to understand money in a Walrasian framework, search models overemphasize the role of money in transactions as an intermediary good. Money is in part a response to information failures; however, the principal failure is not ignorance of where to find goods but the ignorance of what goods we will in fact buy or sell. This latter information failure is the one stressed by Patinkin. And this friction can be overcome by any number of credit arrangements, not just through holding a specialized money good. In any developed economy, the credit system is essential. Money is an essential part of the credit system. But the important thing about money in a credit system is neither its quantity nor the number or value of the transactions in which it mediates.

Rather, the principal modern function of money is the one traditionally regarded as the weak sister of the famous triad (means of exchange, store of value, unit of account). Money is most importantly a unit of account, and the efficiencies of a monetary economy arise not from the services of the particular asset called 'money', but instead from the whole complex of transactions and financial services that use the monetary unit as their principal means of keeping score: 'Men can count, and they do, and that is what makes them have money.'

I have argued in detail elsewhere (Hoover 1988a, 1988b) that a financial system involving nominal paper assets can function only if these are convertible through *direct* or *indirect* chains to a real asset. For these purposes, fiat currency or central bank reserves can be thought of as real assets in the sense that they provide no entitlements to further conversion (unlike, say, a cheque which is an entitlement to receive cash or central bank reserves) and that they are the stipulated means of meeting certain obligations (e.g. payment of taxes or settlement of reserve positions). In practice, most financial assets are ultimately convertible into a narrow class of real assets. This class could be thought of as defining 'money', although that is a narrower definition than common usage. In practice such narrow money is the typical unit of account, although accounts could be specified in units other than the natural units of this class provided that they were related to goods in the class in well-defined ways (e.g. in gold guineas, coins that no longer exist but whose value is defined to be £1.05, or SDRs, which are defined as weighted averages of the values of national moneys).

Stressing the centrality of an accounting system using a unit that is the ultimate good of conversion (or settlement) diminishes the importance of money as a store of value or a means of payment. Narrowly defined money is a very small player in the whole system of credit and finance. When I obtain goods without surrendering a real equivalent, accounts must be kept of what I owe. Some manner of discharging my debt must be, implicitly at least, agreed upon. Narrow money is not important because it is intermediary in most of my transactions: indeed it does not even settle most of my debts, since I mostly pay my bills by cheque, reducing my own demand deposits and raising my creditors' demand deposits with banks transferring but a small proportion of their total clearings of all such exchanges in the form of central bank reserves. Rather, narrow money is important because it defines the unit in which my debts are recorded, and because it provides the ultimate anchor for the convertibility of assets with which I typically discharge my debt.

It is this pervasive engagement with the financial system at every level that explains the peculiar robustness of money. Who has not heard stories of Germans in 1923 paying for bread with wheelbarrows full of money? The story is usually told to illustrate how depreciated the Reichsmark had become during the hyperinflation. I think that it illustrates a much more astonishing point: despite its vast depreciation, despite its high negative real rate of return, despite the vastly increased shoe-leather costs (after all, a wheelbarrow load of paper is heavy) and despite the substitution possibilities into foreign currency or physical assets, the Reichsmark continued to be used.

My first proposal for an alternative monetary theory then is to place the emphasis on the accounting and settlement functions of money. Since these functions have no role in a Walrasian system, it follows immediately that we must seek a non-Walrasian model. We obviously have to give up the auctioneer as a guarantor of the feasibility of trading. Without an auctioneer, the model lacks a price-setting mechanism. The alternative model must therefore supply the gap. The natural alternative is a model of price-setting agents.

My second proposal is to extrapolate from current trends in transactions technology (e.g. credit cards, electronic fund transfers or debit cards), and make the extreme idealizing assumption that no narrow money is needed in advance of purchase. All purchase is on credit, but from time to time uncleared balances have to be settled either at the level of the individual, or at the level of banks or other financial intermediaries, with narrow money. This is to replace the cash-in-advance constraint with a *cash-in-arrears* constraint.

My third proposal is to take the fact that money is dominated in rate of return as a primitive fact about the economy. Monetary theory after Hicks has attempted to explain why that could be an equilibrium result – either by finding some service that makes up the rate-of-return deficit or by introducing some constraint that forces money to be held as the corner solution to an optimization problem. Either way, the goal is to explain why money is held voluntarily. In keeping with the idealized assumption of the cash-in-arrears constraint, I suggest a further idealization. Let us suppose that money is not held voluntarily. Money holdings arise in the process of settlement, and people dispose of their money by purchasing better-yielding financial assets as fast as possible. Clearly all the money in existence must be held by someone, but they need not hold it as part of an optimal portfolio.[5] In taking this view we give up the ideal of static equilibrium. There may, none the less, be something akin to equilibrium in our model, what von Mises (1963: 224–50) has called the 'evenly rotating economy' – an economy in motion, not at rest, but whose rotation is recurring and routine.

One great appeal of the Walrasian model is that it yields nice analytic results. My suggestions force us to give up these results. One might nevertheless answer the main questions of monetary theory in a computer simulation that is founded on the three proposals that I have sketched. Such a model would involve a large number of heterogeneous agents – producers and consumers or producer-consumers. These agents would set prices for the goods that they produce and choose goods for purchase on the basis of the prices advertised in the market. Their behaviour could be forward-looking and consistent with a sort of practical rational expectations. This means that, while we do not endow agents with omniscience about the price-setting structure, we could nevertheless make them efficient learners who do not persist in remediable mistakes.

Demands, supplies or both would be stochastic. This would introduce randomness into purchases and sales. Agents would formulate plans at the beginning of a period for consumption or production in a way not inconsistent with dynamic optimization (e.g. the life-cycle model of consumption), but would find at the end of the period that some expected sales had failed to materialize or that some consumption plans had been frustrated. Agents would then find themselves willy-nilly to be creditors or debtors to other particular agents. (It might be useful to model a separate banking sector, so that the settlement of net imbalances became the specialized task of the banks.)

Transactions are conducted with a higher frequency than settlements: we spend money every day, but pay our bills monthly. Therefore, after a certain number of periods, agents must settle net outstanding balances. Money is needed for this. Agents without money would have to borrow it. Agents who carried money over unwillingly (because it is dominated in rate of return) from earlier settlement periods would use it to settle their own debts and would purchase financial assets with any extra money.

Two different financial markets are presupposed in this story. One, which corresponds to our bond market, is the market for savings. Agents should not be assumed to attempt the impractical Walrasian feat of generating a good-by-good consumption plan for all future periods. Instead, they would choose real savings (and purchase the counterpart financial assets) as part of their general period-by-period consumption decision. This is more Keynesian in spirit: the decision to save is the decision to abstain from current consumption, not the decision to consume some definite thing in the future. The second market is the market for the settlement asset itself. This corresponds to the US Federal funds market, where one bank lends another central bank reserves in order to meet reserve requirements or settlement needs. To obtain sufficient realism it may be necessary to introduce a third financial market – a stock market, where returns are linked to the real yields of productive physical assets.

While such a simulation model would be highly stylized, it is a reasonable portrayal of the future exchange system in developed countries. Moreover, in the context of such a model one could address the classic questions of monetary economics. Does expansion of the narrow-money asset generate proportional inflation? Do changes in the money stock have real effects in the short or long run? Are supply shocks inflationary? Are monetary policies that aim to fix nominal interest rates unstable? Would this model provide different answers than those that try to remain with the Walrasian framework? We cannot know the answer to these questions without actually constructing the model. But as I noted at the beginning of this chapter, this is a prolegomenon to a monetary theory, not a monetary theory itself.[6]

NOTES

1 That Friedman and Schwartz (1963: 649–50, *passim*) characterize money as 'a temporary abode of purchasing power' rather than as a means of exchange does not affect the point here at all.

2 The classic paper on the overlapping-generations model is Samuelson (1958). Wallace (1980) has been the most persistent advocate of using overlapping-generations models to provide a foundation for monetary theory.

3 The *locus classicus* of the cash-in-advance constraint is Clower (1967). Also, see Kohn (1981).

4 The prototypical search model of money is Diamond (1984). Kiyotaki and Wright (1989, 1991, 1993) have been major proponents of this approach.

5 This is the basis of the 'buffer-stock' approach to aggregate money demand; see Laidler (1982).

6 The author thanks Clinton Greene and Steven Pressman for comments on an earlier draft of this chapter.

REFERENCES

Blaug, M. (1990) *Economic Theories, True or False?*, Aldershot: Edward Elgar.

Bryant, J. and Wallace, N. (1979) 'The Inefficiency of Interest-bearing National Debt', *Journal of Political Economy* 87: 365–81.

Clower, R. (1967) 'A Reconsideration of the Microfoundations of Monetary Theory', *Western Economic Journal* 6: 1–8.

Diamond, P. A. (1984) 'Money in Search of Equilibrium', *Econometrica* 52: 1–20.

Feenstra, R. C. (1986) 'Functional Equivalence Between Liquidity Costs and the Utility of Money', *Journal of Monetary Economics* 17: 271–92.

Friedman, M. (1956) 'The Quantity Theory of Money: A Restatement', in M. Friedman (ed.) *Studies in the Quantity Theory of Money*, Chicago: University of Chicago Press.

——(1957) *A Theory of the Consumption Function*, Princeton: Princeton University Press.

Friedman, M. and Schwartz, A. J. (1963) *A Monetary History of the United States: 1867–1960*, Princeton: Princeton University Press.

——(1970) *Monetary Statistics of the United States: Estimates, Sources and Methods*, New York: National Bureau of Economic Research.

——(1982) *Monetary Trends in the United States and the United Kingdom: Their Relation to Income, Prices and Interest Rates 1867–1975*, Chicago: University of Chicago Press.

Hahn, F. (1965) 'On Some Problems of Proving the Existence of Equilibrium in a Monetary Economy', in *Equilibrium and Macroeconomics*, Oxford: Blackwell.

——(1973) 'On Transactions Costs, Inessential Sequence Economies and Money', *Review of Economic Studies* 40: 449–61.

——(1984) 'The Winter of Our Discontent', in *Equilibrium and Macroeconomics*, Oxford: Blackwell.

Hicks, J. R. (1935) 'A Suggestion for Simplifying the Theory of Money', in *Critical Essays in Monetary Theory*, Oxford: Clarendon Press (1967).

Hoover, K. D. (1988a) 'Money, Prices and Finance in the New Monetary Economics', *Oxford Economic Papers* 40: 150–67.

——(1988b) *The New Classical Macroeconomics: A Sceptical Inquiry*, Oxford: Blackwell.

Hume, D. (1742a) 'Of Money', in E. Rotwein (ed.) *David Hume: Writings on Economics*, Madison: University of Wisconsin Press (1970).

——(1742b) 'Of the Balance of Trade', in E. Rotwein (ed.) *David Hume: Writings on Economics*, Madison: University of Wisconsin Press (1970).

Kiyotaki, N. and Wright, R. (1989) 'On Money as a Medium of Exchange', *Journal of Political Economy* 97: 927–54.

——(1991) 'A Contribution to the Pure Theory of Money', *Journal of Economic Theory* 53: 215–35.

——(1993) 'A Search-Theoretic Approach to Monetary Economics', *American Economic Review* 83: 63–77.

Kohn, M. (1981) 'In Defense of the Finance Constraint', *Economic Inquiry* 19: 177–95.

Laidler, D. (1982) *Monetarist Perspectives*, Oxford: Philip Allan.

Lucas, R. E. (1984) 'Money in a Theory of Finance', in K. Brunner and A. H. Meltzer (eds) *Essays on Macroeconomic Implications of Financial and Labor Markets and the Political Process*, Carnegie-Rochester Conference Series on Public Policy, vol. 21, Amsterdam: North-Holland.

Patinkin, D. (1956) *Money, Interest and Prices*, New York: Harper & Row (2nd edn 1965).

Samuelson, P. A. (1958) 'An Exact Consumption Loan Model of Interest With or Without the Social Contrivance of Money', *Journal of Political Economy* 56: 467–82.

von Mises, L. (1963) *Human Action*, 3rd edn, Chicago: Henry Regnery.

Wallace, N. (1980) 'The Overlapping Generations Model of Fiat Money', in J. H. Kareken and N. Wallace (eds) *Models of Monetary Economies*, Minneapolis: Federal Reserve Bank of Minneapolis.

——(1981) 'A Modigliani–Miller Theorem for Open Market Operations', *American Economic Review* 71: 267–74.

——(1983) 'A Legal Restrictions Theory of the Demand for "Money" and the Role of Monetary Policy', *Federal Reserve Bank of Minneapolis Quarterly Review* 7: 1–7.

INDEX